Robert Aldrich is Professor of European History at the University of Sydney. He is the author of *The Age of Empires* and the editor of *Gay Life and Culture: A World History*, both also published by Thames & Hudson.

Robert Aldrich

Gay
Lives

with 20 illustrations

ON THE COVER

Front Portrait of Annemarie Schwarzenbach first published in the
magazine *UHU* in 1933. Photo Atelier Binder/ullstein bild via Getty
Images. *Back* Lionel Wendt, *Photograph of Desk*, date unknown.
Lionel Wendt Memorial Fund, Colombo

First published in the United States of America in 2012 in hardcover by
Thames & Hudson Inc., 500 Fifth Avenue, New York, New York 10110

First compact paperback edition published in 2016
This compact paperback edition published in 2023

Library of Congress Control Number 2022950948

ISBN 978-0-500-29717-9

Printed and bound in the UK by CPI (UK) Ltd

Be the first to know about our new releases,
exclusive content and author events by visiting
thamesandhudson.com
thamesandhudsonusa.com
thamesandhudson.com.au

CONTENTS

PREFACE TO THE NEW EDITION

Queer lives are now more visible, and affirmed more positively, than at any time in history. From western Europe to the Americas to Australasia, marriages between those of the same gender are celebrated. Increasing numbers of public figures, even heads of government, have come out as gay or lesbian. Many young people, and those less young, proclaim the fluidity of their gender and reject sexual binaries of homosexual and heterosexual, as well as male and female. Words such as 'polyamorous' and 'trans' have appeared as self-identifying labels for those who refuse confinement to traditional heterosexuality, homosexuality and monogamy – just as 'queer' emerged in the 1990s to cover a broader range of sexual diversities than implied by 'gay', 'lesbian' and 'straight'. Changes in language, behaviour and attitudes are welcomed by many, decried by some; ideas and words are debated, and readers and writers are sometimes a bit bewildered.

Since this book was written, much has changed for those with same-sex passions and for those whose desires lead them in directions beyond the patterns so long mandated by religion, law and public opinion. In 2012, when the book was first published, provisions for legally recognized marriages between two men or two women had only recently been enacted, and only in very few countries. A decade later, same-sex marriages are lawful in around thirty countries. Some of those same-sex couples also choose to have children. Such arrangements have expanded the very notion of the family.

However, long-term unions with partners of the same gender, even without legal or religious sanction, were practised by several of the historical figures profiled in this volume. Liaisons of the past might well be considered true marriages in terms of the love and commitment, and the sharing of lives, that they embodied. Eva Gore-Booth, Claude Cahun, the 'Ladies of Llangollen' and Edward Carpenter, among others, were involved in partnerships that endured for many years or decades, and they considered themselves linked by bonds as solid as those of legalized marriage. Some, like Oscar Wilde, were legally married and had children, but are best known for the relations they had with partners of the same gender. Such men and women, in theory and practice, were already creating new sorts of relationships, families and unions long before marriage equality appeared on the agenda.

Not so long ago, most commentators would not have predicted that lesbians or gay men would be elected prime ministers of Iceland, Belgium, Ireland, Luxembourg and Serbia, as has been the case in the years since 2009. It is now less and less unusual for a politician, businessperson, actor or athlete to declare a non-heterosexual orientation, despite the challenges and sometimes opprobrium they face in certain quarters. Gender politics are part of mainstream politics, leading in some jurisdictions to laws against discrimination and vilification, though there have been backlashes as well on issues such as reproductive rights. Nevertheless, there is increased recognition, in international forums and nationally, that sexual rights form part of human rights. The modern history of sexual variance is in part one of resistance against discrimination and persecution alongside campaigns for law and social reform, evident from Magnus Hirschfeld's pioneering movement of the late 1800s through the homophile, gay liberation and subsequent movements of the mid-20th century and beyond to the marriage equality campaign.

A striking development over the past decade has been the growing public presence of 'trans' people, those who reject the gender to which they were assigned at birth, some of whom proceed to gender reassignment, and have their new status officially recognized. Identity documents, census reports and questionnaires in some places now give individuals the chance to tick a box other than 'male' or 'female' (or to decline to specify their gender), and the option of using 'they/their' rather than the binary 'he/him' or 'she/her' pronouns has become more common. Gender lines seem now more porous than ever. Yet history, once again, provides examples of those who centuries ago lived between genders, as is notable with the Chevalier d'Éon at the end of the 1700s. In 1906, the Irish woman Eva Gore-Booth and her partner established a journal, *Urania*, that called for the abolition of gender differences and spoke about what we might now consider a 'trans' identity, foreshadowing contemporary discourse.

We are increasingly aware of the varied nature of sexual desire and its expression, even in one person over a lifetime, and there are growing demands for society to validate diversity and transformation in identity and lifestyle. A person may accept or reject the gender assigned to them at birth, pursue sexual desires for someone of the same or a different gender, have casual contacts or enduring partnerships, contract a monogamous relationship or have an open one – and all of the above. Around the world there are now, and have been in the past, men who have sex with men, and women who have sex with women, or with both genders, who have not considered themselves 'sodomites' or 'sapphists', homosexual, gay or lesbian, bisexual or queer. To Renaissance humanists, or those living in some societies outside Europe, notions of an exclusive and life-long sexual preference would have been odd, and terms such as 'heterosexual' and 'homosexual' (only coined in the late 19th century) unknown. As those whose biographies appear in this book suggest, in the past as in the present, sexuality was fluid, desires multiple, relationships malleable, identities defined – by individuals and society – in manifold ways. People even in societies with strict codes of morality accommodated, negotiated with or transgressed social conventions as they searched for emotional and physical satisfaction.

Recent years have seen ever greater attention to issues of sexual abuse and the question of sexual consent, with justified outrage at and condemnation of sexual coercion and violence. There has also been much concern about intergenerational sex and the abuse of minors. Sexual violence and coercion – against women, children, the enslaved and others in subaltern positions – were common in the past, often unpunished by law and uncensored or justified by legal and cultural conventions, and they have not disappeared today. Ideas of what constituted an appropriate age for sexual activity and marriage (and with whom), and notions of consent, differed widely throughout history. Some European countries in the 19th century set the age of consent as low as 10 years of age, or indeed had no legal age of consent at all. In past times and in different places, views about life stages – childhood, adolescence, adulthood – diverged markedly from present-day views. Sexual relations were often asymmetrical in terms of power and consent, as they continue to be in many instances. Types of sexual relationships that now would generally be considered highly inappropriate were tolerated or lauded, for example in the *paiderastia* of ancient Greece, which accepted relations between adult men and adolescent ephebes, and as well as between teachers and pupils. Some of these sexual relationships may make present-day readers uncomfortable. That is understandable, but also a reminder of changing mores, and of the relativity of public opinion, law and private conduct.

The figures profiled here represent only a small sampling of queer lives, and the capacious word 'queer' is inadequate to cover all the sexual differences and diversities of either past or present. The selection reflects my own areas of expertise and interest, and other writers would legitimately make different choices or focus on different groups. For this edition, we have decided to retain the original text and title of the volume, while updating a few details and making a few stylistic changes. New profiles of three people, from an almost infinite number that might have been added, point to issues that have assumed heightened importance at the present day with the case of a British transgender woman, a male African homosexual and a Middle Eastern lesbian. April Ashley, Binyavanga Wainaina and Sarah Hegazi – who all lived well into the twenty-first century – challenged gender stereotypes and social norms, suffered from and fought discrimination, brought their private lives into public view, and worked in favour of sexual rights.

The cases of Wainaina and Hegazi also point to the continued restrictions on sexual behaviours in many parts of the globe. Sixty-nine countries still maintain laws that make homosexual acts criminal, and in Brunei, Iran, Mauritania, Saudi Arabia, Yemen and parts of Nigeria the death penalty can be imposed for same-sex sexual activity. Homophobia is official doctrine in such countries as Russia, where the promotion or defence of homosexuality and other sorts of sexual and gender non-conformity is punishable by fines or imprisonment. Clerics of various faiths as well as politicians and writers who pose as defenders of morality rail against same-sex activity, transgender identities and marriage equality. Discrimination has far from disappeared in countries where it is formally outlawed, and violence against those who have sex with partners of the same gender or do not conform to gender and sexual stereotypes remains prevalent elsewhere. Pride is rightly celebrated at parades and parties, but there is also isolation, castigation and rejection – and for some imprisonment, torture and death.

Gay life stories reveal the variegated mosaic of personal experiences and itineraries. They offer fascinating records of individuals whose lives are by turns fun, moving, inspiring, troubling, cautionary and occasionally exasperating or tragic. This volume is not a 'best of', nor is it a pantheon of heroes and heroines, though certain men and women who feature here may rightly be heralded as pioneers in the quest for social reform. Their personal experiences, their writings and art, their loves and lusts are antecedents for present-day efforts to find pleasure, love and happiness, to construct and express sexual identities and to secure human rights.

INTRODUCTION

This moment yearning and thoughtful, sitting alone,
It seems to me there are other men in other lands, yearning
  and thoughtful;
It seems to me I can look over and behold them, in Germany,
  Italy, France, Spain –
Or far, far away, in China, or in Russia or India – talking other
  dialects;
And it seems to me if I could know those men, I should
  become attached to them, as I do to men in my own lands;
O I know we should be brethren and lovers,
I know I should be happy with them.

– Walt Whitman, Leaves of Grass (1891)

The sex lives of celebrities (and the less famous) always excite the curiosity of others, as the tittle-tattle of gossip magazines, eager to recount the liaisons, the peccadilloes and the romances of film stars, sports heroes and politicians, amply testifies. Accounts provide an extra frisson when bedroom behaviour is tinged with something unusual, and the inside stories move to the front page when there is a whiff of scandal.

More serious writers, however, long shied away from peering into the secret chambers of the lives of public figures, even in the light of Freudian and other psychological theories that underlined the importance of sexuality. Many weighty and otherwise comprehensive biographies, though they might dwell on love and marriage, avoided sex. In some cases, intimate details found no place at all in a biography, being seen as largely irrelevant to the ideas and public activities of the subject. Some writers went to great lengths to deny sexual improprieties, convinced that such conduct would compromise their subject's achievements, or that discussion of the messy business of sex would sully their own scholarship.

The situation changed from the 1960s. Women's and gay liberation movements argued that private life has a public side. 'Gay pride' mandated an open and proud affirmation of sexual orientation, and those who proved too reticent to admit their homosexuality were occasionally outed. Changing laws (at least in the Western world) made it possible for those whose sexual behaviour had previously been criminal to proclaim their desires and practices without fear of arrest, while the outbreak of AIDS made it difficult for those who fell ill to hide what society, notwithstanding the change in the law, often considered reprobate behaviour. The new academic fields of gender studies and the history of sexuality underscored the significance of sex, in its manifold variations, in individual lives and in the collective life of different societies. Queer theory revealed the mutations and ambiguities of sexual identities, and promoted new readings of canonical and obscure texts and images. A consumerist obsession with sexual satisfaction – from pornographic and dating websites to the popular use of medications to enhance sexual performance – made sex an omnipresent theme in the media.

Sex – or the emotions and behaviour associated with sexuality – does not provide the key to everyone's life, but for most people it does form a central part of their sense of their place in the world and their interactions with others. Sex is never entirely a private matter. What individuals feel and don't feel, do and don't do, reflects their acceptance or rejection of social conventions: codes determined by religion, law, medicine, the media, and other standards of authority and opinion. Social and cultural expectations surrounding chastity, virginity, childbearing, monogamy and promiscuity, and 'normal' or 'abnormal' sexual acts influence an individual's expression of his or her sexual desires. And, depending on time and place, the expression of certain desires may be celebrated or condemned.

The figures in this volume illustrate the ways in which those who felt an attraction to those of the same sex lived out their desires across time and around the world. Its purpose is not to offer a compendium of the lives of the 'greatest gays', nor to provide an encyclopedic survey of the different sexual types identified by historians, anthropologists and other specialists. It represents, rather, a richly diverse congregation of figures, whose lives point up the different personal and social experiences of homosexuality through the ages. Some individuals are well known, some less well known, and none is still living. A particular effort has been made to embrace lives from outside Europe: an Arabic painter; a Japanese photographer; a South African activist; a Jamaican novelist; a Vietnamese poet. Other figures – a nun, a priest, a military officer, a criminal – were chosen to show homosexual people in a variety of professional callings. Viewed together, their stories uncover the fashions in which sexual diversity has been expressed, and the connections between private lives and public life – between individuals and their specific historical and cultural environments.

For convenience, the terms 'same-sex' and 'homosexual' are used throughout, but this does not imply an essentialist approach. Indeed, the opposite is true: the lives reveal a great variety of individual and social attitudes towards 'homosexuality': *paiderastia* in ancient Greece; spiritual friendship in the works of the medieval monk Aelred, and the Neoplatonic, humanistic friendship lauded by Montaigne; the ambisexuality of Renaissance figures such as Michelangelo; the women-centred relationships of Rosa Bonheur; and on to Magnus Hirschfeld's idea of a 'third sex', the out-and-proud gay liberation view of Guy Hocquenghem, and so on. The book takes a broad view of experience, without any attempt to find the stains on the sheets or to out any individual. Sexual orientation here is seen as emotional as well as physical – a question of intimate affinities, not just fornication; of love as well as lust.

Several common themes emerge. Close friendship between men, and between women, has often been extolled – in Greek philosophy, Christian humanist treatises, medieval Arabic poetry, and tales of Chinese emperors and Japanese samurai – with a moving boundary between emotional and physical intimacy. Yet men and women with blatantly 'contrary' urges have often battled social censure, from sodomites burned at the stake in medieval Europe to homosexuals harassed by journalists and policemen in McCarthyite America. Despite taboos and interdictions, men who desired other men and women who desired other women, sometimes in the most inhospitable environments, have found spaces in which to pursue partners in love and lust – even in Hitlerite Berlin, gays and lesbians managed to make contact.

Particular images of the sexually dissident – such as the mannish woman or the effeminate man – circulated in different cultures, as did idealized models of the sexually desirable, notably the strong and independent woman typified by Radclyffe Hall or Annemarie Schwarzenbach, and the type of beautiful and muscular young man portrayed by Eugène Jansson. Historical antecedents of 'gay' love from antiquity were passed down, and homosexual men and lesbians (especially before gay liberation) would trace a family tree to the classical civilizations of Europe – allusions that can clearly be seen in the photographs of Wilhelm von Gloeden and in the novels of E. M. Forster. Similarly, in China Chen Weisong referred to the love stories of an ancient emperor and his partner, celebrating a shared culture handed down over the centuries. Ideas spread around the world as well: the photographs of Lionel Wendt, made in Sri Lanka, and of the Japanese Tamotsu Yato, for instance, draw on Western classical and Christian imagery as well as that of Asian cultures.

It is also notable how men and women often sought sexual solace in places far from home, migrating from small towns to big cities, and living for periods in seductive sites from the Mediterranean to distant colonial outposts. Wherever they went, they tried to settle down: consider the cosy domestic arrangements of the Irish-born 'Ladies of Llangollen' in Wales, and of Edward Carpenter and his comradely friends in England, and the succession of residences set up by Donald Friend in Australia, Italy, Ceylon and Bali. In this way they became part of wider national and international cultures: cultures of companionship and 'marriage', of travel and pilgrimage, of wild nightlife and uninhibited passion.

As well as offering an opportunity to recollect lived experiences, then, this gallery of portraits also traces a changing landscape of social mores, cultural contexts and political constraints: it reveals gay lives lived *in* history.

I
ANCIENT ANCESTORS

Khnumhotep and Niankhkhnum *c.* 2400 BCE

What are the earliest 'gay lives' recorded in history? The question is silly. Even a casual reading of scholarship on sex reveals that 'homosexuality' as a term did not emerge until the 19th century. The ways in which people thought about sex and sexuality – and possibly the ways in which they had sex – varied greatly over time and from place to place. It is probable that some men in almost all cultures have experienced emotional and physical desires for other men, just as some women will have felt intimate affection, romance and lust for others of the same sex. Exactly what this meant to them and to others in their societies is seldom entirely clear. A wealth of sources testify to same-sex connections, but the question of how to interpret those documents and artefacts continues to exercise scholars.

One intriguing and ancient instance of intimacy between men dates to 2400 BCE, during the 5th dynasty in Egypt. In 1964 archaeologists discovered an undisturbed tomb in Saqqara: the burial site of Niankhkhnum and Khnumhotep. Several carvings on the walls showed the men looking each other steadily in the eyes, holding hands and locked in an embrace: Khnumhotep's arm was around his companion's shoulder, and Niankhkhnum, in turn, grasped the other's forearm. The inscriptions identify them as 'royal confidants': one man was a manicurist to the king, the other the inspector of manicurists at the royal palace. Other images show the men fowling and fishing, and gathered in the company of their wives and children.

Egyptologists differ in their interpretation of the tomb figures. Some see Khnumhotep and Niankhkhnum as twins, or brothers, or just friends who wished to continue their friendship in the afterlife. There has also been speculation that the carvings reveal a same-sex relationship of a different order. One historian, Greg Reeder, points out that the pose of two men gazing into each other's eyes was uncommon in the iconography of the time; that their embrace is particularly intimate; and that the gestures the two men use follow the artistic conventions that generally unite a husband and wife. Khnumhotep's and Niankhkhnum's spouses seem to play a lesser role in the monument's images than might be expected.

It was assumed that men would marry and procreate, but the Egyptologist R. B. Parkinson has inventoried various references to homosexuality under the pharaohs. Official pronouncements expressed disapproval of sex between men (especially the passive partner), while literary texts were more ambiguous, sometimes revealing good-natured caricature and even humour. 'How lovely is your backside!' remarks Seth to Horus in one tale, in what Parkinson calls a very old 'chat-up line'. Horus's mother, the goddess Isis, warns him against sex with his rival.

Whether Niankhkhnum and Khnumhotep were blood relatives, companionable colleagues or lovers is unimportant. They are worth recalling because of the very indefinable nature of their relationship – an illustration of the porous boundaries in many cultures between affection, friendship, intimacy, and sexual yearning and its realiza-tion. In ancient Egypt, commissioning a tomb and planning its decoration counted among the essential acts of a man's life. In the survival of these carvings for over four millennia, the men's wish to be remembered together has been fulfilled.

David and Jonathan 11th century BCE

Many specialists of biblical exegesis (including believers in the Judaeo-Christian deity), as well as free-thinkers, reject the historicity of the Scriptures. Historians and archaeologists have found so many discrepancies between the narrative and other evidence that, for some, it is difficult to believe what generations of Jews and Christians have considered the inspired word of God, and what fundamentalists still claim as literal truth. Yet even those who do not accept their veracity can read the stories as literary creations of power and drama.

The First Book of Samuel tells of Saul, the first king of the Israelites. After a battle captained by his son and heir apparent, Jonathan, Saul refuses God's order to kill the vanquished – to 'slay both man and woman, infant and suckling, ox and sheep, camel and ass'. In response, God announces to his prophet that he will choose another as Saul's successor, an obscure young shepherd named David. Saul, meanwhile, falls into a great depression and summons the shepherd, who is renowned for singing and harp-playing. The King James Bible describes him as 'ruddy, and withal of a beautiful countenance, and goodly to look to'; Saul 'loved him greatly', and David becomes his court musician and armour-bearer. With battle between the Israelites and Philistines re-engaged, David, though too young to be a regular soldier, distinguishes himself by felling the giant Goliath with a well-aimed stone from his slingshot. Jonathan befriends the hero: 'the soul of Jonathan was knit with the soul of David, and Jonathan loved him as his own soul ... Jonathan stripped himself of the robe that was upon him, and gave it to David, and his garments, even to his sword, and to his bow, and to his girdle'. Saul becomes jealous at the acclaim awarded to David and, again struck with depression, twice tries to kill him; he recovers, however, and gives David command of a thousand men and his daughter's hand in marriage. As bride-price, Saul asks David for a hundred foreskins of the Philistines, covertly hoping that David will die in battle. When a victorious David brings the prize, Saul's daughter weds him.

Saul then tries to persuade Jonathan to kill David, 'but Jonathan Saul's son delighted much in David'. He reveals the plot and ably brings Saul to a change of heart. The good relationship between king and vassal is not to last. Further victories reawaken Saul's ire; he again tries to down David with his javelin, then attempts to have thugs murder him. David takes refuge with the prophet Samuel, but meets secretly with Jonathan – 'thy father certainly knoweth that I have found grace in thine eyes'. Jonathan proposes to sound out his erratic father and, if danger still looms, help David to escape. The two swear loyalty.

When Saul asks after David, Jonathan reports that he has gone home to Bethlehem for a sacrifice. 'Saul's anger was kindled against Jonathan', and he charges: 'Do not I know that thou hast chosen the son of Jesse to thine own confusion', attacking his own son with the handy javelin. The next morning, by a prearranged signal Jonathan warns David, who emerges from hiding for a farewell before his flight: 'they kissed one another, and wept one with another'. David escapes into the wilderness, with Saul's agents in pursuit, but rejoices in the occasional secret meeting with Jonathan. David refuses a chance to kill Saul, only cutting off the bottom of his robe because he will not slay his king, then confronts Saul with deference. Reduced to tears, Saul guarantees his goodwill.

Nevertheless, soon the volatile Saul mounts a further assault. David gives up another opportunity to kill his nemesis, and there is reconciliation. In renewed warfare, the Philistines get the better of the Israelites, take David's two wives captive, kill Jonathan and his brothers, and wound Saul, who commits suicide to avoid capture. A distraught David, hearing of Jonathan's death, rends his clothes, weeps and exclaims: 'O Jonathan, thou wast slain in thine high places. I am distressed for thee, my brother Jonathan: very pleasant hast thou been unto me: thy love to me was wonderful, passing the love of women.'

David fulfilled his destiny to become the Jewish king and to sire a dynasty that supposedly stretched down to Jesus. The tangled story of his relations with the half-mad (or demonically possessed) Saul is the stuff of power politics, conspiracies, warfare, plunder, alliances and rivalries for a crown. Some scholars thus have argued that the oaths between David and Jonathan, the love they declare and the feverish nature of their friendship have more to do with Near Eastern politics and rhetoric than with any homoerotic bond.

Nonetheless, the story has resonated loudly in the homosexual imagination. The shepherd became a figure of legend and art, notably in Michelangelo's larger-than-life marble in Florence, the Renaissance symbol of perfect masculine beauty. The relationship between David and Jonathan, 'passing the love of women', has suggested to many readers of the Scriptures a romantic liaison between two young men sworn to love and parted only by death.

The sex-obsessed Judaeo-Christian tradition has not been kind to homosexuals. The burning of Sodom and Gomorrah, as recorded in the Torah, provided the name for the unnameable sin, and a precedent for God's punishment. In the New Testament St Paul condemned homosexuality as an abomination – a pronouncement followed by later Christian leaders, who damned homosexual acts and sentenced sodomites to repentance or hell, to rectification of their ways or searing punishments in this world and the world to come.

In light of the homophobia of many churches, gay Christians have frequently sought refuge with congregations that do not condemn their yearnings, such as the Catholic Dignity organization, the Metropolitan Community Church or the French group called David et Jonathan. They have also, in amongst the biblical prohibitions against homosexual acts, found some comfort in the story of David and Jonathan, and in the friendship of Ruth and Naomi (Ruth tenderly declared to her mother-in-law and best friend, 'whither thou goest, I will go; and where thou lodgest, I will lodge'). In the New Testament, they find solace and inspiration in the intimacy between Jesus and his 'beloved disciple' – St John, who is often pictured nestling on Jesus' breast at the Last Supper and as witness to his Crucifixion, where Christ confides his follower and his mother Mary to each other's care. Although most biblical scholars and (it goes without saying) traditionalist clerics and scriptural commentators reject the notion of a physical relationship, or even intimacy, between these couples, their tales have often given succour to those who strive to reconcile sexual desires with spiritual beliefs.

Sappho born *c.* 612 BCE

What is known about the life of Sappho fills hardly a paragraph, and her surviving poems, many so fragmentary as to extend to only a few words, cover just thirty or forty pages. Yet she occupies a prominent place in history, as the woman who gave her name to 'sapphism', which today is more commonly called 'lesbianism', after the island of her birth. Well may she have written: 'I think that someone will remember us in another time.'

The facts remain uncertain, but it seems that Sappho was born near the end of the 7th century BCE on Lesbos, in the eastern Aegean; her family was prosperous, though she was orphaned as a child. She lived for most of her life in Mytilene, the island's principal centre, except for a period of exile in Sicily, probably occasioned by her family's political activities. She was married and had a daughter. She had two brothers, and the romantic affair of one of them, who was swindled by a prostitute, troubled her. Legend has embroidered various other details to her biography – that she was unattractive; that she was the head of a school for girls; that she hurled herself off the Leucadian cliff into the sea, suffering unrequited love for a handsome boatman called Phaon – but very little is really known. The suicide, possibly a tardy addition to the Sappho legend, conveniently served those who wished to deny her lesbianism and to suggest that she was a closet heterosexual.

Sappho's poems, even in the truncated form in which they have come down through the ages, speak beautifully of yearning, love, heartbreak and the sensual delights of the Mediterranean. Invocations of the deities remind present-day readers of a classical religion in which the gods could be summoned to bless rather than damn same-sex affections. Images of ambrosia and goblets of wine, the fragrance of myrrh and frankincense, the sound of flutes and lyres, garlands of roses and crocus – even if they were moderately regular accoutrements of daily life in ancient Greece – are romantically evocative.

The poet loved the beauty of young women – 'towards you beautiful girls my thoughts / never alter', she writes in one fragment. She fell in love, and one poem intimates the sexual consummation of her desires. She vividly describes the spine-tingling, sweating, ear-throbbing physical effects of passion. Love also brought pain, and in one of the more complete poems to survive Sappho voices distress that a lover is now drawn to someone else, a man. Elsewhere she addresses a girl several times by name, though with the melancholy of an affair that has come to an end: 'I was in love with you, Atthis, once, long ago'. She calls upon Aphrodite to bring comfort in her lovelorn solitude and to revive a friend's affections. She writes about a wedding, congratulating a bridegroom on his beautiful spouse. Writing as an ageing woman, the poet recalls threading love garlands; she realizes that certain sorts of love have now slipped away, yet mischievously reminds those still in the throes of passion that 'we, too, did such things in our youth'. And she tenderly expresses a hope for her readers in a single-line fragment: 'May you sleep upon your gentle companion's breast.'

Much of our limited knowledge about lesbianism in ancient Greece comes, as the historian Leila Rupp has reminded readers, from a few suggestive images on vases and from the random, sometimes disobliging comments of men often found in Greek comedies. The sexuality of women was of little public import, except where it concerned the pleasures and familial obligations of men, and sex without phallic penetration barely counted as sex at all. Women did not show off their bodies in homosocial settings, as men did in the gymnasiums, and philosophers seldom ennobled passionate feelings between women with the same educative or philosophical mission as that accorded to intercourse between noble men and youths. There is some indication from Plutarch, however, that maidens and older women in Sparta entered into lasting relationships. In one of Lucian's dialogues, a young woman, Leaena, recounts a Sapphic symposium where, after appropriate music-making, she was initiated into a sex triangle with a pair of partnered women, Demonassa and Megilla, the latter of whom happened to hail from Lesbos and took pride in her manliness as she moved to embrace her. For the classical scholar James Davidson, the *mise en scène* implies not only lesbian seduction, but the existence of declared lesbian couples in archaic Greece.

The relative silence about female same-sex love makes Sappho's voice particularly resonant. The shards of her verses offer the first clear expressions of love between women in classical European literature and some of the most tantalizing literary images of lesbianism in the legacy of antiquity. Yet the sentiments painted in her verses are universal. It is no surprise that Sappho has been regularly rediscovered – a lesbian circle in early 20th-century Paris grew so enamoured of the poet that they occasionally dressed in ancient garb and recited her verses in Arcadian gardens, even making a pilgrimage to Lesbos. In the context of the women's movement of the 1960s, Sidney Abbott and Barbara Love wrote a 'liberated view of lesbianism' entitled *Sappho Was a Right-On Woman*. As the classicist Alastair Blanshard has shown, Sappho, like other figures of antiquity connected with love and lust, has become a 'brand', omnipresent in literature and imagery.

Sappho's image appears in many fanciful manifestations. The rather lifeless statue of her in Mytilene, shouldering a lyre, bespeaks pride in the island's native daughter but also discomfort with her sexuality. Indeed, in 2008 the good people of Lesbos mounted a court case, unsuccessfully, to try to ensure that the term 'lesbian' applied only to the residents of the island, not to sapphists. Other statues turn Sappho into an alluring naked seductress, though probably many were meant to lure men rather than women. In other incarnations, she has become a leisured beauty, a stern Victorian bluestocking, a winsome adolescent, an ethereally pastel spirit ascending to the heavens, and a brooding, bare-breasted bard cloaked in mysterious black. The metamorphoses are further proof of Sappho's endurance as honoured poet and lesbian icon.

Socrates *c.* 469–399 BCE

'Greek love' has long been a synonym or euphemism for homosexuality, especially for relations between two males. Much depends on the eye of the beholder, however. Voltaire commented that 'if the love that is called Socratic or Platonic was a virtuous sentiment, then it must be applauded, but if it was debauchery, then one must blush in shame for Greece.' For generations of homosexuals – as illustrated by Oscar Wilde's testimony that love between an older and a younger man, of which he himself was accused, served as the basis of ancient philosophy – the Greek paradigm provided an ennobling model for desires deemed reprobate in contemporary society. Since classical Athens was one of the high points of civilization (so the argument ran), Greek same-sex practices could hardly be ignoble.

Homosexual practices in ancient Greek culture are visible in many forms – figured on vase paintings, described in literature, recorded in history and theorized in philosophy. Those familiar with the Classics (which, until recent times, included most of the Western educated elite) noticed the blatant images of seduction and copulation in Greek art. They knew of the cult of erotic male beauty, developed and displayed by naked athletes on exercise grounds and at athletic contests. They learned of famous male couples in antiquity – Achilles and Patroclus, Harmodius and Aristogeiton, Alexander and Hephaestion – and could retell the feats of the Sacred Band of Thebes, where love between warrior partners steeled their courage. They knew that gods, as well as men, overflowed with homosexual passion, Zeus himself descending to earth to seize the beautiful Ganymede as his cupbearer and lover.

For students of antiquity (especially those who could access unbowdlerized translations), the dialogues of Plato held a special place.

The star of these dialogues was, of course, Socrates, Plato's mentor and one of the most influential of Greek philosophers. Socrates was a 5th-century Athenian who did not write down his words, and biographical information is scarce (the figure who appears in Plato's dialogues is unlikely to be an exact reflection of the real man). He may have been the son of a stonemason and his midwife spouse; scholars are more certain that he performed military service as a heavy-armed infantryman. He married a certain Xanthippe, about whom he was rather critical, and fathered several children. In time he came to dedicate his life to teaching, using the so-called 'Socratic method' to cross-question his students; the resulting dialogues are those recorded by Plato. He eventually incurred the wrath of the city authorities, however, and was arrested on the charge of corrupting the minds of youths and introducing strange gods. In 399 BCE he was condemned to kill himself by drinking hemlock.

Like most men in Athenian society, Socrates would no doubt have had sexual liaisons with young men, and even in old age was said to chase boys. Athenian mores not only tolerated but applauded emotional and sexual intercourse between men, though with certain caveats. In principle this form of sex, known as *paiderastia*, should occur between an adult man and an ephebe, or adolescent from a suitable social class; the older lover (the *erastes*) was meant to play the active role, his partner (the *eromenos*) the passive one, in anal or intercrural sex. The relationship was also ideally one in which the adult oversaw the education and upbringing of his younger friend. When he became an adult, the ephebe would in turn take younger partners of his own. Greek men were expected to marry and to father children, though this did not oblige them to abandon pederastic pursuits.

There has been intense scholarly discussion on the subject of Greek sexuality. David Halperin, for instance, accentuates the penetrative side of sex, emphasizing the unequal nature of the relationship between older and younger men, and its wider context of asymmetrical social relations. James Davidson, however, convincingly finds a much more varied experience of homosexual love and sex in Greece, and focuses on the romantic, emotional and cultural aspects of the relationships rather than the phallic ones. The Greeks, indeed, displayed an intense form of male bonding and male-to-male attraction that was not simply orgasmic – what Davidson playfully refers to as 'homobesottedness'.

Socrates obviously liked young men. One of them was Charmides, who was Plato's uncle and later took part in an oligarchical revolution. The meeting between the philosopher and Charmides, then an irresistible ephebe, is recounted in the dialogue that bears his name. Socrates swoons when Charmides arrives at the palaestra, or training ground: 'I was quite astonished at his beauty and stature; all the world seemed to be enamoured of him ... and a troop of lovers followed him.' After some unseemly jostling to sit near the young man, Socrates continues: 'I saw inside his cloak and caught on fire and was quite beside myself. And it seemed to me that Cydias was the wisest love-poet when he gave someone advice on the subject of beautiful boys and said that "the fawn should beware lest, while taking a look at the lion, he should provide part of the lion's dinner", because I felt as if I had been snapped up by such a creature.' Alastair Blanshard, a scholar of sexuality in the ancient world, comments that the sexual frisson of the anecdote has a very contemporary feel. It illustrates well that Socrates' interests in youth were not purely, as it were, platonic.

In the *Symposium*, Socrates and his interlocutors discuss love – indeed, the work provides Western literature's classic discourse on the topic. Towards its end, the drinking party and debate are interrupted by the arrival of a merrily inebriated Alcibiades. A local celebrity – aristocratic in parentage, heroic in battle, and a would-be student of philosophy – Alcibiades was the very incarnation of masculine strength and beauty. There is some good-natured verbal jousting between Alcibiades and Socrates, with Alcibiades lamenting that he, handsomest of men, has been unable to seduce Socrates, wisest of the pedagogues. Brains do seem to be winning over brawn when Socrates expostulates the theory of love given to him by a wise woman named Diotima; but her argument, it transpires, is that love of the beautiful object can lead to love of transcendent beauty, a means of moving from the physical to the ideal. It goes without saying that the beloved object showing the way is a handsome youth.

The Platonic, and Greek, concepts of love between men cannot be summed up easily, for, in good philosophical fashion, there was much debate. But Socrates' legacy is enormous. His Athenian vision of beauty, as exemplified by Charmides and Alcibiades, established a standard for the Western world, sculpted in Greek statues and the Neoclassical works they inspired: the slender, finely muscled, beautiful-faced young man. Another Platonic dialogue, the *Phaedrus*, offers not only the picture of a teacher and his student happily conversing on love, but also the vision of a charioteer – a metaphor for the soul – trying to control his horses, which represent spiritual and carnal urges. To latter-day homosexuals, the erotic milieu in which Socrates lived seemed a type of paradise: celebration of the appeal of ephebes; open and unashamed seduction between males; a link between manliness and same-sex intercourse; and examples of heroic male bonding. Plato's explanation that the search for love is a search for one's 'other half' – and that the cloven halves may be male and female, or of the same sex – was taken up by 19th-century theorists who saw homosexuals as a 'third sex'. Socrates' evocation of earthly passions as a way to reach divine enlightenment turns pederasty into philosophy.

Hadrian 76–138 CE
and Antinous *c.* 110–130 CE

O f all the love stories between men in history, that of Hadrian and Antinous is among the most poignant: the relationship between a Roman emperor, the most powerful ruler in the world, and the handsome young man who drowned in the Nile and was made into a god by his grieving lover.

Hadrian was one of the greatest emperors of Rome. He secured the empire when it had reached its widest extent, from Scotland, where his famous wall was erected, to the Sahara, and from the Atlantic to the Euphrates. He prided himself on having ruled without a single war of aggression, unlike his predecessors. He reorganized the empire's administrative, financial and military system; his law code endured for four hundred years; and among his most impressive monuments are his mausoleum, now known as the Castel Sant'Angelo, and the rebuilt Pantheon in Rome, and a grand villa at Tivoli.

Historians know little about Antinous. He was probably born around 110 CE in Bithynium (also called Claudopolis), a town in the fairly remote Roman province of Bithynia, now part of Turkey. Antinous, like many residents of the eastern empire, was of Greek genealogy and culture, though perhaps with some admixture of Levantine ancestry. Images show a young man with a strong chest and shoulders, curly hair, a roundish face with sensual lips, and overall startling beauty. Hadrian may have met him while touring the East in 123, but that is uncertain, as are the circumstances in which Antinous went to Rome, though he may initially have been a page at the imperial court. In any case, Hadrian fell in love with the ephebe. A set of bas reliefs suggests that they hunted together (hunting was the emperor's favourite sport), and Antinous may have been initiated into the esoteric Eleusinian mysteries when he travelled with Hadrian to Athens.

The same voyage took Hadrian and his retinue from Greece to Asia Minor, Palestine and on to Egypt, where it ended tragically. After visiting Alexandria, the imperial group sailed down the Nile, where Antinous died in mysterious circumstances. It could simply have been a terrible accident, but one suggestion is that Antinous committed suicide on the anniversary of the death of the god Osiris, sacrificing himself after reports of dire auguries, in order to propitiate the gods of the Nile, prolong the emperor's life and assure his good fortune. Over the course of the centuries, there have also been suggestions that it was a rival for the emperor's favour who had Antinous killed, or even that Hadrian himself had sacrificed Antinous – according to one gruesome interpretation, so that he could divine the future from his victim's entrails.

On the death of his beloved, Hadrian (in the words of a Roman historian writing a century later) 'lamented him like a woman'. The emperor made the small town where Antinous died, Besa, into a new city named Antinoöpolis, complete with a theatre, gymnasium and the other constructions of a Roman metropolis. He proclaimed Antinous a god and promoted his worship with the building of temples. Yearly athletic contests were held in his memory. The emperor had coins minted and medals struck with the image of his friend, and statues of Antinous graced cities around the empire. At Tivoli, Hadrian erected a shrine, and for an obelisk – which perhaps stood first in Antinoöpolis, then was moved to Tivoli, and now can be found in Rome's Pincio Gardens – he composed an epitaph, engraved in hieroglyphics, to 'Osiris Antinous, the just, [who] grew to a youth with a beautiful countenance, on whom the eyes rejoiced'. A new star was declared to be the soul of Antinous flown to the heavens, and a new variety of lotus was said to have bloomed at the moment of his death.

Homosexual relations were not uncommon in the Roman Empire, generally between an older (and free) man and a younger man (or slave), with the convention that the senior partner must play the active role in sexual intercourse. Antinous was apparently not the first of Hadrian's male partners, though Hadrian was also married, but the intensity and longevity of their relationship was remarkable. Roman history offers no other example of the deification of a male lover.

The cult of Antinous spread widely within the empire, perhaps aided by the desire of Greeks to secure the emperor's good graces in honouring their kinsman. For more than two hundred years Antinous was worshipped widely, but in time another god arrived to challenge his popularity. By the late 300s images of the crucified Christ had displaced those of the comely Greek in houses of worship.

Christian commentators, not surprisingly, condemned the worship of Antinous and the sinful relationship that it commemorated, St Athanasius writing about 'Hadrian's minion and slave of his unlawful pleasures', the 'loathsome instrument of his master's lust'. Later generations responded differently to the emperor and his beloved, especially as the wonderful statues, busts, coins and jewels decorated with his features came to light. Indeed, Antinous is one of the most depicted figures of antiquity – as boyish or virile, as the Egyptian Osiris or the Greek god Dionysus, and in many other guises. In the 1700s Johann Joachim Winckelmann, a noted Neoclassicist, the father of art history and a homosexual, described the Mondragone head of Antinous (a sculpture now in the Louvre) as 'the glory and crown of art in this age as in all others'.

For Winckelmann and for others like him, the beautiful Antinous, and the partnership between the Bithynian boy and the Roman emperor, exerted a special fascination. John Addington Symonds's *Sketches and Studies in Italy and Greece*, published in the 1870s, included a learned and evocative essay on Antinous and the enigma of his death. Symonds's view was that 'Hadrian had loved

Antinous with a Greek passion', and he compared the couple to Zeus and Ganymede, Achilles and Patroclus, and Alexander and Hephaestion. He likened Antinous also to St Sebastian, the early Christian whose body pierced with arrows became both a religious and a gay symbol: 'Both were saints: the one of decadent Paganism, the other of mythologising Christianity. According to the popular beliefs to which they owed their canonisation, both suffered death in the bloom of earliest manhood for the faith that burned in them.' In 1915, a long poem by the gay Portuguese Fernando Pessoa painted a picture of the bereaved emperor and the communion of moderns with ancients: 'His love is on a universal stage. / A thousand unborn eyes weep with his misery.' In words of poetic power put into the mouth of the emperor, Marguerite Yourcenar's 1951 novel *Mémoires d'Hadrien* recreates the golden age of Hadrian and Antinous' union.

An exhibition held at the Henry Moore Museum in Leeds in 2006 focused on 'Antinous: The Face of the Antique', and a highly successful show on Hadrian at the British Museum in London boasted a catalogue essay that began, straightforwardly, 'Hadrian was gay'. Both provided a new perspective on the place of Antinous in the life of the emperor, and on representations of the young man in art.

Chen Weisong 1625–1682

In the West, homosexuals looked back to real-life or mythological figures from Greco-Roman times for examples of same-sex love. In imperial China, where homoerotic relations continued to flourish without European constraints, men and women also referred to famous individuals of ancient times, honoured rulers and ancestors who engaged in same-sex practices and loves.

Chen Weisong was not the earliest homosexual figure of repute in China, but verses telling the story of this renowned 17th-century poet use classical figures to celebrate his relationship with a young man – the young man who also forms the subject of Chen's own poems. Chen was born in Yixing (in the present-day Jiangsu province) and completed the arduous examinations to enter the imperial civil service, winning appointment under Emperor Kangxi. One of his major professional accomplishments as a mandarin was to compile a history of the Ming dynasty. Chen also composed 1,600 poems in the *ci* style, which uses a set pattern of characters and tones; he wrote about the common people, national affairs and his feelings of desire.

Chen's great love and life companion was Xu Ziyun (1644–1675), nicknamed 'Purple Clouds', who earned a reputation as the most alluring actor of his age. They met in a garden in 1658, when Chen was 35 years old and Purple Clouds, then still a page boy, was almost 15. It seems to have been love at first sight, and thereafter they lived together as a couple within Chen's entourage (which included a wife, two concubines and several children).

Many of Chen's poems are about his lover. Purple Clouds' departure on a trip to visit his parents inspired a suite of twenty 'Lyrics of Wistful Bitterness' in farewell, recalling their pleasures and bemoaning Chen's empty bed and cold nights. When they were reunited, he wrote happily about 'my soulmate of this life'. He describes the handsomeness of the one whose 'raven locks fall down his jade-white temples', and joins his love for the youth's beauty with his love of art. Artists, too, captured Purple Clouds' image: what the sinologist Wu Cuncun considers the best picture shows him sitting on a rock, a flute close to hand, his long hair coiled in a knot and a touch of rouge on his face, which wears an indolent and contemplative expression.

Chen helped Purple Clouds set up his own family; although he appeared somewhat jealous of the young man's spouse, the relationship between the men did not alter. When Chen was transferred to an administrative post in Henan province, Purple Clouds followed him. When Purple Clouds died, after seventeen years of companionship, Chen mourned him inconsolably and continued writing poems memorializing his lover.

Fellow poets honoured the relationship between Purple Clouds and Chen Weisong. Wu Cuncun quotes from a work by Wu Qing, who contributed to an anthology of poems compiled in honour of Purple Clouds. It reads in part:

> After playing a tune on the pipe,
> Purple-Clouds' cheeks flush.
> Pretending musical appreciation,
> Amorous glances fly between them.
> Keeping intimate company over all these years.
> Every morning and every night their souls firmly embraced,
> A spell of love invaded Chen's romantic verse.
> Never believing a home could not be made by male-love,
> Dreaming of a pillow shared in the fairyland.
> Nothing of 'the cut sleeve' or 'shared peach' has been missed …

The last line establishes a connection between Chen and his lover and the most famous figures of ancient Chinese homosexuality. The reference to the 'shared peach' derives from an anecdote about Duke Ling of Wei (534–492 BCE), a provincial ruler and contemporary of Confucius. A young courtier, Mizi Xia, won his favour. According to an often cited source, one day 'Mizi Xia was strolling with the ruler in an orchard and, biting into a peach and finding it sweet, he stopped eating and gave the remaining half to the ruler to enjoy. "How sincere is your love for me!" exclaimed the ruler. "You forgot your own appetite and think only of giving me good things to eat!"' Although the ruler's passions eventually cooled, Mizi Xia's name became closely associated with homosexuality.

The second famous classical story, that of 'the cut sleeve', also comes from the imperial court, and illustrates the fondness of the Han emperor Ai (27–1 BCE) for Dong Xian. According to Brett Hinsch, who has written a study of homosexuality in China, one short passage about their love 'is the most influential in the Chinese homosexual tradition: "Emperor Ai was sleeping in the daytime with Dong Xian stretched out across his sleeve. When the emperor wanted to get up, Dong Xian was still asleep. Because he did not want to disturb him, the emperor cut off his own sleeve and got up. His love and thoughtfulness went this far!"' The 'passion of the shared peach' and the 'passion of the cut sleeve' thus became bywords for the homosexual behaviour that was commonplace in ancient China. At least ten emperors of the ancient Han dynasty openly engaged in same-sex affairs, male brothels operated for centuries in Beijing and other cities, and male marriages were occasionally celebrated in the province of Fujian. Homoerotic poetry abounded, with the works of Ruan Ji, a 3rd-century poet and one of the most revered authors in the Chinese canon, among the best known. Many scholar–officials like Chen consorted openly with male partners, and jokes and caricatures poked fun at mandarins for losing their hearts to handsome youths.

Wu Cuncun has shown that male beauty and sexual favours were assets that could be traded for social advancement and preferment.

Certain categories of men – actors, opera singers, retainers and disciples – were generally viewed as potential objects of homosexual desire. Homosexual liaisons, like those between men and women, entered into the Confucian pattern of relations between superiors and inferiors – fathers and children, rulers and subjects, elder and younger – on which Chinese ethics rested. Whether a man took a dominant or subordinate role (in both sexual and social terms) was more important than the gender of his partner in structuring intimate relations. Chinese men were expected eventually to marry and to produce children, especially all-important male heirs, but such unions did not impede the keeping of female or male concubines or the enjoyment of more casual encounters. Indeed, to have a young male partner in the late Ming and early Qing periods, Wu adds, was a sign of success and social standing, and many literati considered homosexual behaviour a praiseworthy and romantic practice.

The great changes that overwhelmed China during the 19th century – the Opium Wars, foreign incursions and Westernization – began to break down old ideas and practices, although a major homoerotic novel was published in the late 1840s, and in 1860 the city of Tianjin was reputedly home to thirty-five male brothels with a total of eight hundred employees. Sun Yat-sen's revolution of 1911 and Mao Zedong's of 1949 dealt fatal blows to the sexual traditions of imperial China. Only in recent years has a new gay culture emerged, albeit in the face of opposition from a state ideology that continues to regard homosexuality as deviant. It is more Westernized than traditional, but nevertheless harks back to the affections of Chen and Purple Clouds, and further back to Ling, Ai and their beloveds.

2
FROM THE MIDDLE AGES
TO THE ENLIGHTENMENT

Saints Sergius and Bacchus 4th century CE

In 1994, the year that his life was cut short by AIDS at the age of 47, the gay, Catholic historian John Boswell published *Same-Sex Unions in Premodern Europe*. Basing his work on fifty-odd Greek and Cyrillic manuscripts from the 6th to the 16th centuries, Boswell brought to light ceremonies devised by the Eastern Church for joining together two men, rites remarkably like those of a wedding. The two men came before a congregation, their right hands laid one on top of another on the Gospel book and sometimes entwined in the priest's stole, their left hands holding candles or crosses. Prayers were offered, and they embraced each other and the celebrant, and circled the altar. Although there were often no vows or an exchange of rings, as in heterosexual weddings, Boswell pointed out that these two standard features of marriage did not become common until much later.

Boswell also identified pairs of men who, whether they took part in such ceremonies or not, typified same-sex unions in the early church. Sergius and Bacchus were prime examples of a Christian partnership. The two were officers in the army of a pagan Roman emperor in the 4th century. According to one hagiography, 'being as one in their love for Christ, they were also undivided from each other in the army of the united, united not by the way of nature, but in the manner of faith'. Once their religious heresy was discovered, they were ordered to sacrifice to Jupiter. When they refused, they were ritually humiliated; the emperor 'ordered their belts cut off, their tunics and all other military garb removed, the gold torcs taken from around their necks, and women's clothing placed on them'. The men's continued defence of their faith infuriated the emperor, who had them cast into chains and banished to a distant province.

Strengthened by the visit of an angel when they again refused to recant, Bacchus was flogged to death. Sergius, 'deeply depressed and heartsick over the loss of Bacchus, wept and cried out, "No longer, brother and fellow soldier, will we chant together, 'Behold, how good and how pleasant it is for brethren to dwell together in unity.' You have been unyoked from me and gone up to heaven, leaving me alone on earth, bereft, without comfort."' That night Bacchus, dressed in his military uniform, appeared in a vision to Sergius, saying, 'Why do you grieve and mourn, brother? If I have been taken from you in body, I am still with you in the bond of union.' Once again refusing to deny Christ, Sergius was tortured and beheaded. Posthumously, the two men, 'like stars shining joyously over the earth', became the objects of a cult. For their unflagging faith, and for the miracles they performed, the church canonized them, and their friendship was lauded in stories about the lives of the saints.

Were the saints a gay couple, and were there same-sex unions in early European history? In recent years debate has raged in Western countries about 'gay marriage', a broad phrase encompassing arrangements from civil registration of partnerships to legal recognition and the sacramental union of two individuals of the same sex. Gay men and lesbians now demand the same civil rights enjoyed by heterosexuals in partnerships, such as equal rights of inheritance. Many countries (including most of the western European states and several further east, Australia and New Zealand, a number in South America, the USA and Canada, Taiwan and South Africa) recognize same-sex marriages, although in others acceptance is conceded only by local governments and is limited to partnership agreements, and in still other countries recognition is barely conceivable.

In addition to the state's legitimization, some religiously inclined homosexuals yearn for religious benediction for their relationships. Religious groups other than the more liberal Protestant denominations, however, have refused to accept gay marriage. Clerics, indeed, have lobbied legislators to define marriage as the union of a man and a woman. In the words of the Anglican *Book of Common Prayer*, a wedding ceremony serves 'to join together this Man and this Woman in holy Matrimony; which is an honourable estate, instituted of God, signifying unto us the mystical union that is betwixt Christ and his Church'. A gay union, for conservatives, goes against the laws of God as well as the laws of nature.

It seems likely that Sergius and Bacchus did not exist in reality. The Greek-language *Passion* document that forms the basis of their story – its dating remains uncertain, but it was probably written a century or so after their supposed death dates, and was not translated into English until Boswell appended it to his volume – may have been a composite account of saintly lives and legends. Even if they actually did live, there is little evidence of romantic involvement, let alone that they had a sexual relationship, although Boswell adroitly drew on every shade of meaning to suggest an amorous partnership and church sanction for such a friendship. Churchly blessing of partnerships between men certainly existed, however, even if, as Boswell noted, it was mostly confined to the Eastern Church. These ceremonies of *adelphopoiesis* – 'brother-making' or 'brotherment' – may have been intended primarily to provide sanction for kinship unions or familial adoption.

Boswell's book, not surprisingly, provoked much controversy, its conclusions welcomed by gay Christians but rejected by church leaders and many scholars. Further evidence of religiously blessed unions, of 'brother-making', has since been found in the Latin

Catholic Church. Recent scholarship, in fact, has tended to give more credence to Boswell's interpretation, or at least to the possibility that these rites could in some instances consecrate romantic or sexual partnerships.

Sergius and Bacchus remain emblems, in the religious imagination, of friendship, Christian devotion and martyrdom; to homosexual believers, they can be venerated as gay saints. If one assumes that Sergius and Bacchus were 'gay' – and there is no reason always to assume that a couple of men was *not* – then they provide an interesting model.

Whatever their historical or mythical status, the renewed attention given to Sergius and Bacchus shows the persistence of a desire to identify gay ancestors and to prove that Christianity has not always been as intolerant of same-sex relationships as it would appear. The debates surrounding the publication of Boswell's book, and the story of Sergius and Bacchus, underline the continued role of religion in structuring popular attitudes towards homosexuality and gay unions. The words of the brotherhood ceremonies discovered by Boswell, whatever the exact nature of the unions they hallowed, provide templates for expressions of dedication and loyalty that resonate with modern same-sex couples.

Aelred of Rievaulx *c.* 1110–1167

M edieval monasticism and homoerotic sentiments are not usually seen as conjoined, but a certain type of intimacy between men, including those in holy orders – chaste, in principle – was lauded by Christian writers. St Aelred of Rievaulx is the author of the major philosophical treatise about 'spiritual friendship'. Born into a prosperous family in Northumberland around 1110, he was educated at the court of the king of Scotland and, in his mid-twenties, joined the reformist Cistercian order set up by St Bernard of Clairvaux. In 1147 he became abbot of its monastery in Rievaulx, Yorkshire.

In an early work, Aelred wrote of his close friendship with another monk, Simon, who had recently died, and in *De spirituali amicitia* ('On Spiritual Friendship') he developed his ideas on friendship in the form of three dialogues. In the prologue, he refers enigmatically to a youthful time when 'I gave my whole soul to affection and devoted myself to love amid the ways and vices with which that age is wont to be threatened'; now he understands true friendship, however, and wishes to share his thoughts with his disciples. His interlocutor for the first dialogue, 'my beloved Ivo', died before the second was composed. There, Aelred evokes Ivo's 'fond memory ... his constant love and affection' – one of several intimate friends Aelred recalls, and about whom the symposium participants express great interest. His companion for the second and third dialogues is named Walter; they are joined by Gratian, and Aelred jokes with Walter that Gratian 'is more friendly to you than you thought'.

Aelred divides friendship into carnal, worldly and spiritual. 'Carnal' is not so much defined as physical, however, except by metaphor, since 'the real beginning of carnal friendship proceeds from an affection which like a harlot directs its step after every passer-by'.

It is a lightweight, promiscuous connection inferior to more noble forms of friendship. Worldly friendship seeks advantage and thus has particular self-serving motives, but spiritual friendship aims higher. It is an ideal union between two beings, similar to the union between a believer and Christ. Indeed, Aelred writes that 'man from being a friend of his fellow man becomes the friend of God' – a progression from the terrestrial to the heavenly that recalls the Socratic notion of love for the physically beautiful leading to love for the ideals of Beauty, Goodness and Truth. For Aelred, 'your friend is the companion of your soul, to whose spirit you join and attach yours, and so associate yourself that you wish to become one instead of two, since he is one to whom you entrust yourself as to another self, from whom you hide nothing, from whom you fear nothing.' The spiritual friend is also someone to whom nothing, save a sinful act, must be denied; it is a partnership, based on careful selection and testing, that expresses itself through eternal loyalty and shared affection, 'an inward pleasure that manifests itself exteriorly'.

Aelred's dialogues allude to Cicero's classical treatise *De amicitia* ('On Friendship') and to the Bible, including a couple of extended references to the exemplary friendship that existed between David and Jonathan. It is noticeable that his portrayal of friendship seems to relate exclusively to men: there is only one real reference to a link between a bride and a bridegroom, and an ordinary marital union is never compared to Aelred's model of higher friendship. This is not surprising in the context of a monastic community, but nevertheless implies that his view of true friendship is a relationship achieved between men, not between the sexes.

Nothing in Aelred's dialogues, to be sure, hints at sexual expression. His Christian beliefs would hardly have sanctioned such a suggestion, and neither would the politics of his time, when the sons and the grandson of William the Conqueror were damningly rumoured to be sodomites. Rather, Aelred is talking about a perfect, divine sort of friendship, which he concedes is rarely reachable. The form in which his ideas are voiced in fact describes what many – homosexual or heterosexual – might see as the perfect partnership between two people joined by matrimony or in a similar union. For most, however, his ideal is so pure and abstracted as to be not only near unobtainable, but also bloodless.

Other clerics gave voice in verse and letters to their desire for spiritual and occasionally for physical companionship. Marbod of Rennes, an early 12th-century French bishop, wrote poems about handsome boys, though he would seem, in such works as 'An Argument against Copulation between People of Only One Sex', to reject the physical expression of love for young men. Another, roughly contemporaneous French bishop in the so-called Loire School of poets, Baudri of Bourgueil, wrote more yearningly to one young friend: 'If you wish to take up lodging with me, I will divide my heart and breast with you. I will share with you anything of mine that can be divided; if you command it, I will share my very soul.' Whether such expressions are interpreted as epistolary conventions, spiritual effusions or intimations of a carnal desire, repressed or consummated, may depend both on scholarly analysis and on the empathy of later readers. They remain touching panegyrics of what are, at least, especially close bonds of friendship between two men.

The amorous poems of Hilary the Englishman, who lived in the early 1100s as a canon at Ronceray in Angers, do not embed intimacy with young men in the usual spiritual coverings. 'To a Boy of Angers' includes such lines as 'I have thrown myself at your knees, / With my own knees bent, my hands joined; / As one of your suitors, / I use both tears and prayers'. In 'To an English Boy' he pays a particular compliment: 'You are completely handsome; there is no flaw in you / Except this worthless decision to devote yourself to chastity'. Such lines suggest that the ethereal bonds praised by Aelred occasionally encompassed more earthly desires.

Michelangelo Buonarroti 1475–1564

Michelangelo was born into a society that lauded intimate friendships between men but punished sodomitical activities, a world
in which present-day ideas of gender, sexuality and homosexuality did
not apply. Neoplatonic humanism, which pervaded Renaissance life,
viewed very highly the communion between men in which chaste
love offered a pathway to discovery and appreciation of the good,
the true and the beautiful. Affectionate affinity between men was a
hallmark of learning and culture shared by philosophers, poets and
artists. Church and state nevertheless condemned sodomy, punishing
it with imprisonment or even execution. The city of Florence, where
Michelangelo spent much of his life, had set up an 'Office of the
Night' in 1432 to police sodomy. Nonetheless, a study by Michael
Rocke, a historian of homosexuality in Renaissance Florence, has
shown that the interdiction of same-sex activities between men seems
to have been more honoured in the breach: some 17,000 men were
investigated for sodomy between 1432 and 1502. As many as one
in two Florentine men under the age of 30 came to the authorities'
attention in connection with the vice.

Manly love and sodomitical sex were thus both common in the
Renaissance, and the borders between them were not always apparent.
Michelangelo seems to have had few, if any, sexual relationships of a
physical type, with either men or women. His emotional passion for
Vittoria Colonna, a noblewoman, was an important episode in his
life, but young men dominated as objects of his yearnings, foremost
among them Tommaso de' Cavalieri.

Michelangelo met the handsome Roman nobleman when he was
23, and the celebrated artist already in his late fifties. Cavalieri gave
Michelangelo his friendship and affection, though without the same

intensity that Michelangelo felt, and if Michelangelo craved physical consummation, Cavalieri seems to have withheld it.

Michelangelo was an accomplished poet, and his verses reveal details of their relationship. He was absolutely besotted with Cavalieri, 'he who makes night of day / eclipsing the sun with his fair and charming features'; the poet devised a neat pun to say that 'an armed cavalier's prisoner I remain'. Cavalieri's mere presence ignited a fire in Michelangelo, enchanted by a veritable obsession – 'for whatever is not you is not my good' – and he writes of 'my sweet and longed-for lord'. There is a hint that such ardour violated canons of proper behaviour: 'What I yearn for and learn from your fair face / is poorly understood by mortal minds'; and 'the evil, cruel, and stupid rabble / point the finger at others for what they feel themselves' – Michelangelo did indeed have to defend himself against rumours that he engaged in sodomy. Alluding to Neoplatonic Christian sentiment, he declared: 'A violent burning for prodigious beauty / is not always a source of harsh and deadly sin, / if then the heart is left so melted by it / that a divine dart can penetrate it quickly'. Although Cavalieri's reserved reciprocation brought pain, his intimacy also provided fulfilment: 'I'm much dearer to myself than I used to be; since I've gotten you in my heart, I value myself more, / as a stone to which carving has been added / is worth more than its original rock.'

The art historian James Saslow has shown that Michelangelo put his love for Cavalieri into his art as well as his writing. A homoerotically coded image to which Renaissance artists often returned was the myth of Jupiter and Ganymede, in which the king of the gods swooped down from the heavens in the form of an eagle to capture a beautiful youth as his cupbearer and lover. A series of drawings that Michelangelo made for Cavalieri picture the eagle and the young man in erotic detail. Cavalieri wrote to Michelangelo that the drawings gave him great pleasure, and they also won admiration from the *cognoscenti*. Saslow argues that the drawings were a philosophical gift exemplifying both Neoplatonic and Christian ideals, but they were also emblems of Michelangelo's homoerotic passion and love for Cavalieri, the upward transport of joy with which he burned.

Michelangelo's art is replete with handsome men, from muscular archers to a sensual dying slave. His monumental sculpture of David, completed in Florence in 1504, stands as one of the most dramatic and appealing images of a young man in the history of art, combining the ideal of classical male beauty with an allusion to the strength and courage of the ancient Israelite who was Jonathan's beloved friend. It is not surprising that, by the 19th century, Michelangelo was seen, in the words of the art historian Lene Østermark-Johansen, as a 'patron saint of sexual inversion'.

Nearly four decades after the *David*, Vatican officials were so scandalized by the nudity in Michelangelo's *Last Judgment*, the fresco he painted for the Sistine Chapel in Rome, that they eventually hired another artist to paint in genital-hiding drapery. Research by Elena Lazzarini has suggested that Michelangelo's models for the men who people the painting were rugged manual workers he met during visits to Roman baths, which in addition to providing bathing facilities, massages and rudimentary medical care also served as places of male and female prostitution. In frequenting the rough workmen of Rome, pining with love for Cavalieri, and expressing his attraction for the male through the archetypes of pagan and Judaeo-Christian male beauty, Michelangelo represented much of the homoerotic culture of the Renaissance.

The dome of St Peter's and the *Pietà* inside the basilica, the paintings of the Sistine Chapel, and the Medici Chapel and Laurentian Library in Florence are some of the works that made Michelangelo one of Europe's greatest and most versatile cultural figures. He had an exceptionally long life, and Tommaso de' Cavalieri – by then a married man and Michelangelo's friend for over thirty years – was one of those at his bedside when he died.

Michel de Montaigne 1533–1592

'If you ask me to say why I loved him, I feel that it can only be explained by saying: because it was him, because it was me,' said Michel de Montaigne, simply but profoundly, to explain his friendship for Étienne de La Boétie. The two met at a 'great crowded town festival' in the late 1550s, though Montaigne was already familiar with La Boétie, born in 1530, from his reputation as a brilliant young writer. A few years his junior, Montaigne was the scion of a merchant family in Gascony who would become a councillor in the *parlement* of Bordeaux, the city's mayor, and – with his *Essays* – one of the major literary figures of the French Renaissance. He and La Boétie immediately entered into a relationship that lasted for four years, until La Boétie's death from the plague.

Montaigne's essays range over topics as diverse as cannibals, old age, drunkenness, education, glory and thumbs. One of them, *De l'amitié* (1580), is generally known in English as 'On Friendship', although the editor of one version (for Penguin Classics) renders the title as 'On Affectionate Relationships', thus underlining the particular nature of the friendship on which the work focuses. Montaigne reviews various types of friendship, all of which seem limited, save one. That between father and son is constrained by parental obligations and respect. Love between brothers may be muddled by the clash of different characters or by varying trajectories in life. Love for a woman finds its expression in the passing 'flames of passion', and Montaigne, sharing the views of many of his time, doubts that any woman can really contract the 'holy bond of friendship' that offers a true meeting of minds and is thus the province of men. He then discusses Greek love. Though he characterizes *paiderastia*, the love practised by the ancients, as 'rightly abhorrent to our manners', Montaigne's real concern is the disequilibrium that exists in a partnership between men of different ages and with different levels of experience. He concedes, however, that in its best examples Greek love could lead to an initiation into philosophy, respect for religion and loyalty to the state. He adds that such unions could indeed be good, and he quotes Cicero: 'Love is the striving to establish friendship on the external signs of beauty.'

Montaigne then turns to consideration of the ideal type of love, represented as that between La Boétie and himself: 'In the friendship which I am talking about, souls are mingled out and confounded in so universal a blending that they efface the seam which joins them together so that it cannot be found.' This is a selfless friendship, one man ready to give all for his friend, everything 'genuinely common to them both', an exclusive friendship so strong that it cannot be replicated or divided with other acquaintances: 'One single example of it is moreover the rarest thing in the world.' Thus Montaigne mourned the loss of his own friend, with no consolation possible.

'It is not my concern to tell the world how to behave (plenty of others do that)', Montaigne declares; but he slyly mentions that, 'in my bed, beauty comes before virtue'. In fact, he was married and the father of several children, and nothing suggests that he had a sexual relationship with La Boétie – that he was, in the parlance of his age, a 'sodomite'. Such physical congress would perhaps have been 'abhorrent' – a sin in the eyes of a Catholic – but also a heinous crime that could have incurred execution. However, one should not assume that an 'affectionate friendship' such as Montaigne professed for La Boétie excluded some erotic component.

In the law codes of many countries (in Britain until the 19th century, for instance), conviction for sodomy required that prosecutors prove penetration by one man of another and ejaculation, an awkward piece of evidence to procure. This demand has continued to weigh the argument about homosexuality in the past on lust rather than love, and some writers still insist on finding stains on the sheets: men are guilty of heterosexuality unless it is proved otherwise.

George Haggerty, in a study of friendship in early modern Europe, has suggested another approach that might have won sympathy from Montaigne: refusing distinctions between genital and emotional relations 'to rewrite our understanding of male–male desire, not only in terms of sodomy and sodomitical relations but also in terms of love'. In examining masculinity and heroic friendships, among other sorts of bonding in the 17th and 18th centuries, Haggerty intimates that love between men was commonplace and immensely strong, and that such emotional attachments are actually more threatening to conventional society than sodomitical acts: 'Two men having sex threatens no one. Two men in love: that begins to threaten the very foundations of heterosexist culture.'

Haggerty's work on *Men in Love* finds company with other scholarly treatments of masculine unions, notably Alan Bray's *The Friend*, which also stresses the importance of bonds between men in early modern Europe, emotionally intense relationships not devoid of physical expressiveness and an erotic charge. Fond comradeship, intellectual collaboration, warm correspondence, and occasionally joint burial in the same tomb provided expressions of such friendships as those vaunted in Montaigne's writings and symbolized by his affection for La Boétie.

Antonio Rocco 1586–1653

Antonio Rocco, born in the Abruzzo region of Italy, studied in Padua, Perugia and Rome, and became a friar in Venice, where he lived the rest of his life. He taught philosophy and rhetoric, and published various learned treatises, especially on Aristotelian thought. He also participated in one of the Venetian Republic's major cultural institutions, the Accademia degli Incogniti, whose members were known for their free-thinking views.

Rocco was identified in the 1800s as the author of *L'Alcibiade fanciullo a scola* ('Alcibiades the Schoolboy') – perhaps the most extraordinary dissertation on homosexuality in early modern Europe. Written in 1630 and tentatively published in 1651, it attracted immediate condemnation from the Church, and all but ten or twelve copies of the second edition were destroyed (no copies remain of the first edition). The work resurfaced in a French translation in 1862, only to be banned, then was reissued in Brussels four years later. It was quoted by the homosexual emancipationist and sexologist Karl Heinrich Ulrichs and the explorer Richard Burton, but not fully translated into English until the early twenty-first century.

Rocco's work is a dialogue between a teacher, Philotimos, and a student whom he is trying to seduce, Alcibiades – the name of the youth alluding to Socrates' pupil. Scholars have debated the work's purpose, asking whether it was a parody, satire, a 'carnivalesque' book written for entertainment, an exercise in libertinism and pornography, an exposé, a metaphorical and coded *mise en scène* about the teaching and learning of rhetoric, or a serious discussion and defence of homosexuality.

Alcibiades the Schoolboy opens with a long and detailed description of the beauty of the young man, who is pictured as perfect in almost every sense. Alcibiades' only fault is that, although he gives in to caressing and kissing, he will not consent to the ultimate act of intercourse so desired by his teacher. Philotimos proceeds to provide a convincing argument of why his pupil should relent. He wittily demolishes the idea that sodomy is unnatural; he explains that God punished the wicked cities of Sodom and Gomorrah not for sex but for other crimes; he calls upon historical and mythological examples to show that homosexual sex has won the favour of gods and great men. Taking a misogynistic tack, he demonstrates how male-to-male intercourse is superior to coitus with women. Examples from other cultures show that sodomy is widespread in civilization. Philotimos uses gastronomic metaphors to vaunt the gourmandise of gay sex. He promises the young man that he will experience great pleasure, and – in another wickedly devious approach – says that semen deposited in the anus goes straight to the brain, so sodomy is an ideal method of tuition. Finally the youth drops his robe, and the book concludes with a full-blown description of the student's felicitous lesson in oral and anal intercourse.

The tale of winning Alcibiades' mind and body provides at once a philosophical tale and an example of erotic literature. The genres of erotic literature and pornography – variations on the same theme – play an important part in the history of writing and in the lives of many people. Despite frequently being censored and censured by public authorities and moralists, homosexual erotic literature has always circulated among connoisseurs, albeit often covertly, under 'brown-paper wrappers' and earlier disguises. In the 18th century the Marquis de Sade and his compatriot Restif de la Bretonne penned erotic works portraying a formidable variety of sexual scenarios. The 19th and early 20th centuries proved more puritanical, but erotic literature continued to be passed around by *cognoscenti* and kept under close surveillance in the special collections of libraries.

Only with gay liberation – and the liberation of publishing about homosexuality – did some works come out of the secret libraries. An example from Victorian England is *Teleny, or The Reverse of the Medal*, written around 1890 (and occasionally attributed to Oscar Wilde), which tells the story of a convoluted but sexually intense affair between a Frenchman and a Hungarian. A French parallel is the 1911 novella *Pédérastie passive: Mémoires d'un enculé* ('Passive Pederasty: The Memoirs of a Buggered Man'), like the *Alcibiade* a mixture of philosophy and pornography. The more scabrous passages in Rocco's little book are the ancestors of such works and countless later erotic and 'one-hand' novels.

Rocco's work also contributes to the body of theories surrounding homosexuality. Its dialogue form creates a link between Plato's works and André Gide's early 20th-century apologia for homosexuality, *Corydon* (1924). Like Gide, and such commentators on homosexuality as Edward Carpenter and Magnus Hirschfeld, Rocco as a philosopher of homosexuality is concerned with the historical antecedence of same-sex relations, the debate on whether they are natural or not (and whether they should be banned if *contra naturam*), and the question of pleasure. He boldly challenges scientists, priests and traditional educators. Moreover, Philotimos' rhetoric suggests that a self-assumed homosexual identity, and not just the practice of engaging in sodomitical acts, already existed in the 17th century. Homosexuality was, in his view, natural for the construction of a healthy body and a healthy mind.

Yet another theme – a delicate one – finds illustration in *Alcibiade*. Nowadays, Philotimos could be indicted, and probably convicted, for sexual abuse and for taking advantage of his pedagogical position (even if, ultimately, his pupil consented). Alcibiades' age is unclear, but Philotimos might now be charged with paedophilia as well. However, before passing sentence on sexual crimes, readers and historians must place Rocco and Alcibiades into the context of a time when philosophically intimate relations between master and student were viewed liberally, and of a society with radically different notions of sexual maturity and legal majority. Indeed, even in present-day Italy the age of sexual consent is 14, rising to 16 if the older person holds some position of influence over the younger partner (as a teacher, for instance). Throughout much of history, as Germaine Greer has shown, the figure of the attractive 'boy' – mythological hero, young warrior, schoolboy, scion of an aristocratic family – has attracted artistic attention as the incarnation of beauty on the cusp of manhood. For some men and women, such ephebes also excited sexual desire.

Not enough is known about Rocco's own life to discern whether he followed the practices of Philotimos. There is no record to suggest that he was prosecuted for sodomitical offences in Venice; archival documents record only that Rocco did not attend mass, lived as an atheist, and argued that the soul was not immortal and that infidels could be saved. Despite legislation outlawing the 'crime against nature', homosexual behaviour remained widespread in the most serene republic.

Benedetta Carlini 1590–1661

'For two continuous years, two or three times a week, in the evening, after disrobing and going to bed waiting for her companion, who serves her, to disrobe also, she would force her into the bed and kissing her as if she were a man she would stir on top of her so much that both of them corrupted themselves because she held her sometimes for one, sometimes for two, sometimes for three hours … Benedetta, in order to have greater pleasure, put her face between the other's breasts and kissed them, and wanted always to be thus on her.'

Thus did papal emissaries record the testimony of Bartolomea Crivelli, a nun who revealed her sexual relationship with another sister in 17th-century Italy. Judith C. Brown, who discovered the documents, has reconstructed the 'life of a lesbian nun' in the Renaissance.

Benedetta Carlini was born in 1590 to a prosperous family in the Apennine mountains near Florence. Because mother and child almost died at birth, she was promised to a religious life in fulfilment of a vow, and at the age of 9 joined a newly established convent of Theatine nuns in Pescia. She remained there until her death at the age of 71. The nuns led a contemplative life, spinning silk to pay the expenses of the community. Carlini earned a reputation for piety and, when the Convent of the Mother of God gained full monastic rights of enclosure from the Holy See, the congregation elected Carlini as abbess in 1620.

For several years Carlini had been having visions – not an uncommon occurrence for fervent Christians – in which she saw Jesus and the angels, and a statue of the Virgin Mary that bent over to kiss her.

The visions became more intense and bizarre, and Carlini told others that handsome young men were pursuing and trying to kill her, and that she had visited a garden where a miraculous libation flowed from a fountain. She confessed that she had received the stigmata, the bleeding wounds of the crucified Christ. Falling into trances that lasted for hours, she saw Christ come down to tear out her heart, then return three days later to replace it in her chest with his own heart. When Christ appeared again in order to propose marriage, she convinced the nuns to decorate their chapel for the wedding, and she received a ring – which initially only she could see – from her Lord. She also suffered great pains and had difficulty sleeping, so a young nun – Crivelli – was instructed to share her cell and to comfort her during her spiritual and physical travails.

The nuns seemed to accept Carlini's visions as real, and word of her mystical communion with God spread outside the convent. Clerical authorities, cautious about claims of visionary experiences and the stigmata, sent a priest to investigate. After fourteen visits, in which it seemed that Carlini indeed bore Christ's wounds and that her visions were believable, he decided that she was genuine. Yet doubts persisted: there were contradictions (and signs of possible heresy) in her accounts of the visions, and concerns surrounded the nature of her stigmata. In 1623 officials launched another investigation, sending more inquisitive questioners from Rome. This time the priests decided that, instead of being possessed by God, Carlini suffered from demonic possession. The signs of her sanctity, moreover, were fraudulent: a star that she claimed had been bestowed by heaven was pasted onto her forehead, and the ring that had miraculously become visible was merely painted on her finger. The stigmata, too, were the result of self-inflicted wounds. The inquisitors also discovered Carlini's relationship with Crivelli: kissing, caressing and mutual masturbation on a regular basis, by day and night. There was also a possible improper relationship with a priest.

For thirty-five years until her death, Carlini was confined in prison-like conditions in the convent. Crivelli died the year before the former abbess.

Carlini does not fit the role of a lesbian heroine. Her self-abuse and hallucinations indicate mental illness, and she exhibited predatory sexual approaches. (Although Crivelli may have been involved in a consensual relationship, she testified that she had been forced into sex.) Those who investigated Carlini were, of course, deeply shocked at her behaviour. It is impossible to say at the remove of several centuries whether Carlini's lesbian desires were directly connected with her visions or even what they meant to her. She claimed that she had been possessed by a handsome young angel named Splenditello and had no memory of sexual relations with Crivelli, though her repeated sexual activities clearly gave physical pleasure.

Lesbians in the early modern world attracted less public concern than sodomitical men. Although convents were rumoured to be hotbeds of impropriety, most commonly this took the form of immoral assignations between priests and nuns. Theologians condemned all unholy sensual relationships, but jurists were unclear on legislation against sexual activities not involving men and phallic penetration. Lesbians generally came to attention mostly because of cross-dressing or refusal to adhere to expected standards of gendered behaviour. A situation in which relations between women constituted a *peccatum mutum* ('silent sin'), according to the historian Edith Benkov, left opportunities in which intimacy might blossom.

Convents provided a refuge for women who wished to escape marriage and yet live respectably. Many nuns were literate, and a few extremely learned; and abbesses could become powerful figures. Convents often functioned simply as homes for unmarried women not necessarily called to a deeply pious life. They offered communities of women-only sociability. It is impossible to know how many nuns felt romantic affection or sexual desire for fellow sisters.

Historians have nevertheless discerned traces of lesbian relations, or at least intimate affinities between women, in monastic worlds long before Carlini. The 11th-century abbess, mystic, poet and composer Hildegard of Bingen, for instance, was much attached to another nun, Richardis of Stade. After ten years together, Richardis' nomination to head her own abbey brought such distress to Hildegard that she sought to prevent the departure of the 'deeply cherished' Richardis, who 'had bound herself to me in loving friendship in every way' and whose leaving would 'disturb my soul and draw bitter tears from my eyes and fill my heart with bitter wounds'. When Hildegard learned of Richardis' death, she confided tenderly: 'My soul had great confidence in her, though the world loved her beautiful looks and her prudence, while she lived in the body. But God loved her more. Thus God did not wish to give his beloved to a rival lover, that is, to the world.' These fragmentary messages, a possible homoerotic reading of her poems, and Hildegard's comment that a woman 'may be moved to pleasure without the touch of a man' suggest to the scholar Susan Schibanoff that love flourished between the women.

Hildegard and Richardis, and Carlini and Crivelli, joined in religious vocation but separated by half a millennium, illustrate different experiences of love and lust between women, a history of the 'erased lesbian' that is now becoming better known. That the convent continued to be a place where some women, happily or with difficulty, experienced lesbian yearnings is shown by the publication in 1985 of a volume of contemporary memoirs.

Michael Sweerts 1618–1664

The life of Michael Sweerts would provide good material for a novel (and indeed inspired Dominique Cordellier's *Le Peintre disgracié* (2017)). He was born in Brussels, then under Habsburg rule, in 1618, at the beginning of the Thirty Years War. His father was a prosperous merchant in Flanders, a hub of international business. Sweerts was baptized a Catholic, but little more is known about him until he shows up in Rome around 1646, one of the northern artists who journeyed southwards to study the works of antiquity, enjoy Mediterranean culture, and paint. Although a loner, he established himself in the community of expatriate artists, and found in Pope Innocent X a patron. Sweerts stayed in Rome for almost a decade. He then appears in Brussels (though it is unclear why he returned to Flanders), where he set up a not entirely successful art school.

At the beginning of the 1660s, Sweerts unaccountably volunteered to join a missionary expedition to the Far East. The Paris-based Société des Missions Etrangères, under Bishop Pallu, recruited priests and lay people for a journey to Siam and China; among them were doctors, pharmacists and one painter. Three men would die in the Middle East, and two more in India, before the survivors arrived as one of the pioneering legations to the Siamese court in Ayutthaya. Sweerts helped supervise the building of the society's ship in Amsterdam, then headed to Marseille, where the travellers set out for Palestine. In a letter to superiors, Bishop Pallu praised the Flemish artist's piety, but along the way trouble occurred. Pallu revealed that Sweerts had become a busybody, meddling even in ecclesiastical affairs; he hinted that the artist had lost his mind. The conflict was resolved when Sweerts and the missionaries separated amicably, somewhere in Turkey or Persia. The artist moved further eastwards, making his way to the Portuguese colony of Goa, where he died in 1664.

Sweerts' paintings, few in number but generally high in quality, span several genres. He left just one work in the grand style: a panoramic view of the plague in a classical city. There are many commissioned portraits of merchant princes. His only series of religious paintings catalogues the Seven Acts of Mercy, while another cycle depicts the five senses. Sweerts excelled at views of life among the common people, following in the footsteps of the Bambocci-anti – a group of northerners who specialized in lowlife scenes set in the South. Men cast dice, play cards and smoke pipes, drinkers quaff wine, a ragged workman warms himself at a brazier and an old peasant woman spins thread. A prosperous-looking couple relax in a Roman garden filled with classical statuary. Neapolitan musicians give an impromptu concert, and a grand voyager disembarks. Several paintings show people delousing each other or their clothes.

Handsome men often appear in Sweerts' works. In one portrait, a beautiful, melancholy young fellow sits at a worktable piled with books and coins, an inkwell and a velvet moneybag before him; a Latin motto warns that every man must give an account of himself. Another shows a debonair gentleman with long russet hair and a red cloak, perhaps the portrait of a Flemish patron. Elsewhere, two Caravaggio-style young men in bright hose play draughts. A man with fine features stands in a shop selling artworks; he looks at a small *putto*, but an artist or apprentice points him towards a plaster cast of a robust male torso. An Orientalist touch comes in a portrait of a pretty, androgynous youth, sporting a silk turban and holding a nosegay.

Nude or semi-nude men make their way into Sweerts' scenes. A bare-chested adolescent sits quietly while a mother minds her two young children. A boy in a fez plays cards with a partner, oddly undressed except for a white head-cloth and an indigo wrap around his buttocks. Roman wrestlers encircle each other with strong arms as they joust. One, his creamy back to the viewer, is completely naked; the other, ruddier of hue, wears a demure posing strap. On the sidelines another splendid male specimen, perhaps next in line for a match, raises his hands to pull off a shirt. Spectators abound, a young woman looking outwards with a naughty smile as she witnesses the tussle of male muscle. Kneeling on the ground are two other men, one watching intently, the other stretching his hands in the air, as if moving out of the way or warding off the crowd: images of attraction versus concern.

Manly contact and homoerotic imagery are more brazen in Sweerts' paintings of bathers. One, completed after his return from Rome but suggesting memories of the South, shows nine men near a pond; one is nearly underwater, with another immersed just far enough so that his buttocks and back become the focal point. Behind them, three nudes lounge stiffly on the bank as river gods. A background figure pulls his shirt over his head. Another, in bourgeois cloak and hat, stares with intent at a tall, slender man next to him, naked except for a loincloth; he looks happy to show himself off as he gesticulates while making some comment to his interlocutor. There is a hint of intimacy, voyeurism and exhibitionism – even homosexual cruising.

The hints become flagrant in the small, dark *Young Men Bathing*. A group of well-built men congregate around a river at sunset, the last light shining on bodies silhouetted against dense vegetation. Several disport themselves on the shore while others stare at the handsome bathers. The youths resemble classical statues, with well-proportioned physiques and gleaming flesh. A bather raises his hands to wipe his dripping face. Another perches on a rock, stripping off his shirt. Next to him a bare-backed man lowers his trousers, his bottom and genitals exposed with the flair of a strip-tease artiste. He looks towards a bystander, this one wearing cloak and hat, and he returns the gaze of the exhibitionist. Another man sits untying his shoelaces, his head bent at crotch level before the disrobing figure.

Does such a scene reveal homosexual magnetism between the men standing in the shadows and bathers baring their bodies? One element to suggest this interpretation is the presence in the middle ground of two completely naked men in the shallows, one behind the other, pulling towards him the partner who leans forward, bracing his arms against a tree or a rock. The men could pass for a couple preparing for intercourse. Is this what one art historian brands 'horseplay'?

No one knows how Sweerts intended his paintings to be seen, and his young blades and lusty swimmers could simply represent academic conventions and scenes of everyday life. The scant contemporary documents about Sweerts record no romantic or sexual affairs, bordello-going, brushes with authorities for sexual misbehaviour, or honest marriage and fatherhood. The scholar Albert Bankert repeats sympathetically the conclusion of Vitale Bloch, an earlier authority, that Sweerts was homosexual – a judgment based on the painting of Roman wrestlers – while Thomas Röske has focused on the homoeroticism of Sweerts' paintings as an example of 'queer' art. Sweerts himself stares out of a self-portrait: immaculately dressed in a black outfit trimmed with brilliant white collar and sleeves, he is a foppish gentleman with long jet-black hair and a carefully trimmed moustache. He wears an enigmatic smile.

Katherine Philips 1631–1664

'For thou art all that I can prize
My joy, my life, my rest.'

These lines come from a poem entitled 'To my Excellent Lucasia, on our Friendship', addressed by Katherine Philips to Anne Owen who, like other members of Philips' 'Society of Friendship', had taken a name inspired by the Classics. Both women were married, but the words bespeak an intense emotional bond that is repeated in other verses. 'To the dull angry world let's prove / There's a Religion in our love,' she wrote in 'Friendship's Mystery, To my Dearest Lucasia'; and in a poem on 'Content', about the pleasures of their intimacy, she declaimed, 'Then, my Lucasia, we have / Whatever Love can give or crave ... / With innocence and perfect friendship fired, / By Vertue joyn'd, and by our Choice retired.' Lucasia was only one of the women in her circle with whom Philips, or 'Orinda', developed such ties. Another poem, for instance, is 'L'Amitié: To Mrs M. Awbrey', also known as 'Rosania': 'Soule of my soule! My Joy, my crown, my friend!' The poems describe a mystical, all-giving friendship, a 'sacred union' in which all secrets are known and happiness shared, away from the common concerns of the world.

Philips was born in London, the daughter of a Presbyterian merchant (though she later became a keen royalist and supporter of the established church in the struggle between king and parliament). After her father's death, she moved with her remarried mother to Wales. She herself was married in 1648 – to a husband whom sources variously describe as only a few years older than his bride, or more than twenty years her senior – and gave birth to two children, one of whom died in infancy. Philips was well educated, and translated several of Corneille's plays from French. She succumbed to smallpox on a trip to London in 1664, at the age of 32.

Are her verses lesbian? Philips and her friends were all married, and her poetry bears traces of a lack of interest in the 'fevers of love'. There is no evidence of physical consummation in the poems, which speak of the rewards of friendship in terms of trust, confidence and communion. Finding lesbians – in the sense of women whose romantic attachment joined with sexual intercourse or who clearly affirmed their physical yearnings for other women – in early modern Europe is very difficult. Some scholars argue that seeing signs of lesbian attraction in Philips' poetry amounts to a misreading of her work. Claudia A. Limbert, for example, rejects any notion of lesbianism, conceding only that in Philips' verses the 'emotional level has been turned up to an almost excruciating pitch', and claiming that Philips has a 'spotless sexual reputation'.

Other commentators beg to differ, retorting that the interest women held for other women, especially in Philips' age, ought not to be seen in narrow terms of genital connection. They stress the importance of women-centred affinities in life and letters, and discover what they suggest are coded erotic references. Harriette Andreadis, for instance, points out that one distinction of Philips' poetry was that she adapted a platonic but homoerotic language of male friendship to relationships between women.

Andreadis also finds some intriguingly circumstantial biographical details. Philips largely abandoned her friendship with Mary Aubrey ('Rosania') after the latter's marriage in 1652, transferring her affections to Anne Owen ('Lucasia'). When Owen married and moved to Ireland in 1662, Philips, with the ostensible reason of looking after her husband's business interests and overseeing the production of her translation of a Corneille play, followed the couple to Dublin. When she returned to Wales, she bemoaned in a letter: 'I have now no longer any pretence of Business to detain me, and a Storm must not keep me from Antenor [her pseudo-classical name for her husband] and my Duty, lest I raise a greater within. But oh! That there were no Tempests but those of the Sea for me to suffer in parting from my dear Lucasia.' She continued to suffer grief and disappointment about the separation caused by Owen's marriage and move: 'I now see by Experience that one may love too much … I find too there are few Friendships in the World Marriage-proof.'

Andreadis contrasts Philips' mention of 'Duty' in the single extant poem about her husband with the effusive emotions expressed in the many works dedicated to women friends. If, in her poems to Rosania and Lucasia, she had been writing about a man, no one would assume that she was not speaking of romantic and erotic love. After her friend's marriage, she reacted as a lover scorned. The scholar concludes: 'There is no question that Katherine Philips produced lesbian texts, that is, texts that are amenable to lesbian reading in the twentieth century.'

Philips' writing invites continued rereading as sexual or political – as revealed, respectively, by Arlene Stiebel and Graham Hammill. This demonstrates not only the suggestive power of her work, but different academic approaches to female same-sex love in early modern Europe.

Perhaps the last word might be left to a contemporary: Sir Charles Cotterell, the mentor who encouraged Philips' writing. He pronounced judgment in 1667: 'We might well have call'd her the English Sappho, she of all the female Poets of former Ages, being for her Verses and her Vertues both, the most highly to be valued'.

Frederick the Great 1712–1786

Frederick II, the Great, was born in Berlin, the son of Frederick William I and his Hanoverian wife, whose father became George I of England. Frederick William, known as the 'soldier-king' and characterized by his son as a 'severe father and rigid tutor', has earned a reputation as brutish, interested primarily in military glory, miserly, indifferent to the arts, and an absolutist in politics and in his family life. The young Frederick had the opposite temperament: it was remarked that seldom did father and son less resemble each other. In an autobiographical poem Frederick II would make reference to the Spartan virtues extolled by his father and the 'gentle manners of Athens' that beckoned him. His French governess taught him rhetoric, music and poetry, all disciplines depreciated by his father, and he became an ardent Francophile. Frederick displayed a gift for music (even when his disapproving father broke his flutes), and composed dozens of flute sonatas and four symphonies. Architecture was another passion, and towards the end of his reign he would endow Berlin with a series of magnificent buildings.

When he was around 16, Frederick became attached to a younger page boy, Peter Keith (the name testimony to his Scottish ancestry); Frederick's beloved sister spoke of Keith's devotion, but let slip, 'Though I had noticed that he was on more familiar terms with this page than was proper in his position, I did not know how intimate the friendship was.' An even more intimate friend was Hans von Katte, eight years Frederick's senior, a nobleman who had studied law and French before entering the Prussian army, where he held the rank of lieutenant. In 1730, Frederick, Katte and Keith devised a plan to flee Prussia for France or England, leaving behind the despotic reign of its king. Their plan was foiled, and they were charged with treason, though Keith managed to escape to Holland. The king ordered Katte to be executed outside the window of the cell where the crown prince was being held: Katte was brought to the window and bowed to Frederick, who extended his hand. The crown prince was so distressed that he fainted as his friend was beheaded. Twelve days later his father finally granted him a reprieve. It will never be known whether Frederick and Katte's relationship was sexual. It seems that Frederick was in love with him, and his execution was a trauma, perhaps leaving Frederick incapable of forming another attachment of similar depth.

In 1733 Frederick was forced into marriage by his father; he wrote to his sister that between him and his Austrian bride 'there can be neither love nor friendship'. In fact, his wife was fond of him, though they never produced children and Frederick generally saw her only once a year.

Frederick's own reign as monarch, beginning in 1740, provided a change of direction from his father's rule. He nevertheless proved a heroic military leader, fending off enemies leagued against Prussia and scoring victories in the Seven Years' War. He dramatically enlarged his realm with the acquisition of Silesia and part of Poland, almost doubling its size. He made significant reforms to the state and the economy, ended torture, allowed freedom of worship and reduced censorship. In so doing, he was putting into practice the ideas of the Enlightenment that had nourished him since his schooldays.

Frederick had long corresponded with the greatest of the *philosophes*, Voltaire, and in 1750 he invited the French thinker to his residence at Potsdam. The stay lasted almost three years, as Frederick granted Voltaire a court position and comfortable lodgings. Their personal relationship did not always run smooth – Frederick even had Voltaire placed under arrest at one moment – but this was a meeting of minds, the philosopher and the philosopher-king.

After leaving Prussia, a disgruntled Voltaire composed a brief and somewhat scurrilous work on *La vie privée du roi de Prusse* ('The Private Life of the King of Prussia'); it was only published decades later. Voltaire noted that Frederick 'liked handsome men' and that he 'had no vocation for the [second] sex'. The philosopher also recollected the history of Katte's execution and painted a sketch of a soldier who had befriended the crown prince when he was incarcerated by his father and who remained a faithful companion: 'This soldier, young, handsome, well built, and who played the flute, managed in more than one way to amuse the prisoner.' A French minister of the time commented, in jolly versification, that Frederick found the inebriation of *amour* only in the arms of *tambours* (drummers).

Frederick became close to several soldiers, courtiers and other visitors to the grandiose palace of Sanssouci that he constructed, among them the dashing Francesco Algarotti. A bisexual writer and diplomat and a quintessential Enlightenment figure, Algarotti travelled to England (where he had dalliances with Lord John Hervey and Lady Mary Wortley Montagu), France (where he befriended Voltaire) and Prussia. He lived there for eight years, was made a count and court chamberlain, was awarded various decorations and possibly was Frederick's lover for several years as well. (Voltaire noted, however, that Algarotti was inconstant; spying him hugging a French attaché, he said, 'I seem to see Socrates reinvigorated on Alcibiades' back.')

Frederick commissioned a fresco of Ganymede for his palace, and had his 'Temple of Friendship' at Sanssouci ornamented with medallions of classical couples, including Pylades and Orestes, Heracles and Philoctetes, and Pirithous and Theseus. He also penned a verse wondering why St John was taken as the Ganymede of Jesus – a neat linking of homoerotic classical and Christian mythology. The references show the cultural influences that could be used both to hide and to reveal the sexual proclivities of an Enlightenment potentate.

Chevalier d'Eon 1728–1810

The categories of male and female have traditionally provided ways to classify individuals according to physiology and expected types of behaviour. However, some people did not conform to the categories assigned to them at birth or during childhood. They and others often rejected norms of dress, personal and professional pursuits and choice of sexual partners. They consciously adopted new identities that historically encompassed labels such as 'hermaphrodite', 'transvestite', 'transsexual', 'transgender' and 'intersex', among others. 'Trans' has come to be an accepted term to cover various sorts of gender non-conformity, and 'trans' people have come into more prominent view in the early 21st century.

Such transgressive behaviour is not new, as the example of the 18th-century Chevalier d'Eon shows. Born in a Burgundian town to a minor royal official and a noblewoman, Charles-Geneviève-Louise-Auguste-André-Timothée d'Eon de Beaumont confesses in a not always trustworthy autobiography that, since his sex was unclear at birth, he was given 'the names of both male and female saints in order to avoid any error'. Raised as a boy, he received a fine education at an elite Paris school, took a degree in law, and in his mid-twenties published a tome on French finances, the first of fifteen volumes he authored. Intellectual achievement and personal connections brought him to royal attention, and he won appointment to a diplomatic mission to Russia. During the Seven Years' War, he served as an officer in the dragoons, sustaining injuries in battle, and in 1763 was sent, ultimately with the rank of Minister Plenipotentiary, to London for negotiations on the peace treaty between France and Britain. For his efforts, he received France's highest decoration, the Order of St Louis. Unknown even to most of the king's ministers, d'Eon also worked secretly as a spy for Louis XV in London, continuing to send reports back until the monarch's death in 1774 – intelligence intended for a possible French invasion of the British Isles.

Soon after his arrival in London, to his uncontained anger d'Eon was passed over for appointment as permanent ambassador in England – partly because of official annoyance at his huge expenses (especially the bills for Pinot Noir), and partly because his patron had lost favour at court. The foreign minister recalled d'Eon, but he refused to leave London, reminding the king of his secret mission. The conflict between d'Eon and his masters placed the French government in a delicate position – especially since d'Eon was flirting with British radicals – and continued without solution for almost a decade. D'Eon, now deprived of an official post but still gathering intelligence, all the while feuding with the new French ambassador, gave journalists and caricaturists a chance to make merry with depictions of court intrigues and supposed conspiracies.

Around 1770 rumours began to circulate that d'Eon was in fact a woman, adding to his notoriety and leading people to place bets totalling tens of thousands of pounds on his true sex. D'Eon mounted a lawsuit against the wagering, but remained coy about settling the matter. The scandal made news on both sides of the Channel, until a court emissary worked out an agreement. In return for a pension, d'Eon would return to France as a woman, wear only women's clothing, relinquish all secret documents and take no further role in politics.

D'Eon went home but made great efforts, in vain, to be allowed to wear the uniform of a dragoon captain, though the king conceded that she could wear the Order of St Louis. Banished from court, d'Eon lived at the family house in Burgundy. Her patroness counselled: 'If Louis XV armed you as a Knight of French soldiers, Louis XVI arms you as a *chevalière* of French women.' Her request to raise a company of women soldiers to fight in the American War of Independence met with refusal.

In 1785, bored with life in rural France and chafing at her treatment by Versailles, the *chevalière* returned to London, championing the British political system and soon applauding the revolution unfolding at home. She lived as a woman, sharing lodgings chastely with an admiral's widow. The French no longer paid her pension, and she sold a vast library, then earned money through fencing tournaments, to make ends meet. From the mid-1790s, she lived in virtual seclusion, composing memoirs and religious writings that articulated what her biographer calls 'Christian feminism'.

At this point of her life, d'Eon admitted that she had been born a female and was now happy to assume her true gender. However, when d'Eon died in 1810, her octogenarian housemate announced, after preparing the body for burial, that d'Eon was physiologically male. Physicians confirmed the finding, even though in the 1770s magistrates and doctors had pronounced d'Eon a female. The fact that various people, including medical professionals, categorized d'Eon's body in different ways demonstrates that biological sex is more fluid than some might believe.

In a study of d'Eon's remarkable life, the historian Gary Kates has showed how d'Eon fashioned a persona for himself/herself, and explored the reasons why d'Eon decided to lead the second half of his life as a woman. The change came not from gender confusion or sexual dissidence; rather, d'Eon's metamorphosis was a conscious intellectual decision. Faced with the ruin of a political career, financial difficulties and alienation from French life, d'Eon found in the transformation a way to confront an awkward future. It was, perhaps, d'Eon himself who had planted rumours that he was a woman, although his slight build, absence of facial hair and lack of amorous affairs had already raised eyebrows. Long interested in the status of women – his library included many volumes on the subject – d'Eon made a dramatic, radical life choice. There is, incidentally, no record of any romantic or sexual entanglement with man or woman.

The public greeted the d'Eon *affaire* with fascination but neither horror nor outrage; d'Eon was never considered a pariah or a freak. As Kates points out, although gender divisions were clearly demarcated in Enlightenment Europe, sex and gender were not considered synonymous. 'D'Eon's life', he adds, 'was played out against the backdrop of other kinds of gender experiments that tested and challenged relations between the sexes and the nature of manhood and womanhood.' Writers from Jean-Jacques Rousseau to Mary Wollstonecraft philosophized about upbringing, sexuality and gender. There existed a fluidity in terms of gendered clothing, behaviour and activities. Figures such as William Beckford – known for sexual encounters with young men, and for playing with gender in the novel *Vathek* – challenged traditional notions. Increasing urbanization and social mobility helped swell the sexual subcultures of cities such as London and Paris, each of which also hosted thousands of prostitutes. In London, 'molly houses' provided ample opportunities for men who sought their own sex, where they nevertheless often adopted female names and personae during their merriment. D'Eon was part of this changing culture, including that of individuals who would now be called 'trans' people.

D'Eon's story has inspired novels, plays, a film, an opera and a Japanese *anime* series. Moving between countries, professions, dress and gender, d'Eon occupied various interstices of Enlightenment life, thwarting gender assignment by jurists and doctors, rejecting easy categorization by contemporaries and historians, and engaging in impressive self-fashioning. A suitable epitaph comes from d'Eon's autobiography: 'For I who have neither husband, nor master, nor mistress, I would like to enjoy the privilege of obeying only myself and good sense.'

3
FOUNDING FATHERS AND MOTHERS

Walt Whitman 1819–1892

In the pantheon of great gays, Walt Whitman certainly ranks, alongside Oscar Wilde, as one of the most famous and most influential figures. After the two met in 1882, Wilde said of Whitman: 'He is the grandest man I have ever seen. The simplest, most natural, and strongest character I have ever met in my life. I regard him as one of those wonderful, large, entire men who might have lived in any age, and is not peculiar to any one people. Strong, true, and perfectly sane: the closest approach to the Greek we have yet had in modern times. Probably he is dreadfully misunderstood.' The differences between the two are great – the cosmopolitan British dandy, the rather rustic and proudly simple American – and they typify varying 19th-century attitudes towards homosexuality. Despite a common harking back to antiquity, one approach drew its inspiration from the traditions of the Victorian metropolis, while the other was rooted in a new-world sense of democracy, egalitarianism and camaraderie. They bequeathed these strands of homosexual culture to the next century.

The New York poet, in his life and writings, provided great inspiration for homosexuals in America and overseas. Edward Carpenter (who visited Whitman in America, and intimated that their meeting included a sexual encounter), André Gide, Yukio Mishima and many others invoked his name as kindred spirit and precursor. Later homosexuals named after him a long-lived gay bookshop in Manhattan. Yet Whitman had such broad resonance through-out American culture that he became a national hero, the nation's poet; the more conservative of his admirers carefully bowdlerized sexual passages in his writing and passed over his homosexuality as they christened streets, schools and other public institutions in his memory. Many who heard in Whitman's verses the authentic voice of the American would have been – and may still be – horrified to think of him as a sodomite.

Reading Whitman's work today, it is difficult to believe that anyone could have ignored its homoerotic aspects. In 'Song of Myself', he confesses to 'the hugging and loving bed-fellow [who] sleeps at my side through the night', and he enjoins a friend to 'Undrape! You are not guilty to me …'. A single stanza of exaltation merges a man's body with the landscape, the 'firm masculine colter', 'beard, brawn', 'fibre of manly wheat', 'broad muscular fields' and 'your milky stream'. Certain scholars find even more blatant references to sexual acts coded into his words. In the 'Calamus' poems of the 1860s, Whitman's statements are particularly bold as he describes the 'adhesiveness' of comradely love: 'I am the new husband and the comrade', he declares to a friend, inviting him to commune 'if you will, thrusting me beneath your clothing, / Where I may feel the throbs of your heart or rest upon your hip'. In another poem, he recalls a night spent with 'my dear friend my lover': 'In the stillness in the autumn moonbeams his face was inclined toward me, / And his arm lay lightly around my breast – and that night I was happy'.

Whitman's writing exudes joy at intimate friendship. 'I myself am capable of loving', he affirms, holding aloft a phallic calamus root as a token of his desires. As a greybeard, he takes pleasure in the kiss of a young man, and finds supreme contentment just in a friend's simply holding his hand; he recollects with sad fondness a departed one who is yet never separated from him. And in 'Among the Multitude', he spies the 'lover and true equal' who is his heart's ideal.

The self-styled 'poet of comrades' fashioned a vision of manly love between friends that would be the leaven for a new age and a new spirit, embedded in the nature that Whitman evoked – the busy life of Manhattan, the quiet of the prairies, the earthy smells of the soil. 'COME, I will make the continent indissoluble, / I will make the most splendid race the sun ever yet shone upon, / I will make divine magnetic lands, / With the love of comrades, / With the life-long love of comrades.' There is utopianism in Whitman's work, a great communitarian vision of society as eroticized companionship writ large, built on the adhesion of individuals.

Singing of himself, a prophet of personal and political liberty within this desired comradely cosmos, Whitman's verse also bespeaks refusal of norms, a rejection of social expectations. Musing in 'As I Lay with My Head in Your Lap, Camerado', he challenges: 'I confront peace, security, and all the settled laws, to unsettle them; / I am more resolute because all have denied me, than I could ever have been had all accepted me; / I heed not, and have never heeded, either experience, cautions, majorities, nor ridicule.' Elsewhere, he declaims: 'I am the sworn poet of every dauntless rebel the world over.' Here is a confession of difference, and a manifesto for action: no wonder Whitman's voice echoed for later generations of activists.

Whitman was born on Long Island, in New York, in very modest circumstances, and grew up in the borough of Brooklyn. He received only a simple formal education, though his work testifies to interest in literature, opera and history. He worked in various jobs, from apprenticing as a compositor and editor in a printing office to school-teaching and journalism. He held several posts in the civil service, losing one position in the Department of the Interior because his boss considered his collection of poems *Leaves of Grass*, first published in 1855, to be obscene (the book was banned in certain American cities). During the Civil War he went to Washington, where he worked as a volunteer in Union hospitals, the war service and his frequenting of the young soldiers (such as the 'Tan-Faced Prairie-Boy' of one poem) leaving a lasting impression. The assassination of the greatly admired Abraham Lincoln also much affected him and inspired poems in his memory.

Whitman formed 'adhesive' relations with several young men. The most significant of his partners was Peter Doyle, a bus conductor, whom he met in 1866: 'We were familiar at once – I put my hand on his knee – we understood. He did not get out at the end of the trip – in fact went all the way back with me,' Doyle remembered. A series of letters that Whitman wrote to 'dear boy Pete' from 1868 to 1880, full of expressions of affection, recounted Whitman's daily life, commented on political developments, and proffered fatherly advice to his protégé.

Some aspects of Whitman's poetry jar with present-day readers – the utopianism, a naïve American boosterism, a stylistic tendency to catalogues of places or allusions. Yet in his transcendental (and now, as we see it, very ecological) appreciation of landscape, his pleasure in friendship and love, his celebration of unbounded sexuality, his taking up of the cause of the outcast (in, for instance, a poem addressed 'To a Common Prostitute'), and his rejection of the dictates of God and religion, the patriarchal Whitman remains a profoundly modern bard.

Edward Carpenter 1844–1929

More than a century after his death, Edward Carpenter, like Walt Whitman, seems a remarkably contemporary figure for our own times. Although his understanding of homosexuals – or 'Urnings', as he termed them – as an intermediate sex is now antiquated, and some of his views appear quaintly utopian, his presence remains strong. An advocate of manly 'homogenic love' in theory and practice; an apostle of a simple, proto-environmentalist life; a promoter of socialist democracy; a spokesman for women's rights; a scholar of international gay cultures – Carpenter was broad and sympathetic in his reach.

Born in Brighton to a former naval commander turned barrister and successful railway investor, and a mother who looked after her large family (he was one of ten children), Carpenter was educated at Trinity Hall, Cambridge. After finishing his undergraduate studies, he was elected to a fellowship at his college and ordained as an Anglican minister. Within a few years, however, he had lost his faith, and in 1874 resigned religious orders and his fellowship. He moved to the north of England, to take up a position in a newly created university extension scheme for the education of workers and women. In 1880 he found lodgings with a scythe-maker named Albert Fearnehough, who, though married, became Carpenter's lover.

Several encounters proved particularly significant for Carpenter, but none more so than his friendship with Walt Whitman, who was his lodestar. Carpenter had written in admiration to the poet in 1874, and in 1877 he visited him in New York; a second trip a few years later confirmed their deep affinities. *Leaves of Grass* provided a model for Carpenter's book-length poem *Towards Democracy*, first published in 1883 and later expanded; and Whitman's ideas about an egalitarian, mutually supportive attachment between men – spiritual, emotional and physical – formed the basis of Carpenter's notions of homogenic love. Whitman's influence is also clear in Carpenter's writings on homosexuality. These took the form of a privately printed pamphlet later reissued as *Love's Coming of Age* (1896) – his courage in addressing the subject at the time of the Oscar Wilde affair is remarkable – and *The Intermediate Sex* of 1906. The works constitute the first straightforward defence of homosexuality in Britain.

While still at Cambridge, Carpenter had met Ponnambalam Arunachalam, a student from Ceylon. They became good friends (though, it seems, not lovers), and Arunachalam, later both a highly placed colonial civil servant and an early nationalist leader, introduced Carpenter to the *Bhagavad Gita* and other classic Indian texts – sparking an interest in Eastern philosophies that endured. Carpenter visited Arunachalam in 1890–91, and his journey to Ceylon and India, chronicled in *From Adam's Peak to Elephanta*, proved a grand experience, for the attractive exoticism of the landscapes, religions and culture, as well as for the beauty of the young men. Carpenter came back with firm opinions about the wrongs of colonialism. The two friends also conversed about sexuality in Asia: a posthumous publication brought together some of their writings on the subject, and in 1914 Carpenter published a book on *Intermediate Types among Primitive Folk*, an explanation of same-sex traditions in the classical world, among indigenous peoples, and in the Japanese samurai caste.

Soon after his return from Asia, in a chance encounter in a railway carriage, Carpenter met an unemployed 20-year-old from the Sheffield slums, George Merrill. They began an affair, and Merrill moved into the farm, Millthorpe, that Carpenter had bought in Derbyshire. They remained together until Merrill's death in 1928, one year before Carpenter himself died. (The two are buried together in Guildford, Surrey.) Merrill was the ideal partner, and Carpenter felt that such an attachment as his own, between someone from the working classes and another from the middle classes, could help breach the enormous social and cultural divides that he considered one of the evils of European society.

Carpenter and Merrill pursued an intentionally simple life at Millthorpe, engaged in what Carpenter termed the 'exfoliation' of unnecessary layers of social practice. They did not eat meat or drink alcohol, wore plain clothes (with sandals something of a fashion fetish), and supported William Morris's artisan-based Arts and Crafts movement. Carpenter took an active role in the Progressive Association, the Sheffield Socialist Society, the Fabian Society, the Humanitarian League (which campaigned against blood sports and vivisection), the anti-war movement at the time of the Great War, and the British Society for the Study of Sex Psychology, which he helped to found in 1913. Alongside these other activities, he continued to write: a mischievously titled book on *Civilization: Its Cause and Cure*; a memoir about Whitman; and a collection of homogenic poetry through the ages, called *Ioläus: An Anthology of Friendship*, to name but three. His writings, and those of his interlocutors John Addington Symonds and Havelock Ellis, articulated an apologia for homosexual life and rights. Carpenter became a well-known figure for disciples of the 'counter-culture' (though the term is anachronistic) and for homosexuals, and his house a place of pilgrimage for such men as E. M. Forster, who sought his wisdom and his encouragement.

André Gide 1869–1951

André Gide was one of the towering cultural figures of the first half of the 20th century. That he won the Nobel Prize for Literature in 1947 is only one of the attestations to his place in the modern pantheon. He typified some of the swirling currents of his lifetime. Born into comfortable circumstances, the son of a professor of law, he pushed against the boundaries of social conventions. Like many people, he wrestled with religion (in his case, the Protestant beliefs that he ultimately jettisoned). He dabbled with Communism, a creed he rejected after a visit to the Soviet Union. He journeyed to equatorial Africa to witness France's *mission civilisatrice*, and returned to write a searing critique of colonialism. He moved in the hothouse world of the Parisian intelligentsia, adopting and contributing to the ideas and styles of modernism. His sexual horizons were broad: he was married (though the union was almost certainly unconsummated) and the father of a child by another woman, but he also was one of the best-known homosexuals of his time.

Homosexuality appears in much of Gide's life – he claimed a number of young disciples and lovers, from young street-boys and peasants he met in Algeria and Egypt to gifted French protégés. Homosexuality also appears regularly in his protean writings. His own homosexual initiation in the Maghreb is recounted in the autobiographical *Si le grain ne meurt* (1924) and fictionalized in *L'Immoraliste* (1902).

Two works can be taken to represent Gide's perspectives on homosexuality. Written in 1911, *Corydon* earned canonical status as an apologia for same-sex desire. A few copies were privately published and distributed to friends by Gide, but the book did not publicly appear until 1920 – itself an indication of Gide's concern (or his friends' fear, as he noted in the preface) about its likely impact on his reputation. The book is a set of imagined dialogues between a homosexual doctor, Corydon (who takes his name from one of Virgil's shepherd lovers), and a rather homophobic narrator. Corydon tries to develop a theory about homosexuality in nature, attributing its existence to a surfeit of males and an over-abundance of male sexual urges, and drawing a distinction between 'normal' (that is, masculine) and effeminate homosexuals.

The argument is hardly convincing, and Gide was no scientist, but the couching of the debate in scientific terms relates it to other diagnostic efforts to explain homosexuality as the biological phenomenon of a 'third sex', as an arrested stage of psychosexual development, or (much later) as the product of a 'gay gene'. But setting aside the dubiousness of Gide's theory and its tedious and pedantic exposition, the importance of *Corydon* lay in positing homosexuality as a natural thing, a result of nature, and present even in the animal world; it is therefore not, as the moralists argued, *contra naturam*. Gide's book also adduces the ancients as evidence of the social benefits of homosexuality, suggesting (as did many later apologists) a link between homosexuality and creativity, and between sex and art. Finally, he refers to many of the prominent homosexual figures and scandals of the modern world – Whitman and Wilde, Sir Hector Macdonald's suicide and the Krupp scandal in Germany. For all its flaws, therefore, *Corydon* remains a historically significant commentary on medical, historical, aesthetic and contemporary debates on homosexuality, and a bravely straightforward statement by a homosexual luminary.

In 1907 Gide wrote *Le Ramier*, less than twelve pages long in the published version, which did not appear until 2002. It recounts one late July night in the south-west of France, where Gide celebrated a village festival and the election to local government of his friend Eugène Rouart, the engineer son of a wealthy industrialist, and a future senator. On this evening, Gide made the acquaintance of the handsome son of a farm worker, Ferdinand, a 17-year-old (though

Gide erroneously said he was 15). After the fireworks and dancing, they walk together, and Gide's flirtation and caresses meet with a mixture of bashfulness and eagerness on Ferdinand's part. They end up in Gide's bedroom, the windows thrown open to the summer breezes. Their lovemaking is simple. Gide describes his extraordinary happiness in lyrical prose that captures both the moments of pleasure and his recollection of them. The encounter reminded him of earlier assignations, one with Luigi in Rome, and one with Mohammed, a young man introduced to him by Oscar Wilde in North Africa. Here the scene is the French countryside, the partner is a peasant lad, the sentiments evoked are pure and natural – Gide nicknames Ferdinand the 'wood-dove' for the cooing sound he makes during their embraces.

Gide's short piece is rich in details: his attraction to ephebes; Rouart's apparent cultivation of a whole flock of young partners; the sense of complicity between the two men; Ferdinand's pretensions to sexual experience and knowledge, contrasted with his manifest innocence; his ardour and willingness to engage in sexual relations with a man twenty years his senior, though without declaring himself homosexual. Rouart later had his own intimate encounters with Ferdinand, and even planned, as he told Gide, to write a novel about the young man. But Ferdinand succumbed to tuberculosis and was confined to hospital, where Rouart visited him, keeping Gide informed of his illness until the boy's death in 1910.

Corydon and *Le Ramier* record theory and practice, the intellectual and the emotional experience of homosexual attachment, a debate in a Paris drawing-room and a chance encounter in the French countryside, an attempt to grasp the condition of the homosexual as a species and the memorialization of a particular type of desire and its satisfaction. Today Gide may seem somewhat fusty, his theories outmoded, his encounters tentative and coy and his liaisons problematic, but in his own day he was a sexual and literary revolutionary.

E. M. Forster 1879–1970

When Edward Morgan Forster was born, Queen Victoria still had more than two decades to reign; when he died, Queen Elizabeth had been on the throne for almost twenty years. In 1879 a man convicted of buggery could still be punished under English law with life imprisonment: only three years before Forster's death did Parliament hesitatingly and incompletely repeal laws that made consensual homosexual acts a crime.

Forster lived through the Wilde affair of the 1890s, offered to testify on behalf of Radclyffe Hall's *The Well of Loneliness* when it was declared obscene in 1928, and followed with concern a homosexual scandal of the 1950s involving several English gentlemen arrested for public indecency. He met Edward Carpenter in 1912, negotiated the complex sexual relationships of the Bloomsbury set in the years around the First World War and, from a distance, witnessed the beginnings of gay liberation in the 1960s.

The convoluted sexual history of British society helps readers understand the pattern underlying both Forster's long private life and his writings. Shortly before his death, speaking to a potential 'official' biographer, William Plomer, Forster emphasized his attitude towards his sexual experiences and their importance: 'M[organ] said he wanted it made clear that H[omosexuality] "had worked".' The centrality of homosexuality to Forster's life and work is not a topic that all commentators have highlighted, although Wendy Moffatt's biography is noteworthy for giving it due place.

Forster was a product of the Victorian middle class. His father, who died when Forster was a child, was an architect. His mother was a headstrong and cloying companion with whom he shared a house and who dominated Forster until her death in 1945 – a major reason for his lack of public openness about his homosexuality. Forster studied at King's College, Cambridge, between 1897 and 1901, returning as a fellow for his last twenty years. He lived by writing, eventually amassing enough wealth to fund his generosity to friends and protégés. His friends encompassed a *Who's Who* of the cultural aristocracy of his day, including many of a homosexual disposition. Among early acquaintances were Virginia Woolf, Lytton Strachey, Duncan Grant and John Maynard Keynes, and Forster later became a mentor to Christopher Isherwood, who received the unpublished manuscript of *Maurice*, his gay-themed novel, after his death. Though shy and awkward, Forster claimed many great figures as his admirers. He received fame and honours: he was awarded the Order of Merit, was made a Companion of Honour, and was offered a knighthood, which he declined.

Forster's romantic and sexual passions were not for those who shared his background. (He told Plomer it was important for biographers to note that 'none of his intimates had been eminent'.) Forster's sexual apprenticeship had been long and painful. He really had no sexual experience as a young man, not even the erotic horseplay of adolescents. At Cambridge he fell in love with a fellow student, Hugh Meredith, and a few years later met Syed Ross Masood, a robustly handsome, debonair Muslim from a grand Indian family who was studying in England. Masood returned his affections – although not sexually – and Forster considered him his closest friend for many years afterwards. They remained correspondents when Masood returned to India, and after Masood's death his children continued to visit Forster in England.

Forster's real sexual initiation came in Alexandria, where he had gone in 1915 to serve with the Red Cross during the First World War. This experience took the form of a quick encounter with a soldier on the beach, but Forster soon met a striking young tram conductor, Mohammed el-Adl. Despite their social and cultural differences, they drew closer and entered into a sexual relationship – Forster's first consummated affair. Forster was in love, but the end of the war spelled the end of his sojourn in Alexandria. He remained in contact with el-Adl, just as he had with Masood (in whom he confided about his Alexandrian romance). El-Adl married, fathered a child – whom he named Morgan – and saw Forster again when the writer travelled through Egypt on his way to India to visit Masood. El-Adl died from tuberculosis, in 1922, while still in his twenties. Forster never forgot him, carefully preserving his letters – the final messages from Mohammed, with 'I love you' repeated in a shaky hand, remained powerful mementos – and each year on the anniversary of his death he put on a ring that el-Adl had given him.

By the time he returned to England, in 1919, Forster was sexually freer, and in the middle of the 1920s estimated that he had had sex with the respectable number of eighteen men. Other relationships followed, sometimes simultaneously, and always with men from the working classes. The most important was with Bob Buckingham, a police officer who was Forster's lover for years, and occasionally slept with him even after his marriage. Buckingham and his wife proved Forster's most loyal companions in his later years.

Homosexuality makes only veiled appearances in Forster's early published writing. However, he intimated that he stopped producing novels after the 1920s because social disapproval meant he could not treat the topic that was central for him. The last novel to appear in his lifetime, *A Passage to India* (1924), provides perhaps the clearest portrayal of a bond between two men, an Englishman and an Indian – a relationship doomed by colonialism and mores, possible (in Forster's poignant phrase) 'not yet … not there'. The book, dedicated to Masood, drew on Forster's own rather rocambolesque adventures as a short-term secretary to a maharajah in the 1920s, and spoke deeply of his love of India and his discord with the tenets of British colonialism.

Forster wrote his gay-themed novel, *Maurice*, before the First World War, and occasionally showed it to friends, but considered the manuscript unpublishable. The story, of a relationship between a stockbroker and a gamekeeper – 'ordinary affectionate men' – now seems sentimental and dated, but it perfectly captures the homosexual mood of its time and place. Forster was determined that his sole true novel about homosexuality should have a happy ending. After his death, the publication of *Maurice* (1971) and of a sheaf of short stories with homosexual themes written over the years focused attention on the gay aspects of his life and his other literary works.

Forster's writings and loves reveal ways in which a homosexual man could 'connect' (to 'connect' intellectually, emotionally and in other ways was the hallowed directive of the Bloomsbury Group) across boundaries of social status and race, and even across the boundary between homosexual and heterosexual. Though he felt constrained by law, family pressure and the regard of society, Forster illustrated the many fashions in which gay lives could be constructed and sexual desires moulded – from the common rooms of Cambridge to the London suburbs, from England to the Italy and America that figure in his travels and stories, and on to Egypt and India. It is not surprising that literary critics, biographers, historians and readers return time and again to his works.

Radclyffe Hall 1880–1943

Radclyffe Hall's *The Well of Loneliness* is the most important lesbian work in modern literature. Today her view of lesbianism as 'inversion' – a common conclusion in the early 1900s – is no longer credible, and the book's somewhat overwrought writing and dark ending hardly make it a joyful read. For decades after its publication in 1928, however, the novel provided one of the few forthright and affirmative depictions of love between women, and thus exerted enormous influence internationally. The daring nature of Hall's work is also significant. The British government banned it as obscene: despite the support of many literary luminaries, it was not again on sale in the United Kingdom until after the Second World War.

The Well of Loneliness tells the story of Stephen Gordon, a provincial woman from the upper classes (given her first name by a father who had hoped for a boy) who shows no interest in men as companions or suitors, or in typically feminine pursuits, but is drawn to manly activities such as hunting and fencing. She struggles to establish her identity, takes to wearing men's clothing, reads about sexuality in her father's library, and falls scandalously in love with a woman neighbour, declaring the nobility of her love when her family discovers her sentiments. She moves to London to write novels, then travels to Paris and discovers a lesbian coterie in the French capital. As an ambulance driver in the First World War, she meets and falls in love with another woman, Mary Llewelyn; Gordon eventually gives her up to a man, however, which seems the only way to secure for Mary the happiness that she herself cannot provide. The book concludes with Gordon's plea for recognition: 'God, we believe … Acknowledge us, oh God, before the whole world. Give us also the right to our existence!'

Various aspects of the novel, if not the exact plot, mirror Hall's own life. She was born into a prosperous family in Bournemouth, but her parents separated when she was very young. Her childhood was not entirely happy: she did not get along with either her mother or her stepfather, who may have abused her, though her beloved grandmother provided comfort. Hall was educated privately, as was usual for girls of her background, and went on to study briefly at King's College London and in Dresden. At the age of 21 she inherited a fortune (the equivalent of many millions of pounds in present-day terms) from her grandfather, who had been a physician, sanatorium-owner, magistrate and alderman.

Hall, or 'John', as she was later known to her friends, had her first lesbian infatuations and affairs as a young woman, and did not doubt that she had been born an 'invert'. She was well versed in the sexological theories of the early 20th century, including the writings of Havelock Ellis, who contributed a foreword to *The Well of Loneliness*. Such theorists explained homosexuality as 'congenital': some people felt the emotions and desires of one sex while trapped in the body of another. Homosexual desires were, therefore, natural to them, though society generally took the opposite view. Homosexual men and women, they argued, were often drawn to mannerisms and styles of dress (for example) more common to the other gender. Photographs of Hall, who was always elegant, show her attired in Savile Row-tailored masculine suits and in hats of the sort sported by Stephen Gordon in her novel.

In 1907, when she was 27 years old, Hall fell in love with the 50-year-old Mabel Batten, known as 'Ladye', whom she had met at a spa resort in Germany. The daughter of the British Judge Advocate General of India, Batten was a fashionable singer and a pianist. She was married and had children and grandchildren, but after her husband's death, in 1911, she moved in with Hall. Batten was a Roman Catholic, and the following year Hall converted, and was soon received by the pope during a trip to Rome; she never saw a contradiction between her sexuality and her religion, or between Catholicism and an interest in spiritualism.

Through Ladye, in 1915 Hall met her cousin Lady Una Troubridge. Margot Taylor, who owed her married name and title to an ageing admiral, was a Royal Academy-trained sculptor, singer and translator. She and Hall began an affair, and after Batten's death in 1916 – and Troubridge's separation from her husband – they lived together as partners, in a relationship of almost thirty years. They divided their time between London residences and Paris, which they increasingly preferred after the obscenity trial connected with *The Well of Loneliness*. In both cities Hall made friends with many of the prominent lesbian figures of her day, from Ethel Smyth to Natalie Clifford Barney (the model for a major character in *The Well of Loneliness*). Late in life Hall had one further relationship, with Evguenia Souline, a Russian nurse she had engaged to care for the ailing Troubridge. After Hall's death in 1943, Troubridge, who lived for a further twenty years, wrote a memoir detailing their life together. Hall and Batten are buried in the same vault in Highgate Cemetery, London; Troubridge died in Rome and was buried there, her tombstone describing her as 'the friend of Radclyffe Hall'.

By the time of the First World War, Hall had published half a dozen well-received volumes of poetry. Yet where her novels are concerned, *The Well of Loneliness* has overshadowed all her other works, including *Adam's Breed* (1926) – the story of a misfit among a group of Italian migrants in Soho that won literary awards in both Britain and France. The early novel with the most overtly lesbian theme is *The Unlit Lamp* (1924), in which a girl falls in love with her female tutor, a learned and assertive 'New Woman'; she proves incapable of realizing her desires, however, caught between family obligations and her lack of resolve, and ends up defeated and unfulfilled. Fortunately, many later lesbians had a happier fate.

Christopher Isherwood 1904–1986

Christopher Isherwood had three lives. His first, and most forma-
tive, was that of an English gentleman born in the Edwardian
age. The second – as an expatriate in early 1930s Berlin – provided
experiences that made him and his writing famous. His third, and
longest, life, covering almost five decades, saw him settled in the
United States as an acclaimed author, a student of Hinduism and a
California celebrity.

Isherwood was born into the upper-middle class, his father a
lieutenant-colonel killed in the battle of Ypres in 1915, his mother
from a family of wine merchants. At Repton, a venerable independent
school, he met W. H. Auden, a life-long friend, literary collaborator and sometime lover. Isherwood read history at Cambridge, but
intentionally failed his tripos examinations – writing humorous
and facetious answers – which resulted in his expulsion in 1925 and
put paid to his mother's hope that he would become a don. Enrol-
ment to study medicine in London was an even more abbreviated
encounter with academia. In the meantime Isherwood was involved
in a sustained relationship with the violinist André Mangeot and was
working on his first novel, *All the Conspirators*, published in 1928.

Auden had gone to live in Berlin in the late 1920s, attracted by
Europe's most dynamic gay life, which included numerous bars
and cabarets, Magnus Hirschfeld's sexology institute, and readily
available men. He encouraged Isherwood (and Stephen Spender,
the third in the triangle of literary comrades) to follow, and so he
did. 'To Christopher, Berlin meant Boys,' Isherwood wrote neatly
in his autobiography. Weimar Germany provided a liberation from
inter-war England, and Isherwood indulged happily in its pleasures,
ultimately falling in love with a young man named Heinz Neddermeyer, the type of rough diamond extracted from the working class

to whom he felt attracted. On the horizon, however, was Nazism, and Isherwood's novels *Mr Norris Changes Trains* (1935) and *Goodbye to Berlin* (1939) deftly capture the oncoming menace that would bring the 'divine decadence' to an end. The novels scored an enormous success, and the works were eventually transformed into a play, a musical, and then, in 1972, the movie *Cabaret*. That film – with the handsome Michael York perfectly playing Isherwood, and Liza Minnelli singing memorable songs with more talent than the real *chanteuse* that she incarnated – is arguably the most popular gay-themed movie ever made, even if the gay adventures of Isherwood form only part of the plot.

The rise of Nazism forced expatriates such as Isherwood out of Germany. Isherwood and Neddermeyer went first to Greece, though the ruin-strewn land of antiquity so seductive to other homosexuals held little magic for men nostalgic for the boulevards of Berlin. England, too, proved uncongenial, and the Canaries provided only an interlude, since Neddermeyer was obliged to return to Germany, where in 1937 he was arrested for committing sexual offences and avoiding military service. Separated from his partner, the following year Isherwood went to the Far East with Auden, writing *Journey to a War* (1939) about their travels during the Sino-Japanese conflict.

In 1939 Isherwood, along with Auden, arrived in America as a refugee from a Europe on the verge of war. He settled in sunny southern California, as did many other expatriates. Isherwood adapted rapidly to American life, earning money as a scriptwriter and finding easy sexual contacts. He became keenly interested in the Indian Vedanta religion and philosophy, and retreated to a monastery set up by Swami Prabhavananda. They worked together on translations of the *Bhagavad Gita* and other texts, and Isherwood continued to study the scriptures, though without converting to Hinduism, after he left the monastery, confessing that sexual abstinence proved impossible.

In 1953, on a beach in Santa Monica, Isherwood met Don Bachardy, an attractive 16-year-old. Two years later they began an affair – a love story that lasted, despite the thirty-year age difference and occasional difficulties, for the rest of Isherwood's life. Isherwood nourished Bachardy's interest in art: after four years of study at art school, Bachardy developed great skill as a portrait painter and held his first one-man show, at the Redfern Gallery in London, in 1961. Over the years, Bachardy painted and drew countless portraits of the famous actors and writers who were the couple's friends, handsome young men who disported themselves around Hollywood and on the beaches of the Pacific, and those who commissioned his work. His favourite subject, however, was Isherwood, whose many portraits lovingly show him through the decades.

Isherwood appears as a key figure in his own works, from his autobiographical writings and Berlin stories (produced in the 1930s and long afterwards) to books about his parents and his guru. His life is also reflected in *A Single Man*, published in 1964. A story primarily about middle age (according to Isherwood), it centres on an academic trying to remake his world after the death of his lover. Isherwood wrote the novel when he and Bachardy were going through a rough patch in their relationship, and he was imagining what life would be like without his long-time partner. The 2009 film adaptation did much to revive interest in Isherwood's writings, and in a life that is uncommonly revealing about experiences of homosexuality over much of the 20th century.

4
THE FIN-DE-SIÈCLE AND BELLE ÉPOCH

Maximilian von Schwartzkoppen 1850–1917
and Alessandro Panizzardi 1853–1928

Homosexuals have at times been figures of scandal, and have been placed on trial, because of prohibitions against homosexual acts and solicitation. They have faced imprisonment and public shame, on some occasions so great as to ruin careers or lead to suicide. In other instances, they have been drawn into political scandals where sexuality was not of central importance, yet entered into the public consciousness – scandals involving treason, for instance. The Dreyfus case provides an illustration.

The Dreyfus Affair involved charges in 1893–94 that a Jewish captain in the French army had been selling military secrets to a German official: espionage and treason. A military court convicted Alfred Dreyfus and sent him to prison on Devil's Island, the 'tropical hell' of a French colony in South America. Despite efforts by family and supporters, he was reconvicted when the case went to appeal. Only after several more years was it proven that some of the documents used to convict Dreyfus had been forgeries, and that another person had been providing the secrets to the Germans. Dreyfus was eventually exonerated. For a decade, the case divided France between two camps bitterly debating the place of Jews, the honour of the military, and France's international reputation. Anti-Semitism, not surprisingly, played a large part in proclamations of Dreyfus' guilt.

There was a little-known homosexual side to the story. The initial memorandum used to indict Dreyfus was found by a cleaner in the rubbish bin of Captain Maximilian von Schwartzkoppen, a military attaché at the German embassy in Paris. Born in 1850 in Potsdam, the aristocratic Schwartzkoppen had served in the Westphalian infantry, and fought in the 1870–71 war in which Prussia dealt an ignominious defeat to the French. In the early 1890s, he took up the sensitive post in Paris.

Schwartzkoppen's counterpart at the Italian embassy was Alessandro Panizzardi. Probably unknown to most associates, because of their great discretion, was the fact that Schwartzkoppen and Panizzardi were engaged in an affair. However, in addition to the document used against Dreyfus, the French secret agents working in the German embassy also discovered letters from the Italian to Schwartzkoppen. Panizzardi wrote in slightly fractured French, sometimes signing himself 'Alexandrine' in letters to 'my dear friend' 'Maximilienne' (in the female form), or 'my little dog'. Panizzardi expressed his eagerness for meetings, cooing, 'Am I still your Alexandrine? When are you going to come to bugger me ... I'll come soon so you can bugger me anywhere. A thousand salutations from her who loves you so much.' One letter made a vague reference to a 'dangerous situation for me with a French officer', and a passing remark about maps of Nice that this 'scoundrel D.' had given him.

'D.' turned out not to be Dreyfus, but his prosecutors nevertheless felt that they had turned up useful evidence. Complicit officials compiled a dossier falsely suggesting that a homosexual circle including Schwartzkoppen and Panizzardi, and extending to Spanish and American attachés, was involved in espionage. The prosecutors did not make the information public, since they thought the revelations indecent. They also feared the effect that disclosure would have on French relations with Italy, which were growing uneasy because of Italy's alliance with Germany and Austria-Hungary. Furthermore, there had been riots against Italian migrants in France in 1893, and in 1894 an Italian anarchist had assassinated the French president. The prosecutors did, however, submit the secret dossier to the military tribunal (without sharing it with Dreyfus' lawyers), which inspected it in camera with some distaste.

Jews and homosexuals were both regarded with suspicion: they were considered sexually predatory and vice-ridden, but also effeminate and unmanly, lacking in bravery and honour. They were thought to be deracinated, potentially traitorous and criminal. The Dreyfus Affair, which unfolded in a country still chafing from military defeat and worried about its declining birth rate, posed challenges to established sexual and gender roles and contributed to a general crisis of French manhood. Revelations about two homosexual military attachés would have shocked the public, and to the court-martial panel even an indirect link between homosexuals and Jews could not but reinforce notions of moral and military danger to *la patrie*. One scholar has suggested that the guilty verdict imposed on Dreyfus represented not only a punishment of French Jews, but in some ways struck a surrogate blow against homosexuals.

There was a further homosexual twist to the complex Dreyfus Affair. Panizzardi, upset at Dreyfus' conviction, since he knew from Schwartzkoppen the real identity of the spy who had sold French documents, contacted a friend named Carlos Blacker, a wickedly handsome Englishman in Paris. Blacker was also a friend of Oscar Wilde (his best friend, according to some). Panizzardi and Blacker discussed releasing information to the press to show that Dreyfus was innocent, while presumably also taking care to ensure that Panizzardi's and Schwartzkoppen's identities (and their relationship) remained hidden. Wilde and Blacker had fallen out when Wilde briefly took up with Lord Alfred Douglas after his release from prison, but they were reconciled in Paris when Wilde claimed that he and Douglas had parted company. At that juncture Blacker told Wilde about

1 Suzuki Harunobu, 'The Evening Bell of the Clock', from *Eight Views of the Parlour*. Woodblock print, *c.* 1766. A subtle sensuality pervades this intimate scene of mistress and maid.

11 Walt Whitman, photographed *c.* 1860. 'The grandest man I have ever seen. The simplest, most natural, and strongest character' – Oscar Wilde.

III Domenico Beccafumi, *Saint Catherine of Siena Receiving the Stigmata*, *c.* 1513–15. Benedetta Carlini claimed that she too received Christ's wounds.

IV Joshua Horner, *Portrait of Anne Lister*, 1830. A 'female rake', Lister subverted traditional gender norms in work and love.

v Unknown artist, *Frederick II (1712–1786), King of Prussia*, 18th century. As Crown Prince, he had a doomed romance with Hans von Katte, and later clearly preferred the intimate companionship of other men.

VI Léon Bakst, *Portrait of Sergei Diaghilev and his Nanny*, 1906. Diaghilev's Ballets Russes transformed ballet with provocative and highly influential new pieces, and the impresario had affairs with several of his male dancers.

VII Eugène Jansson, *The Naval Bathhouse*, 1907. Swimmers and gymnasts were frequent subjects for the Swedish painter's studies of male beauty.

VIII Wilhelm von Gloeden, *Cain*, c. 1902. Von Gloeden combined classical ideals of Mediterranean beauty with homoerotic image-making.

IX Alair Gomes, *Beach*, *c.* 1970–80. Gomes' genre-defying photographs were often shot from his sixth-floor flat overlooking the beach in Rio.

x Bhupen Khakhar, pioneering Indian artist, photographed in 2002.

XI Bhupen Khakhar, *Yayati*, 1987. Khakhar's work embeds homosexual eroticism within Indian cultural life.

Panizzardi's revelations. He subsequently fell out again with Wilde, who had importuned him for money. But the Dreyfus-related information was now in circulation. Wilde passed it on to Chris Healey (also homosexual, and the lover of a correspondent for *The Observer* and *The New York Times*), and Healey, in turn, gave it to Émile Zola, from whom it was transmitted to the press. Publication of an anonymously signed article in a Paris newspaper in 1898, soon after Zola was convicted for his *J'accuse* attack on the anti-Dreyfusards, set in train the process that eventually led to Dreyfus' release and pardon.

Neither Schwartzkoppen nor Panizzardi seems to have suffered permanent damage. Their correspondence shows no shame or fear of repercussion over their relationship. In 1896 the Italian did break with the German, explaining enigmatically that 'an unsurmountable barrier will rise up between you and me'. Among later correspondence discovered by the French was a letter from a woman with whom Schwartzkoppen was sexually involved, a liaison that may have precipitated the rupture (though Panizzardi knew that Schwartzkoppen was bisexual). Panizzardi continued in his career, and a photograph taken in 1899 shows him as a debonair mustachioed and bemedalled officer; by the time of the First World War he had attained the rank of general. Schwartzkoppen, also much pained by Dreyfus' conviction, returned to Germany, where he served in the First World War and died of wounds in 1917.

Oscar Wilde 1854–1900

If there is any figure in the history of homosexuality who needs no introduction, it is Oscar Wilde. The patron saint of modern homosexuals, Wilde has occupied an unrivalled place in the pantheon of gay lives. Wilde is many things: raconteur, poet, novelist, playwright, man-about-town, celebrity, Irish nationalist and victim. Those multiple facets of his personality explain his continuing appeal: he is the subject of biographies, memoirs, plays and films; the British Library's catalogue lists 2,856 works under the keywords 'Oscar Wilde'; and a Google search turns up some 59 million results (Walt Whitman manages 16.5 million).

Wilde was born in Ireland in 1854. As the son of a prosperous surgeon, he enjoyed a background of bourgeois comfort, but his mother supported Irish nationalism, neatly placing him within the paradoxes of Victorian life. Wilde's provocation of society began very early, when as a child he was baptized twice: once into the Anglican Church of Ireland – his father's denomination – and then, several years later, as a Roman Catholic, at his mother's insistence.

Wilde studied at Trinity College, Dublin, and then went on to read Classics at Magdalen College, Oxford, between 1874 and 1879. It was a time when Hellenism, and the homosexual expression integral to classical culture, suffused Oxford, inspiring Walter Pater's theory of 'art for art's sake' and the celebration of male sociability and affection. Wilde cultivated a flamboyance that, both at Oxford and afterwards, contributed to his fame and would be mimicked by many 'camp' homosexuals for years to come. He sought and won celebrity in the drawing rooms and theatres of London, and during a wildly successful year-long tour of America delivered 150 lectures on topics ranging from Irish poetry to the decorative arts. Wilde travelled to other countries as well: he visited Baron von Gloeden in Sicily (like many other homosexuals), fixed up André Gide with a native bedpartner in North Africa, and frequented the *beau monde* in Paris. His 'posing as a somdomite' (as the Marquess of Queensberry, father of Lord Alfred Douglas, misspelled the accusation) foreshadowed what postmodernists call 'the performance of sexuality'.

Like many eminent Victorian homosexuals, and those of other eras, Wilde was married (to Constance Lloyd) and had children (two sons, Cyril and Vyvyan), but his homosexual tastes were manifest and protean. He felt attraction to men of all types and backgrounds – strong soldiers, Arab boys, the tousled-headed but feckless young aristocrat 'Bosie', and the gentle Canadian Robert Ross. He transgressed boundaries of sexual desire and of age and class.

As is well known, in 1895 Queensberry's allegation prompted Wilde to take out a warrant for criminal libel. At the Old Bailey, evidence of Wilde's frequentations led to Queensberry being found not guilty. Subsequently Wilde was arrested for offences under the 1885 Criminal Law Amendment Act, which had extended buggery legislation to criminalize any sexual acts between men. Wilde's oft-quoted words at his trial deserve to be repeated yet again, for they gave his loves a genealogy – the gay lives of antiquity and the Renaissance: '"The love that dare not speak its name" in this century is such a great affection of an elder for a younger man as there was between David and Jonathan, such as Plato made the very basis of his philosophy, and such as you find in the sonnets of Michelangelo and Shakespeare. It is that deep, spiritual affection that is as pure as it is perfect. It dictates and pervades great works of art … It is in this century misunderstood, so much misunderstood that it may be described as "the love that dare not speak its name", and on that account I am placed where I am now. It is beautiful, it is fine, it is the noblest form of affection. There is nothing unnatural about it. It is intellectual, and it repeatedly exists between an elder and a younger man, when the elder man has intellect, and the younger man has all the joy, hope and glamour of life before him. That it should be so, the world does not understand. The world mocks it, and sometimes puts one in the pillory for it.'

The world – or at least the British court system – did put Wilde in prison. After his release, his health and spirit broken, he wandered around the Continent for three years. He died in a shabby hotel in Paris in 1900, in his last moments, and with a final burst of wit, famously remarking that either the wallpaper or he had to go. The room, minus the wallpaper, is preserved in his memory and can be rented at an eye-watering rate.

Wilde was a literary phenomenon, and his works almost get lost in the personality cult. The repartee of comedies such as *Lady Windermere's Fan* (1892) and *The Importance of Being Earnest* (1895) pokes fun at the conventions of British life. *Salomé* (1891; originally written in French) remains a shocking representation of the biblical heroine–villain who demands the head of John the Baptist. *The Picture of Dorian Gray* (1891), arguably the most famous novel of its time, paints a darker portrait of vice and its rewards. His essay 'The Soul of Man under Socialism' (1891) suggests an aesthetic approach to anarchism, while *The Ballad of Reading Gaol* (1898) offers a meditation on life and death, man and his fate, and the tragedy of crime and of punishment.

Wilde's martyrdom is of great importance. Arrest, scandal, conviction and ignominy loomed as the possible fate for men in Britain, Germany, the United States and other countries where homosexual acts were illegal, and where even the finest words about love, the ancients and natural desires could not convince constables, jurors and legislators. The spectre of the dapper Wilde wearing tattered convict-clothes, the clever Oxonian on the treadmill of forced labour, haunted homosexuals.

Wilde shows up in gay culture around the world: both Yukio Mishima in Japan and Ugra in India, for instance, invoked him in their writings. An apposite quotation from Wilde's work (not to mention a well-placed lily) in the early decades of the 20th century indicated – to those who could read the signs – membership of the homosexual fraternity. One of the first openly gay bookshops in the world, opened in New York in 1967, took Oscar Wilde's name; and on the internet, the curious can hear what purports to be a scratchy recording of his creaky voice reading from *The Ballad of Reading Gaol*. He is memorialized in a rather lurid statue ('the fag on the crag', as Dubliners have affectionately dubbed it) in Merrion Square, near the house where he was born. The tomb in Père Lachaise cemetery in Paris where Wilde's remains were transferred in 1909 – in the presence of his son and Robbie Ross, faithful friend and former lover, whose own ashes would be buried there, too – seldom lacks for a flower, or a visitor cheerfully photographing and reverently touching the monument. Since 1998 Londoners have had Maggi Hambling's memorial, a bench-like sculpture in Adelaide Street where passers-by can sit to chat with Wilde, whose shoulders and head (smoking a cigarette, with consummate political incorrectness) rise as if from a coffin, or a bed, or perhaps (to paraphrase Wilde) just from the gutter, looking at the stars.

Wilhelm von Gloeden 1856–1931

Victorians knew Wilhelm von Gloeden for his photographs, often distributed as postcards, of Italian landscapes and genre scenes, shaded courtyards and picturesque peasants. He is now known primarily for the countless shots of naked Sicilian youths collected in albums destined for a gay audience. Although these seem quaint to the modern eye, von Gloeden remains the most important homoerotic image-maker of the late 1800s and early 1900s.

Born in northern Germany in 1856, von Gloeden moved to Italy as a young man, hoping the warm climate would cure his tuberculosis, and he took up photography as a hobby. Financial need turned the avocation into a profession, and the new market for picture postcards provided him with an income. He lived in Taormina until his death (except during the Great War, when he was forced, as an enemy alien, to leave Italy). The town is one of the most beautiful sites in Sicily: its hilltop houses looking over a well-preserved Greek theatre, the peak of Mount Etna and the 'wine-dark' Mediterranean. Taormina's residents were modest fisherfolk and artisans, but von Gloeden helped turn their town into a tourist attraction, visited by the kings of England, Spain and Siam, the German Kaiser, Eleonora Duse, Richard Strauss and Oscar Wilde.

Taormina provided the young men who posed for von Gloeden. Most stripped off their clothes, though the photographer sometimes costumed them with a mock toga or crowned them with a wreath of leaves. A few were perilously young, but the majority were ephebes, teenagers displaying the attributes of sexual maturity. Some pictures are stiff *tableaux vivants* of antique or modern Mediterranean life, and the occasional one exhibits a cheeky sexual innuendo. Others are simply portraits of shapely young men standing before the camera.

Von Gloeden's pictures provoke interest for several reasons. They embody an ideal of the beauty of Mediterranean youth that stretches back to antiquity. That ideal was revived in the work of Johann Joachim Winckelmann, father of art history, Enlightenment traveller to the Mediterranean, papal librarian, and victim of a rough male partner who murdered him in Trieste. Winckelmann saw statuary of the classical Greek male as the epitome of both beauty and artistic accomplishment. Male beauty, antique and contemporary, drew many visitors to the Mediterranean in the 19th century, and in Northern Europe Hellenists such as Walter Pater, working in Oxford in the late 1800s, promoted the Platonic vision of truth and beauty (even when colleagues applied real and metaphorical fig-leaves to the Classics). Von Gloeden's young men incarnated the ideal; even if they sometimes look a bit grubby, these *ragazzi* are dark-headed, finely muscled and seductive gods. This image of Mediterranean manliness remained the recurrent dream of many classically educated homosexuals until the early 20th century and beyond. Physical and emotional longing mixed easily with a romanticized nostalgia for the ancient world, where such desires flourished, and Italy had a special resonance as the place where sexual and cultural tourism went hand in hand.

Von Gloeden's experiences also make us wonder how he did what he did. After all, posing dozens of near-naked young men around the gardens of a small town in a Catholic country might have proved a provocation to the locals. Von Gloeden and his faithful major-domo Pancrazio Bucini (Il Moro, 'the dark one') apparently organized trysts that went well beyond the exigencies of photo sessions. Under different conditions, von Gloeden could have been indicted as a pornographer, a sodomite or possibly a paedophile. Homosexual acts, however, were not criminal in Italy; von Gloeden seems to have been a generous patron (he established bank accounts for some models and set up several young men in business); and his fame attracted tourists to Taormina. Perhaps the *mises en scène* of peasants and fishermen as classical heroes proved flattering to local sensibilities, and the youths probably enjoyed strutting around for the friendly foreign man and his new-fangled picture-taking apparatus. Southern mores, preserving the Madonna-inspired chastity of young women while encouraging expressions of male virility and camaraderie, allowed space and time in a young man's life for erotic games of the sort that von Gloeden played.

If von Gloeden's photos now appear risible to those accustomed to a more raw and explicit form of imagery, it is easy to forget the subtle ways in which they questioned the attitudes of their time. Villagers in Sicily, regarded even by many Italians as a wild, savage place, were cast as the inheritors of the classical world. Antique settings made homosexuality – sin, crime and illness, to moralizing contemporaries – noble. The idyllic outdoor compositions of ordinary adolescents and seaside landscapes made 'unnatural' desires look very natural. Taormina was far removed from the dens of urban depravity associated in the common view with homosexual vice. The easy comradeship of boys with their arms thrown around friends' shoulders, or lounging together on a terrace, suggested a utopia of happy and affectionate bonding, not the sordid backstreet couplings denounced in the yellow press. The gamut of ages in von Gloeden's pictures suggested the dawning of sexual awareness in adolescence and earlier. The full-frontal exuberance of the models presents an image of sexuality that in the hands of some of von Gloeden's contemporary painters and photographers looked coy and abashed. Even if they are often pseudo-classical, the themes of his pictures allude to artistic conventions – the figure study, the ages of man, the Three Graces, the odalisque, bathers, the good Samaritan, a haloed saint, mythological characters – that set him within the curriculum of art history. His most famous image, echoing a painting by Hippolyte Flandrin, shows a boy sitting on a rock with his head on his knees; it offers an existential statement about youth, sexuality and the individual in the world.

Other photographers, such as Vincenzo Galdi and Guglielmo Plüschow, imitated von Gloeden, but their work was more blatantly pornographic. Some of their images no doubt served as tourist brochures, and the Mediterranean pilgrimage that had begun before von Gloeden continued. The German industrialist Friedrich Krupp and the French writer Jacques d'Adelswärd-Fersen were denizens of Capri, Italy's other homosexual hideaway, while John Addington Symonds and A. E. Housman formed liaisons with gondoliers. Thomas Mann's fictional Aschenbach met his death in Venice, even if the lad he longed for, Tadzio, was a blond Pole rather than a swarthy Italian.

Von Gloeden and Il Moro lived a contented life in Taormina; only after the German's death did Fascists destroy many of his photographic plates. By that time, other venues for homosexual fantasy beckoned, but the Mediterranean had occupied the centre of the homosexual map for centuries, the place where, it was hoped, antique statues came to life and the quest for beauty found its fulfilment. The reality in the technicolour landscape might be less romantic – an impecunious young man bargaining pleasure for a few coins – yet no other travelogue proved so seductive.

Sergei Diaghilev 1872–1929

It is difficult to overstate the importance of Sergei Diaghilev's Ballets Russes in early 20th-century European culture. His troupe reinvigorated an effete, moribund art form and became great celebrities of the age. But his reach extended far beyond the world of dance: Diaghilev introduced exotic Russian themes to the West and contributed to burgeoning interest in Orientalism, primitivism and a revival of classical motifs. The Ballets Russes had an immense influence on the visual arts, bringing together a star-studded ensemble of composers and artists – Stravinsky, Picasso and Cocteau, among the most famous – in the process contributing to the birth of modernism. In terms of gender, Diaghilev's works challenged stereotypes and elevated the male dancer to the central role previously occupied by women. The homosexual ethos of the impresario's circle, both dancers and audience, made the Ballets Russes a vital arena of gay life.

Diaghilev came from the provincial gentry. His was an aspirational and cultured family, which would lose its wealth (earned from vodka distilleries) through financial mismanagement. Sergei studied law at the University of St Petersburg, travelled widely in Europe – calling on Oscar Wilde in London – and in 1898 set up a pioneering journal, *Mir iskusstva* ('World of Art'). This established Diaghilev as a promoter of culture, although he was also a writer and composer in his own right. Diaghilev gained entry to the tsar's court and organized art exhibitions in the Russian capital and, later, in Paris. He secured appointment as an administrator at the Imperial Theatres, which managed the Bolshoi in Moscow and the Mariinsky in St Petersburg – a role that sparked his interest in ballet.

Before long Diaghilev turned from ballet administrator to impresario, and decided to take a troupe of Russian dancers to Paris. After several years of preparation, the Ballets Russes arrived in 1909, presenting a season of works that showed off Russian culture, abstract-style choreography and the principals' dancing prowess.

Although a financial drain, these first performances in Paris scored an enormous triumph. The poet Anna de Noailles summed up the effect: 'It was as if Creation, having stopped on the seventh day, now all of a sudden resumed.' Over the next twenty years, the troupe performed annually in Paris, London and other capitals, and also toured the Americas. The Ballets Russes became the most important ballet company in the world, presenting some traditional works but specializing in provocative new pieces – such as *The Rite of Spring*, which, with its innovative dance vocabulary and avant-garde music by Stravinsky, ignited a riot in Paris in 1913. Later works, such as the first Cubist ballet, *Parade* (1917), which boasted sets by Picasso, a libretto by Cocteau and music by Erik Satie, continued the company's flair for confrontational brilliance.

Diaghilev filled his private life with handsome young men – dancers, choreographers and assistants who became his lovers. Although his father had taken him to a prostitute for sexual initiation, Diaghilev was exclusively attracted to men. Despite homosexual acts being criminal in tsarist Russia, the upper echelons of society proved tolerant of such proclivities, and his circle included many homosexuals, such as the poet Mikhail Kuzmin, who like Diaghilev cruised around St Petersburg's parks and artistic salons for cadets and students. Diaghilev's first lover was his wealthy cousin and the co-editor of *Mir iskusstva*, Dmitry Filosofov. Their relationship ended after a decade when Diaghilev learned that Filosofov was trying to steal his own current lover-on-the-side; Diaghilev made a scene in a restaurant, but parted with Filosofov in tears when he left for France. He then marked time sexually with a new companion, Aleksei Mavrin, whom he took for a honeymoon to the Mediterranean.

Diaghilev's meeting with the 17-year-old Vaslav Nijinsky in 1907 provided him with a new lover and gave the Ballets Russes its greatest star; he would become the world's leading male dancer. It was a former partner, Prince Pavel Lvov – homosexual, aristocratic and artistic circles were intimately linked – who passed Nijinsky on to Diaghilev. Count Harry Kessler, a homosexual habitué of the ballet, remarking on Nijinsky's extraordinary agility and strength in soaring above the stage, wrote that he was like 'a butterfly, but at the same time he is the epitome of manliness and youthful beauty'. Nijinsky was now the focus of both Diaghilev's private and professional activities. Diaghilev required loyalty from his protégés, however, and when Nijinsky unexpectedly married in 1913 Diaghilev was left distraught and bitter, dismissing him from the company.

Soon Diaghilev found another budding dancer, the darkly seductive 18-year-old Léonide Massine. Kessler again commented: 'Nijinsky was a Greek god, Massine a small, wild, graceful creature of the Steppes.' Soon they were cavorting on a trip to Italy. Less dramatically gifted as a dancer than Nijinsky, Massine became the much-applauded chief choreographer for the Ballets Russes. Although bedded by Diaghilev, he went his heterosexual way in 1921 (he, too, was sent packing from the ballet company). Next for Diaghilev came an affair with another teenager, Boris Kochno – a former lover of the composer Karol Szymanowski who would later have a fling with Cole Porter. Diaghilev's interest eventually waned, even if they continued to work together. His new flame was a tall, elegant English dancer who performed under the name Anton Dolin; Lydia Lopokova, one of Diaghilev's dancers and John Maynard Keynes' future wife, noted succinctly: 'Shadow of Oscar Wilde'. Then came another grand dancer and choreographer, Serge Lifar, also young and beautiful. ('I don't like young men over twenty-five,' Diaghilev conceded.) Diaghilev's last 'official' lover was Igor Markevitch, a sweet 16; he subsequently earned a reputation as composer and conductor, and married one of Nijinsky's daughters.

Diaghilev died in Venice during a holiday with Markevitch; Lifar and Kochno soon arrived to pay their tribute. Nijinsky was mentally ill, suffering from the schizophrenia that would confine him to clinics until his death in 1950.

Diaghilev's loves were central to his life and to that of the Ballets Russes. Those who attended performances also appreciated the dancers. The gay Bloomsbury artist Duncan Grant painted pictures of the performers and enshrined a photo of Nijinsky on his mantelpiece; and Keynes admitted that he first attended the Ballets Russes to 'view Mr Nijinsky's legs'. Homosexuals such as Cocteau, Ravel and Reynaldo Hahn flocked around the company for artistic stimulation and for the homoerotic pleasures of its ambiance.

The Ballets Russes' productions were sexually charged, and often homoerotic. Early in his career, the Bolshoi had dismissed Nijinsky for wearing a too-revealing costume, and his later outfits showed off his fine body even more than was common in ballet. In the notorious *L'Après-midi d'un faune* (1912), Nijinsky, clad in a tight bodysuit, mimed masturbation on the scarf of a paramour. In *Schéhérazade* (1910), one of the most famous of Diaghilev's creations, Nijinsky's rather feminine-looking costumes and camp movements bent expectations of gender; other performances showed him off varyingly as masculine or androgynous. *Narcisse* (1911) presented the ancient story of the hunter who fell in love with himself, and ballets featuring sailors played on a homosexual obsession of the time. Writing about a seduction scene featuring two girls and a young man in *Jeux* (1913) – a ballet set on a tennis court that he choreographed – Nijinsky revealed how 'Diaghilev wanted to make love to two boys at the same time and wanted these boys to make love to him … I camouflaged these personalities on purpose.' Few productions passed up on the chance to reveal the physiques of such dancers as Massine and Dolin, making the Ballets Russes a very gay spectacle.

Jacques d'Adelswärd-Fersen 1880–1923

Jacques d'Adelswärd-Fersen (or simply 'Fersen', as he sometimes signed himself) was blessed by the gods. Tall and slender, with a shock of blond hair, he personified a type of handsome elegance. His pedigree was grand, and he had the title of baron, though he later promoted himself to count. A Swedish nobleman in his ancestry had been Marie-Antoinette's lover. His paternal grandfather had served in the Paris constituent assembly of 1848 (and briefly gone into exile with Victor Hugo), and was the founder of a steelworks in Longwy, in Lorraine, while an ancestor on his mother's side founded the Paris newspaper *Le Soir*. Fersen was wealthy, having inherited a fortune from the Lorraine factories. He was well educated in the best Parisian *lycée*, and briefly continued his studies at the elite École des Sciences Politiques and at the University of Geneva. He was also talented, in his short life publishing almost twenty novels and books of poetry. He lived luxuriously in a Paris apartment near the Arc de Triomphe, and in a clifftop mansion he had built on Capri.

Fersen's life incarnates several key aspects of gay history. He was a dandy who moved in a cosmopolitan and cultured homosexual milieu of the Belle Époque. He ran afoul of the law, and was sentenced to six months in prison for inciting youth to debauchery. Like many homosexuals of the time, he experienced the magnetic attraction of Italy and the East. He edited the first French literary journal to treat homosexual themes, and his own writings evoke antiquity, aestheticism, exoticism and male loves.

By the dawn of the 20th century, when he was only in his early twenties, Fersen had already published a *Conte d'amour* (1898), *Chansons légères* (1900), *L'Hymnaire d'Adonis, à la façon de M. le Marquis de Sade* (1902), and a book on Venice, *Notre-Dame des mers mortes*

(1902). A habitué of aristocratic salons, he also organized soirées at his residence, attended by members of Paris society, at which young men – students whom he recruited from secondary schools – dressed in mock classical garb for *tableaux vivants*, and where Fersen and others recited poetry. He also had sex with many of the boys – behaviour that brought him to the attention of the police and led to his arrest and sentencing on morals charges. The *affaire Fersen*, and the incarceration of the author and a fellow aristocrat, fed rumours of orgies and black masses; they filled the pages of Paris newspapers, which caricatured the manners and morals of these devotees of antiquity and young men. For good measure, in 1905 Fersen himself wrote a novel about the scandal, *Lord Lyllian*.

Once released from jail Fersen fled to Capri, which, along with Taormina in Sicily – where Fersen visited the photographer Wilhelm von Gloeden – was already becoming a mecca for those who found Italy more congenial than northern countries to their tastes. Fersen also travelled to Rome, where he met Nino Cesarini, a 15-year-old newspaper vendor who became his life-long companion. While Fersen's Neoclassical Villa Lysis was being constructed on Capri, near the ruins of one of Tiberius' palaces, he journeyed to Ceylon, where he discovered opium and became enamoured (in Orientalist fashion) of the mysteries of the East. He also found houseboys to bring back to Capri.

To present-day readers, Fersen's writings are hothouse in style and feverish in emotion. The poems of *Ainsi chantait Marsyas*, published in 1907, are illustrative. The opening poem maps the lover's body: 'Warm breast on which opals fade / Armpit, golden vapours deep in light and shade / Burnished heels, sinewy calves, the odours of the male / Belly whence the rose incense stifles the voice that moans.' A dedication to Nino vows: 'Nothing can ever tear you from my arms / God himself could not unseal our lips … / You are my blood, you are my flesh, you are my fever! And you are the sole good which will never be taken from me.' In a poem entitled 'Nino', 'Your name is the light / And the blue sky / A ray of prayerful sun / In the depths of your eyes … / It is Italian languor / In a kiss / Around which my soul agonises … / It is the soft and sweet perfume / Of the death of flowers.' Other poems fear the loss of the beloved – one is a vicious text explicitly inscribed to a woman who had been pursuing Nino – or the loss of beauty with the ravages of age. Alcibiades and Antinous are summoned, and the landscapes of Italy and Asia invoked, in the celebration of love and its lingering memory.

Few authors dared to voice their homosexual sentiments as clearly as Fersen. And relatively few would write a novel such as *Et le feu s'éteignit sur la mer* (1909), in which a sculptor enamoured of Classics leaves his wife for a male companion, braving social opprobrium and Christian sanction: 'For twenty centuries this monstrous doctrine of sacrifice prevailed by its cowardice in the face of imaginary tortures and the fear of a ridiculous hell.'

Fersen's work merits rereading. *Et le feu s'éteignit sur la mer* offers mordant comic portraits of *arriviste* Americans, pretend Russian nobles, precious pedants, and what he called 'tea-caddy' Englishmen; and his overwrought poems nevertheless contain lines of great beauty. Fersen's last work, *Hei Hsiang* (1921), with its evocation of China and India, its poems about Oscar Wilde and Lord Alfred Douglas, and its description of ideal youths, is a testimony to a certain early 20th-century homosexual sensibility.

In Paris in 1909, Fersen began publication of a splendidly produced literary journal, *Akademos*, which he described as a monthly review of art and criticism. Although it managed only twelve issues, its articles included pieces on aestheticism, the renaissance of paganism, paintings of St Sebastian, the poetry of Sappho, and androgynous love; in addition there were translations of Javanese legends and Arabic poems. Artistic engravings of many comely men – the canonical Antinous and St Sebastian among them – underlined the review's orientation, as did its contributors: the homosexual authors Georges Eekhoud and Achille Essebac, for instance, and luminaries such as the bisexual Colette.

Fersen weathered occasional attacks (his novel on Capri riled many local people), continuing to travel, write and entertain a *Who's Who* of visitors to the Villa Lysis. His weakness was drugs, however – one room at the villa was set aside for opium-smoking, and he also used cocaine. His death – caused by a heart attack, according to autopsy reports – was probably provoked by an overdose of cocaine mixed into a glass of champagne, prepared during a meal with Nino after he had returned, ill, from Naples. In his poem 'The Last Supper', a clairvoyant Fersen foresaw the scene of an antique love in the modern world: 'Pale, dazzled by the moon's ardour / Which spreads through the heavens in mystic splendour / United for the last twilight on earth / On the edge of a Greek bay consumed in light / Here, marmoreal, the gods resuscitated …'. Fersen's tomb overlooks the Bay of Naples, and his life was memorialized in Roger Peyrefitte's novel *L'Exilé de Capri* (1959). Nino Cesarini, to whom Fersen left shares in the family steelworks, bank accounts and use of the house in Capri, died in Rome in 1943. The Villa Lysis is now a museum.

Karol Szymanowski 1882–1937

O ne of the most intriguing early 20th-century composers, Karol Szymanowski was born into the Polish gentry, growing up on his family's estate in the Ukraine, where many Poles had settled after their country's absorption into the Russian Empire. As well as speaking Polish, he learned Russian, French and German as a child, and studied music with his father and tutors before enrolling in a musical academy in Warsaw. While there, he became associated with the Young Poland group of intellectuals, who, greatly influenced by Symbolism, agitated for a revival in the Polish arts. Over the next few years Szymanowski travelled around Europe, returning to the family house to compose. Exempted from military service in the First World War because of a childhood injury that left him lame, he experienced some of his most creative years composing in the Polish countryside. The idyll would not last, however: with the arrival of the Bolshevik Revolution the family home was destroyed, and in the midst of violence and bloodshed Szymanowski and his family fled to Warsaw.

Szymanowski's outpouring of works in the postwar years – concertos, settings for poems, symphonies, religious compositions – brought him fame in Poland and abroad, but his finances were never healthy, and sometimes dire. A period as director of the Warsaw Conservatory (1927–29) and then as head of the Polish Academy of Music (1930–32) proved neither happy nor successful: there were conflicts with colleagues, and the Polish state was becoming increasingly authoritarian. Alcoholism and tuberculosis precipitated his death, in a Swiss sanatorium, at the age of 54. After a state funeral, he was buried in Kraków.

Although a proud Pole, Szymanowski espoused what he termed 'pan-Europeanism' – a type of cultured cosmopolitanism – and criticized the provincialism of compatriots and of the independent Poland that emerged in 1918. He was particularly drawn to Italy, where he had travelled regularly before the war, visiting Florence, Rome and other cities. His real magnet was Sicily: he was enamoured of the seaside town of Taormina and the antique ruins of Syracuse. The Islamic world and its culture also beckoned, prompting visits to Tunisia and Algeria, where he borrowed themes for his settings of erotic and mystic poems by Hafiz and Rumi.

Like many others of his age and inclinations, Szymanowski thus followed the pathway to the Mediterranean. The pianist Arthur Rubinstein recollected one conversation: 'After his return he raved about Sicily, especially Taormina. "There," he said, "I saw a few young men bathing who could be models for Antinous. I couldn't take my eyes off them." Now he was a confirmed homosexual, he told me all this with burning eyes.'

Although Szymanowski's orientation is beyond doubt, there are few published details about his private life. From what we know, it seems that his most important relationship was probably his summer affair, during 1919, with Boris Kochno, a 15-year-old Russian with literary aspirations. Rubinstein quoted Szymanowski's recollection: 'I found the greatest happiness – I lived in heaven. I met a young man of the most extraordinary beauty, a poet with a voice that was music, and, Arthur, he loved me. It is only thanks to our love that I could write so much music.' Owing to the chaos of warfare in Poland, they lost contact after the holiday; several later meetings in Paris were made awkward by Kochno's new relationship with Sergei Diaghilev. Little is revealed about Szymanowski's other loves. Alistair Wightman, the author of a 400-page biography of Szymanowski, acknowledges the composer's sexuality but is coy about his emotional life, providing only tidbits: Szymanowski spent part of a trip to New York 'in pursuit of' a man the composer described as 'the young (and beautiful) Lord Allington'; and in his last years, 'a string of young men' apparently came to his retreat in the Tatra Mountains, the 'first of whom was the novelist Zbigniew Unilowski, who was passed off as the composer's secretary'.

Szymanowski expressed his sexuality most clearly in a two-volume novel, *The Ephebe*, written soon after the First World War. It was never published: the manuscript remained in the hands of his friend (and sometime librettist) Jarosław Iwaszkiewicz, but was destroyed in the German bombing of Warsaw in 1939. In 1981 a Polish musicologist in Paris discovered some miscellaneous commentaries on the book, as well as one long chapter that Szymanowski had translated into Russian for Kochno. Several French-language poems that the composer had appended speak of his search for love and the pleasure he took in a young partner's caresses, even in the face of social disapproval.

The surviving chapter of Szymanowski's novel, finally published in 1993 in German, is a dialogue on homosexual and heterosexual love, with arguments advanced by a classically educated German nobleman and a Frenchman resident in Florence, who argues the superiority of love between men. The main protagonists in the full novel, as remembered by Iwaszkiewicz, are a beautiful young Polish prince and aspiring writer, and his companion, an older composer, the two characters representing different aspects of Szymanowski's persona. The setting is Italy. In one section, called the 'Tale of the Saintly Youth Enoch Porfiry, Iconographer', a rebel artist creates a fresco for a Byzantine church that shows not a dying Christ but a handsome youth; he is killed by outraged priests, foreshadowing the duel between Christianity and antiquity in Szymanowski's opera *King Roger* (1924).

The musicologist Stephen Downes has argued that Eros is a unifying theme in Szymanowski's work. It appears most homoerotically in *King Roger*, the composer's masterwork, which was influenced by his memories of Italy and his reading of Nietzsche, Walter Pater and Euripides. The opera is set in the early 12th century, at the court of

King Roger in Sicily – a crossroads where Greek, Arabic, Latin and Norman influences blended. The work concerns the pull between Christian asceticism, represented as the opera opens by the grandeur of the Orthodox liturgy, and Dionysian hedonism, personified by a beautiful young shepherd – 'My God is as beautiful as I,' he tells the king. The queen and courtiers are seduced, but at the end of the opera Roger neither follows the shepherd nor returns to the world of tradition – even if his lyrical greeting of the sunrise nevertheless suggests a step towards personal emancipation. Szymanowski planned to readdress the conflict in another work, on the Renaissance sculptor Benvenuto Cellini; it was never written, although he summarized the scenario as one in which 'mankind abandoned the harsh, cold churches, forgot about the scent of incense, about priestly psalmodies to find himself in the bright light of the sun, surrounded by beautiful figures'.

5

WOMEN WHO LOVED WOMEN

Eleanor Butler 1739–1829
and Sarah Ponsonby 1755–1831

'Sisters in Love, a love allowed to climb,
Even on this earth, above the reach of Time!'

Thus did William Wordsworth, after a visit to their house in north Wales, describe the 'Ladies of Llangollen', two women who lived together for fifty years. Eleanor Butler and Sarah Ponsonby were born not far from each other in rural Ireland. Both boasted aristocratic connections: Butler was the daughter of an earl, while Ponsonby's great-grandparents included an earl and a viscount. When she was a child, Butler's Catholic family dispatched her to France for a convent education, but it was back in Ireland, in 1768, that she met Ponsonby, an orphan sent by her guardian to boarding school. The two became fast friends, visiting and writing to each other. As she matured, Ponsonby resisted suggestions that it was time for her to marry, and Butler refused to fulfil her mother's desire that she become a nun.

The two women conceived a plan to elope to England, but were foiled by their families, who separated them and confined them to their homes. The persistence with which they continued to demand to live together eventually persuaded the elders to give in, perhaps fearing some greater scandal if they tried again to elope, or if Ponsonby's claims to have suffered the unwanted advances of her guardian became public. Reluctantly, Butler's brother provided a small annuity. Accompanied by a woman servant, Butler and Ponsonby left Ireland and finally settled in Llangollen. There they purchased a cottage, which they enlarged and remodelled into a mock-Gothic folly filled with old woodcarvings, thousands of books (in English, French, Italian and other languages), and keepsakes ranging from antique clocks to a letter from the king of France and a lock of Mary Queen of Scots' hair, as well as the silver and glassware on which their joined initials were engraved.

The ladies lived a quiet life, reading, writing, playing music, doing embroidery and engaging in similarly genteel pursuits. A gardener, a footman and two female servants attended to their needs. Neighbours became accustomed to the sight of the two strolling about the village, often wearing long coats and hats described as mannish. Their situation and their literary interests made celebrities of them, and among a long list of personalities who came to call were Edmund Burke, Lord Byron, Sir Walter Scott and the duke of Wellington. Even if they were apparently occasionally annoyed by the procession of visitors, the ladies offered tea and conversation.

In 1790 the Llangollen couple reacted angrily to a newspaper article hinting that their relationship was perverse. On hearing the news, Burke wrote, 'I trust that the piety, good sense, and fortitude that … make you the mark of envy in your retreat will enable you on recollection perfectly to despise the scandals', consoling them by pointing out that 'you suffer only by the baseness of the age you live in … the calumny for the virtues that entitle you to the esteem of all who know how to esteem honour, friendship, principle, and dignity of thinking'. Occasional rumours continued to circulate about the impropriety and debauchery of their attachment, but the ladies remained eminently respectable in their behaviour.

When Butler died, at the age of 90, the inscription that Ponsonby chose for her tombstone paid tribute to 'an almost unequalled excellence of heart', 'manners worthy of her illustrious birth' and 'brilliant vivacity of mind'. 'Her various perfections, crowned by the most pious and cheerful submission to the Divine will', it continued, were most fully appreciated by God 'and by her, of whom for more than fifty years they consisted in that happiness which, through our blessed Redeemer, she trusts will be renewed when this tomb shall have closed over its latest tenant'. On Ponsonby's neighbouring gravestone, two years later, was written: 'She did not long survive her beloved companion, Lady Eleanor Butler, with whom she had lived in this valley for more than half a century of uninterrupted friendship.'

During their lifetimes and afterwards, the ladies' visitors and writers generally viewed them with sympathetic, if sometimes bemused, curiosity. An 1847 volume brought together some con- temporary accounts that provide illustrations: a newspaper in 1796 noted that 'Miss Butler and Miss Ponsonby are now retired from the society of men into the wilds of Llangollen', and reported that one caller 'found not in them the gravity, formality, and demureness of virgin recluses, but the ease of liveliness, and animated conversation of happy, cultivated, and polished minds'. An actor whose perfor- mance they attended in 1820 referred to them as 'the dear inseparable inimitables'; at a dinner the 'dear antediluvian darlings' arrived in 'manified [*sic*] dress, with the Croix de St. Louis, and other orders, and myriads of large brooches, with stones large enough for snuff-boxes, stuck in their starched neckcloths!'. (Dressing up, and pinning on would-be decorations, seems to have been a hobby.) A gentleman who had visited in the company of Sir Walter Scott described the situation of the women 'who having been one or both crossed in love, forswore all dreams of matrimony in the heyday of youth, beauty, and fashion, and selected this charming spot for the repose of their now time-honoured virginity'. A German prince who had met 'the most celebrated virgins in Europe' when he passed through Wales also reflected on the peculiar life of women who 'took it in their heads to hate men, to love only each other'. For one Englishwoman, the hermits (as she called them) 'devoted their long lives so romantically to friendship, celibacy, and the knitting of blue stockings'. A French woman tourist saw in them the 'model of perfect friendship since their early life', as 'they had no difficulty to persuade themselves that heaven had formed them for each other'. Anne Lister, a contemporary whose diaries record her ardent lesbian relationships, said of their union: 'I cannot help thinking that surely it was not Platonic.' Butler and Ponsonby referred to each other simply as 'my better half', 'my sweet love', and 'my beloved'.

Present-day historians such as Martha Vicinus view Butler and Ponsonby as brave and learned women who challenged the expectations of their families and of society. Together they epitomized the 'romantic friendship': the type of partnership – often called a 'Boston marriage' in the United States – that women sometimes formed in the 19th and early 20th centuries. It would be unreasonable to assume that erotic desires and gestures were not part of some of these unions.

Anne Lister 1791–1840

A contemporary of the Ladies of Llangollen, Anne Lister was one of the most active lesbians of the early 19th century. The daughter of a Yorkshire doctor, she recorded her sexual desires and encounters in a numeric, algebraic and Greek code she devised for secret sections of a 4-million-word diary. She also adopted a vocabulary for her sexual notations: 'kiss' for orgasm, 'connection with the ladies' for lesbianism, and 'going to Italy' for sexual relations accompanied by full commitment.

Lister's romantic and sexual liaisons have the makings of a novel, and Leila Rupp, in a study of lesbians in history, calls her a 'female rake'. Lister had her first lesbian experience, with a half-Indian fellow student, at her boarding school. At the age of 19, she began an affair with Isabella ('Tib') Norcliffe, with whom she enjoyed several trips to Italy. In 1812, through Norcliffe (whom she jettisoned two years later), Lister met the woman who would be the love of her life, Marianna Belcombe, one of five sisters and the daughter of a doctor. Four years later, for financial and family reasons, Marianna married an ageing widower named Charles Lawton, though the women did not intend this to be the end of their relationship. Indeed, Marianna presented the ring that her fiancé had given her to Lister, who replaced it with one on which she had her initials engraved. The two women continued to see each other, though they were pained by the separation that matrimony brought. Marianna's husband then discovered a letter from Lister to his wife musing on how they could live on Lawton's inheritance when he died. He barred his house to his wife's friend. Later he relented, and the women were able to keep regular company, with Lister writing of the women's union as a true marriage; their intimate encounters were apparently common knowledge.

Lister's attentions, after a time, wandered. She took up again, erotically, with Norcliffe. But at a women's country weekend, attended by Belcombe's sisters Anne and Harriet, other possibilities occurred. Within a short time, Lister had seduced Anne, as she related: 'Talking ... but then got more loving. Kissed her, told her I had a pain in my knees – my expression to her for desire – & saw plainly she likes me & would yield again, without much difficulty, to opportunity & importun[ity]'. Several days later, she was flirting with Harriet, and may have had some sort of sexual relations with her as well.

In 1824, now financially secure because of her effective management of the family's estates near Halifax, on which she had opened a profitable colliery, Lister went to Paris. In the *pension* where she lodged, she met and began an affair with another Englishwoman, Maria Barlow, who would refer to herself as both Lister's 'husband' and her 'mistress'. They rented an apartment together, and for several years Lister commuted between her two partners, Barlow in France and Marianna Belcombe in England. On one occasion, Lister even introduced the two women to each other. Barlow liked the mannish persona Lister affected (which Belcombe did not), and even considered the possibility of their being married, with Lister cross-dressing as the bridegroom. Lister and Belcombe, meanwhile, continued to wear each other's rings, and in 1825 they carried out another private partnership ceremony: 'Marianna put me on a new watch riband & then cut the hair from her queer [genitals] & I that from mine, which she put each into the little lockets we got at Bright's this morning, twelve shillings each, for us always to wear under our clothes in mutual remembrance. We both of us kissed each bit of hair before it was put into the locket.'

Lister persisted with her dual relationships, and her recurrent flirtations with Norcliffe and the other Belcombe sisters, but she also had an affair with a French noblewoman during her stay in Paris. In 1832 she fell in love with yet another woman, a widowed heiress (her wealth a not inconsequential attraction) who was a neighbour in Halifax, where Lister lived at her family seat, Shibden Hall. Anne Walker soon moved in. They swore vows of love on a Bible, exchanged rings and, a day after having sex, took Holy Communion together at the parish church and rewrote their wills to each other's benefit.

Their life together was somewhat troubled by Walker's melancholy and depression; Lister sent her to none other than Belcombe's brother, a doctor, for treatment. The two women occasionally travelled, and Lister was the first woman to scale several high peaks in the Pyrenees. It was on another journey, to the Caucasus Mountains in Georgia, that Lister died of a fever. Walker returned to England with Lister's embalmed remains, which were buried at her local church in Halifax. Walker ended her days in a mental asylum.

Lister's life, and her various sexual engagements, are particularly revealing. For Martha Vicinus, a historian of 19th-century Britain, Lister's story says something important about women's sexual desire (and Lister's was clearly strong) as well as their yearnings for friendship. It addresses questions of gender, in terms of Lister's self-modelling as mannish and the way she often played a more stereotypically masculine role in sexual assertiveness, ambition and business dealings. The ceremonies that Lister performed with her partners replicated the rituals of a wedding, and Lister thought of herself, in her unions with Belcombe and Walker, as being united in marriage, though obviously not monogamously. The rounds of flirtation and bed-hopping chronicle the homosocial environment (even in its international dimensions) of women who loved women. For Anna Clark and Jennifer Frangoes, Lister in her life and diaries was not only living a lesbian life, but defining a lesbian identity.

'I love and only love the fairer sex,' said Lister, an affirmation of her desires and her sexual identification. Lister – 'Fred', as lovers called her, or 'Gentleman Jack' to her Yorkshire neighbours – has been called the first modern lesbian, and in 2010 formed the subject of a television documentary and a dramatization of her diaries. They provide a different perspective on the Regency England of Jane Austen, and bring to public view an important chapter in the history of lesbian lives.

Eva Gore-Booth 1870–1926

The Gore-Booths were Anglo-Irish gentry, with landholdings of 25,000 acres and a stately home, Lissadell, in County Sligo. Eva's father, the Eton-educated fifth baronet, managed the family estate (earning respect for his humane treatment of the peasants who farmed his lands) and served as chairman of the local railway. He also took part in four expeditions to the Arctic, which involved a mixture of hunting, fishing, natural history, navigation, and even a search for an explorer lost at sea. Eva's mother was a cultivated gentlewoman with aristocratic connections.

Educated at home, Gore-Booth learned French, German, Latin and Greek from a governess. As a young woman, she was presented at court to Queen Victoria. She travelled with her father to America and the West Indies in 1894, and the following year attended the Wagner festival in Bayreuth. Figures of the Irish cultural renaissance came to dine at Lissadell, including William Butler Yeats, who composed a poem about Eva and her sister. Since she suffered from periods of illness, family and doctors hoped that a trip to the warmth of Italy would help restore her health. The journey would change her life.

In Italy Gore-Booth met Esther Roper, a woman born in 1868 in Cheshire, whose parents had served as missionaries in Africa. She became Gore-Booth's life partner, and they remained together for some thirty years, until Gore-Booth's death. It was Roper who sparked Gore-Booth's interest in the social question, having worked for the trade unions and campaigned in city slums. The two women soon moved in together in Manchester – whose industrial grittiness made a dramatic change from leafy Lissadell – and devoted themselves to social activism. They became prominent figures in the Manchester University Settlement, an institution that provided education and welfare for impoverished workers. The trade unions were a particular focus, especially those that represented women workers both in the local textile industry and elsewhere. In this context it was perhaps natural that the campaign for women's suffrage should attract their efforts, and Roper became secretary of the Manchester National Society for Women's Suffrage. In their collaborative work Roper favoured a behind-the-scenes position, organizing meetings, petitions and publications, while Gore-Booth played a more public role. The Irishwoman earned accolades for her efforts with working-class women – lecturing, setting up a theatre troupe, and working for the rights of barmaids, florists' assistants and 'pit-brow' lasses in the mines.

In 1913, partly because of Gore-Booth's health, the couple moved to London. Gore-Booth was now a published poet, writing volumes that were well received as exemplars of the new Irish poetry. She published on other subjects as well, including a study of the Gospels based on her reading of the Greek-language texts. In addition to the Christian scriptures, Gore-Booth was attracted to theosophy, the esoteric religion that combined the 'wisdom of the East' with occult practices. Among her writings – ten books of poetry and seven plays – are several collections of spiritual essays.

During the First World War, Gore-Booth and Roper joined the pacifist movement, campaigning on behalf of conscientious objectors. They were also drawn into the Irish nationalist movement, mostly on account of Gore-Booth's sister Constance, who played a key role. Constance Markievicz had helped found the nationalist Sinn Féin organization in 1908, as well as the first nationalist journal for women, the Irish Neutrality League, and the Irish Workers' Cooperation Society. Unlike her pacifist sister, Markievicz favoured an armed fight for Irish independence – often wearing military uniforms – and was arrested on numerous occasions. She took an active part in the Easter Rising of 1916, commanding nationalist forces on St Stephen's Green in Dublin. Arrested yet again, she was convicted and sentenced to death – a sentence that was commuted to penal servitude only because she was a woman. Released in an amnesty in 1917, Markievicz was soon rearrested for participation in Sir Roger Casement's plot to secure German support for the Irish cause.

Gore-Booth and Roper travelled to Dublin to visit Markievicz in prison and undertook efforts to secure her release. Later they tried also to gain a pardon for Casement, who had been condemned to death for treason (Gore-Booth even secured an audience with the king to plead for his life). The refusal of a reprieve was assured when Casement's diaries, detailing his energetic homosexual life, were handed to the authorities. When Casement was hanged, Gore-Booth and Roper were among supporters who fell to their knees in prayer outside the prison, later setting up a League for the Abolition of Capital Punishment.

Another interest for Gore-Booth and Roper was gender politics. In 1916, along with three others, they founded and edited a journal called *Urania*, which continued until 1940. The masthead of the eighty-four issues proclaimed: '*Urania* denotes the company of those who are firmly determined to ignore the dual organisation [into male and female] of humanity in all its manifestations. They are convinced that this duality has resulted in the formation of the two warped and imperfect types. They are further convinced that in order to get rid of this state of things no measures of "emancipation" or "equality" will suffice, which do not begin by a complete refusal to recognise or tolerate the duality itself. If the world is to see sweetness and independence combined in the same individual, all recognition of that duality must be given up.'

Urania thus called for abolition of gender differences. 'Sex' (a word that the historian Sonja Tiernan interprets as 'gender', a term not current until the 1960s), declared Gore-Booth, 'is an accident'. The radical idea of *Urania* was that male and female must be collapsed into one. The editors strongly opposed heterosexual marriage and promoted couples' refusal to have children. Instead, they identified companionable and egalitarian partnerships, of the sort embodied by Gore-Booth and Roper, as the model for a future society free of distinctions between the sexes.

Despite the openness of Gore-Booth and Roper's relationship and their advocacy of a genderless social order, the sexual nature of their lives and politics, and the significance of *Urania*, have been downplayed. The *Dictionary of Irish Biography*, for instance, refers only to a 'life-long friendship' between the women. Gifford Lewis's biography of Gore-Booth is at pains to avoid any suggestion of an erotic, or even a romantic, union, and stresses the mystical bent of Gore-Booth's writing rather than its sexual radicalism. Sonja Tiernan's research has restored these dimensions to the women's lives and writings.

Gore-Booth died of cancer in 1926; Roper survived her by twelve years. They are buried together in a London cemetery.

Sylvia Townsend Warner 1893–1978

In 1930, the up-and-coming writer Sylvia Townsend Warner met Valentine Ackland, by happenstance, in a village in Dorset. The two women did not immediately hit it off, but when Warner decided to buy a cottage in the village she asked Ackland if she would mind the house while she was away. Before long the women became lovers, and would remain together for almost forty years.

Warner's father had taught history at Harrow, one of England's grandest schools, and it was from him and his fellow schoolmasters that she received her education. Her real passion was for music, which she would have studied in Vienna had the First World War not thwarted her plans. In the event, she served on the editorial board of a ten-volume series of Tudor church music between 1923 and 1929. Small, handsome and bespectacled, she had an early and serious affair with Percy Buck, an organist and noted musicologist, but otherwise was attracted to women.

The convent-educated Ackland had been married by the time she was 19, although the marriage was annulled a year later for lack of consummation (her husband was homosexual). She was immensely tall and slender, and often dressed in men's clothing; her choice of the name 'Valentine' over her Christian names (Mary Kathleen) highlighted her ambiguous nature.

By the time she and Ackland met, Warner had published several volumes of poetry and a novel, *Lolly Willowes* (1926), featuring a spinster who becomes a witch. She followed it up with a stream of short stories (mostly destined for *The New Yorker*) and six other novels notable for the variety of their themes, some of them homosexual. Her second novel, *Mr Fortune's Maggot* (1927), set on a South Pacific island, tells the story of a clergyman who falls in love with his sole convert, a robust and attractive lad. The Reverend Fortune learns that he cannot, and should not, try to impart 'civilisation' to the 'natives' and loses his own faith, but sees, too, that a future with Lueli, his 'maggot' (meaning 'whimsical fancy'), cannot be realized.

A later novel, *Summer Will Show* (1936), portrays a lesbian romance set in England and France. Sophia Willoughby jettisons her philandering husband and goes to Paris, where she meets Minna, a Jewish performer, *salonnière*, rebel, and her husband's sometime mistress. Minna tells her that she has run away:

> 'But what have I run away from?'
> 'From sitting bored among the tyrants. From Sunday Schools,
>   and cold hearted respectability, and hypocrisy, and prison.'
> 'And domesticity,' she added.

The two women begin a passionate affair, and Sophia declares that she has never before known such happiness. As the novel advances, events draw Sophia and Minna dramatically into the revolutionary tumult of 1848.

Ackland, too, was a writer and a poet, although relatively few of her verses were published during her lifetime. Lesbian love appears in her work as well, and in an experimental joint work with Warner, *Whether a Dove or a Seagull* (1933), to which they both contributed poems (none was individually signed). Collections of Ackland's poems and the reissue of Warner's novels have allowed a rediscovery of their works.

In addition to their literary collaboration, Warner and Ackland were jointly involved in other public activities. Concerned about the direction of European politics in the early 1930s, they signed up to the British Communist Party and contributed articles to its journals, but their enthusiasm eventually faded. They twice journeyed to Spain during the Civil War to take part in a conference of writers and to express support for the Republicans, and they also participated in a leftist writers' congress in New York.

The letters between Warner and Ackland, published with a commentary by Warner after her partner's death, form a touching chronicle of what they termed their 'marriage'. They wrote frequently when they were separated (they were often away looking after their ageing mothers), and sometimes even penned notes to each other when they stayed together at their house in East Chaldon. The letters speak of quotidian matters – their various cats and dogs, the garden, visitors, food – but also of intense love and sexual pleasures. Early in their romance, Ackland teasingly wrote, 'You must *desire* the pleasures I am devising for you,' and Warner certainly did so. She recounted: 'When she [Ackland] came to London' – where Warner was working – 'I reversed the sun. My day began when I went to spend the night with her ... The nights were so ample that there was even time to fall briefly asleep in them.' The letters to 'my most dear love' recorded their deepening commitment, joy and oneness – 'we are one flesh, one spirit'.

The relationship was not completely untroubled. Warner felt monogamous, but Ackland sometimes strayed into extramarital liaisons. 'She was so skilled in love that I never expected her to forego love-adventures. Each while it lasted (they were brief) was vehement and sincere,' Warner recalled. In 1937, however, Ackland fell in love with Elizabeth Wade White, a wealthy American visitor to England. With remarkable outer equanimity, Warner let White stay in their house and share a bed with Ackland; she even once agreed to vacate their home for a month so that the two could spend time together. Remorseful, but expressing her love for both women, Ackland separated from White (though the affair would be rekindled a decade later). Her love was torn between the two, but her loyalty to Warner was never in doubt.

Once Ackland's affair with White had finally concluded, she and Ackland drew even closer together. Their last decades were troubled only by Ackland's problems with alcohol, and by her losing, regaining and relosing her Catholic faith, a religious interest that Warner did not share.

The two women continued to exchange letters filled with the same endearing tone and pledges of love that marked their early correspondence. 'I love you with a most true, most *married* love: that I feel as I have done always, since we first lay together, a deep and absolute responsibility for you – which was my greatest joy and happiness,' wrote Ackland in 1956. In 1968, as she lay dying of breast cancer, she summed up her sentiments: 'There is indeed nothing at all but pure love. Not less pure because it is trimmed with boundless gratitude, the deepest and most ardent admiration[,] respect and delight in you … I have, to my capacity, stood with you.' Thinking forward to life without her partner and referring to herself by an affectionate nickname Ackland had given her, Warner promised to 'be sensible, take care of myself … eat an orange a day, and take care of your possession, your Tib'. She concluded: 'Never has any woman been so well and truly loved as I.' Warner lived for nine years after Ackland's death, and their ashes are interred together in the graveyard at East Chaldon.

Claude Cahun 1894–1954

The primary subject for Claude Cahun's photography was her own image – an infinitely changing, theatrically projected and obsessively observed visual persona. In perhaps her most famous self-portrait, she stands in front of a mirror, sporting closely cropped hair and wearing a chequerboard coat, and her handsome face looks out in a doubled view to the spectator.

In other shots she appears lying on a bed, Medusa-like with her hair – long and unruly on this occasion – spread out behind her, or as a prim schoolgirl with neatly waved coiffure, sitting and reading a book. Sometimes she is dressed as a harlequin, the fringes of her hair arranged in jaunty curls on her forehead. Elsewhere, her head completely shaved, she sits in the cross-legged pose of a Buddhist monk. In another work, she is dressed in a bulky sweater, her head covered by a sailor-type cap, and she stands with her hands in her trouser pockets against a silk backdrop. One photo shows her dressed in a vampishly modernist dress and what can only be described as an extraterrestrial headdress. More surrealistically, she takes a picture of herself with her head – her hair pulled tightly back – enclosed in a glass dome on a tabletop. There are images of her wearing glasses or goggles, hair dyed appropriately. And there is a self-portrait as a much older woman, standing in a garden, her hair enclosed in a demure scarf.

Cahun was born Lucy Mathilde Renée Schwob in Nantes in 1894, into a prosperous and literary Jewish family. Her father was the proprietor of a newspaper, her great-uncle the head of a grand Paris library, and an uncle a novelist and co-founder of one of France's most innovative cultural journals. Growing up in the *fin-de-siècle* in such a milieu meant a certain familiarity with avant-garde artistic currents, but it also meant exposure to the anti-Semitism catalysed by the Dreyfus Affair. The 12-year-old Schwob, whose mother suffered from psychological illness, was sent to school in England for two years to insulate her from exposure.

A few years after her return to Nantes, in 1909 Schwob met Suzanne Alberte Eugénie Malherbe, a fine-arts student two years her junior, whose father was a professor of medicine and member of the Nantes city council. The two became intimate friends, and at some point lovers; they began living with each other in 1917, and stayed together for the rest of their lives.

Claude Cahun (as Schwob now called herself) and Malherbe (who assumed the name Marcel Moore for her work as an artist and illustrator) made a formidable couple. They set themselves up in Paris, where Cahun studied letters at the Sorbonne, and eventually they settled in Montparnasse, at that time one of the world's major artistic centres. In the 1930s they mixed with Surrealists such as André Breton (who became Cahun's mentor), Georges Bataille, Henri Michaux and the homosexual René Crevel, with whom Cahun had a particularly affectionate friendship. Cahun became the most prominent woman in the cliquishly male Surrealist circle, and helped to organize an early Surrealist exhibition in London. While in Paris, Cahun occasionally went on stage, playing several roles with experimental, anti-naturalist theatre troupes. She belonged to the Association of Revolutionary Writers and Artists, and signed a declaration 'Against Fascism and Against French Imperialism'. She also wrote in support of a pioneering homosexual journal, *Inversions*, and translated work by the sexologist Havelock Ellis into French.

Exhausted by life in Paris, and concerned about Cahun's delicate health, in 1937 Malherbe and Cahun moved to the Channel island of Jersey, where they had spent several summers. There they lived as two sisters – indeed, by this time Cahun's widowed father had married Malherbe's widowed mother. The two were living in Jersey when the Second World War began, and they remained, refusing to flee to England. The Channel Islands were the only part of Britain to be occupied by the Nazis, and Cahun and Malherbe, at great risk, took part in the Resistance. They listened, illegally, to BBC broadcasts, and on tiny sheets of paper Cahun typed out news and anti-war messages that Malherbe then illustrated. They left the flyers in restaurants, on cars, or in other places where German soldiers would find them. Eventually the women were discovered; they were arrested and sent to a military prison while the Gestapo ransacked their house. A German court sentenced the women to death, and only a stay of execution, followed by the Allied liberation, saved them.

Cahun and Malherbe formed a highly creative partnership, appearing in each other's works. In 1919 Malherbe drew the illustrations for Cahun's *Vues et visions*, a remarkable collection of essays and images that touch, in part, on same-sex attraction in antiquity and modern times. They later collaborated on photomontages for Cahun's *Aveux non avenus* (sometimes known in English as 'Cancelled confessions'), published in 1930.

Cahun's work plays with perspective, makes use of props such as masks and mirrors, employs the techniques of collage and assemblage, juxtaposes curious objects, and overlays multiple exposures. But alongside the more Surrealist imagery, her photographs encompass portraits of the couple's friends and colleagues, and of their cat. Her writings include *Héroïnes* – a collection of witty essays on prominent women in history and literature. Ulysses' wife, Penelope, is a tease; Cinderella is the desired object of a foot fetishist; the biblical Judith, who beheaded Holofernes, is a sadist; and Delilah – famous for shearing the hair of the strongman Samson – takes revenge on the High Priest, 'the natural enemy of woman. On him will I avenge all my sisters.' The Virgin Mary, happily rid of her virginity, is a proud but petulant mother who feels that she is misunderstood by all. Sappho jokes that all women chase her and try to bed her, and that since she wears a short chiton she has become the 'arbiter of lesbian elegance' – though she harbours thoughts about having an affair with a man and bearing a child.

After the end of the war, the two women continued to live on Jersey. Cahun died in 1954; Malherbe survived until 1972. They are buried on the island, in St Brelade's cemetery, where their grave is marked with their names and with two Stars of David.

Cahun was playful, provocative and subversive, interested above all in representation and performance. She was a manipulator of history and image, and shifted the construction of gender and sexual stereotypes. For these reasons her work, and that of her partner, have been rediscovered as a herald of postmodernism. For their creativity, for their lives as a lesbian couple, and for their heroic resistance against the Germans, they deserve to be celebrated as remarkable women.

Suzy Solidor 1900–1983

T he singer Suzy Solidor was born Suzanne Marion in a village near
Saint-Malo, Brittany. Her surname was that of her unmarried
mother, who worked as a chambermaid to the Surcouf family, one
of whose sons had fathered the child. The Surcoufs were of grand
Breton lineage, tracing their fortune back to explorers and corsairs.
Once she had moved to Paris, Suzy chose a stage name, Solidor, from
a 14th-century tower in her home town.

Solidor had a hard and poor childhood, but the First World
War provided an opportunity to leave school and volunteer as an
ambulance driver and mechanic on the home front. After the war,
she hoped to become a model in the capital: she possessed a slender
figure, height, blonde hair, angular good looks and an androgynous
style that were much in favour in the *années folles*. That ambition
changed when she encountered Yvonne de Bremond d'Ars (like
Solidor the illegitimate daughter of a nobleman), one of Paris's
most important antique dealers and the author of several books on
antique collecting. Solidor became Bremond d'Ars's protégée and
lover, remaining with her for eleven years.

According to Solidor, it was Bremond d'Ars who turned the Breton
peasant into a stylish *Parisienne*. Solidor began to move in celebrity
circles on account of her partner's connections and her own charms.
The 1920s saw the triumph of the boyish girl – a type represented
by Victor Margueritte's novel *La Garçonne* (1922) and portrayed by
Solidor in a 1935 film adaptation. A bobbed hairstyle, form-fitting
dresses, long cigarettes and fast cars were the accoutrements of the
liberated young woman, and Solidor fitted the bill perfectly. Among
those whose attention she attracted were artists: called the 'most
painted woman in Paris', she sat for 225 portraits, including ones by

Foujita, Cocteau, Van Dongen and the lesbian Tamara de Lempicka. Lempicka's image of Solidor – her hair a blond helmet, one breast exposed, an arm dramatically raised and her torso posed against a Cubist cityscape – captures her spirit.

Bremond d'Ars was a possessive partner, but Solidor's sexual and romantic interests were not exclusive. An affair with Maurice Barbezat led to an acrimonious break between the two women, who never saw each other again. Solidor's lover helped set her up in her own antique business on the Left Bank, and remained a close friend after their ardour had cooled. Solidor soon had another woman lover, Daisy Bartholoni, whose marriage of convenience to a gay man gave her the title of Baroness Vaufreland.

Solidor had occasionally entertained friends by singing and reciting poems, and in 1932 she took the step of opening a cabaret. Located in the Rue Sainte-Anne (coincidentally, the centre of Paris gay life in the 1960s) and lined with her rapidly multiplying portraits, La Vie Parisienne became a popular nightspot, frequented by a crowd of lesbians, artists and bohemians over whom Solidor presided as host and entertainer.

As well as holding her own cabaret, Solidor sang at other venues, was an early radio performer, appeared in several films, and was chosen for an experimental television programme. With her substantial earnings, she bought a house in Brittany and rented smart apartments in Paris. She pursued numerous lesbian affairs, though she never entirely abandoned Bartholoni.

In the 1930s Solidor became the lover of Jean Mermoz. The dashing aviator had earned his wings in the French Air Force in Syria in the 1920s, and a pioneering transatlantic voyage in 1930, from Senegal to Brazil, had turned him into a hero. Mermoz and Solidor made a glamorous couple, but their romance came to a heartbreaking end when Mermoz's plane was lost over the Atlantic in 1936. Solidor took refuge in her women friends, the cabaret, and a new interest in writing: she published several novels and volumes of stories, which often featured sexually ambiguous characters.

Solidor's songs, delivered with impeccable diction in a husky voice, sometimes bespoke her Breton origins. 'Les Filles de Saint-Malo' and 'La Belle d'Ouessant' evoked port cities, sailors and their women. Solidor also sang about love between women: 'I want every woman / From her heels to her hair / … Under her heavy skirts / My unquiet dreams / Slip a sly kiss / Onto her naked skin…'. In another song, entitled 'Ouvre', she sang: 'Open your eyes, wake up … Open your legs, take my flanks / Into these white and smooth curves / Open your two trembling knees / Open your thighs' – perhaps the most risqué evocation of lesbian sex in the repertoire. Although women often performed songs as if they were men singing to women, the combination of such lyrics and Solidor's personal proclivities no doubt gave a particular *frisson* to lesbians who heard her renditions. A worldy audience, among whom gay singers and their so-called *chansons interlopes* ('illicit songs') were in favour, applauded her performances and easily accommodated her loves. As the historian Tirza True Latimer has suggested, Solidor brought lesbianism out of refined and avant-garde Sapphic circles into popular culture, from the intellectuals' salon to the cabaret.

One piece of music for which Solidor became particularly famous was a French version of the German torch song 'Lili Marleen', which she sang even after Paris had come under Nazi occupation in 1940. She had made several tours to Germany and continued to mix with Germans, even once performing at a reception for the Nazi ambassador to Vichy France. In 1943 the Germans closed her cabaret for ten days because of a song that seemed to voice opposition to German rule, but in the eyes of the Free French Solidor's reputation had nevertheless been damaged. During the postwar purge of collaborators, Solidor – despite testimony that she had covertly supported the Resistance – was formally disgraced and forbidden to perform for a year.

Effectively banished from the Paris stage, Solidor went on a successful tour to New York and Montreal. By the time she returned, in 1949, she was permitted to open a new cabaret, which operated until 1958, even as musical tastes turned away from the tradition of the *chanteuse*. She then moved to Cagnes-sur-Mer, accompanied by a cohort of women friends, and started a cabaret where nostalgia for the old songs blended with the glitz of the Côte-d'Azur.

Solidor died in 1983. Three years later came the death of Daisy Bartholoni, who was living in Paris; following Solidor's wishes, her remains were buried next to Solidor's in the Mediterranean village where the singer had made her home. Solidor had donated the many portraits made of her to a museum in Cagnes. A compilation of Solidor's recordings, including songs from the remarkable *Paris Lesbien* album, appeared a quarter-century after her death.

Annemarie Schwarzenbach 1908–1942

Adventurer, reporter, novelist, poet, anti-fascist, heiress, drug addict – many words describe Annemarie Schwarzenbach. She was born in 1908 into one of the wealthiest families in Switzerland; her father was a silk manufacturer, her mother the daughter of a general. As a child she acquired the expected social graces – including musical skills good enough to make her a concert pianist – and joined the Wandervögel movement of nature-lovers, but at school she came into conflict for her unruliness and her crushes on fellow pupils and women teachers. Schwarzenbach continued her education at the Sorbonne and the University of Zurich, where she wrote a doctoral thesis on the medieval history of the Engadine region and produced her first novel. With money, connections, education, creative talent and an androgynous beauty that mesmerized men and women, Schwarzenbach seemed blessed by fate.

In 1931, driving the car she had received as a graduation present, Schwarzenbach travelled to Berlin to join her friends Klaus and Erika Mann, the children of Thomas Mann. She was desperately in love with Erika, and they were to share a stormy life-long friendship. She dived into the nightlife of the German capital, which forms the backdrop of her second work of fiction, *Lyrische Novelle* (1933). It portrays an ill-fated passion between an actress and the narrator, to whom Schwarzenbach gave the persona of a man, even though the short work is patently a story of a lesbian infatuation. While in Berlin, Schwarzenbach was introduced to morphine, to which she developed an addiction that continued to the end of her life – she made many painful and unsuccessful attempts to wean herself from drugs, alcohol and tobacco.

Alarmed by the rise of Nazism, Schwarzenbach and the Manns founded an anti-fascist journal that attracted contributions from

Brecht, Einstein, Gide, Huxley and other luminaries. In 1934 Schwarzenbach and Klaus Mann attended an international workers' conference in Moscow. The scion of the *haute bourgeoisie* was fascinated with the place of writers in the Soviet Union, though she never subscribed to Marxism or joined the Communists. Soon Hitler's government forbade her to live in Germany. Her political ideas did not sit well with her family, who applauded Hitler's rise to power, and her private life also caused concern, even though her mother had a long-term amorous relationship with a female opera singer. What Schwarzenbach would do with her life was not clear, but already *Wanderlust* had emerged as its major theme.

In late 1933 Schwarzenbach set off for a six-month trip to the Middle East, traversing Turkey, Lebanon, Syria and Iraq on the way to take part in an archaeological dig in Persia. The trip inspired articles that she published in Swiss newspapers, a travelogue and a series of short stories. The following year she again journeyed to Persia, where she met Claude Achille Clarac, a French diplomat posted to Tehran. They were married in 1935, although they remained together for only a few months before Schwarzenbach continued her peregrinations. Indeed, they would almost never see each other again, even if they remained friends and spouses.

Schwarzenbach's personal life continued to be nightmarish: she was frequently confined in drug-treatment clinics and made several suicide attempts. Yet in spite of her problems she proved capable of periods of extraordinary energy and productive work. In 1936 and 1937 she made two trips to the United States, travelling from Maine to the Deep South and writing incisive features on the effects of the Depression on factory workers and sharecroppers. In Europe, she filed reports from the Baltic countries, from Vienna on the eve of the *Anschluss*, and from Prague, chronicling the advance of Hitler's supporters. In 1939, with the Swiss travel-writer Ella Maillart, she made an even more ambitious and fantastic voyage. With

Schwarzenbach at the wheel of her brand-new, specially equipped Ford, the two women drove from the Adriatic to Afghanistan, an expedition recounted by Schwarzenbach in her *reportages* in Swiss and foreign newspapers.

In 1940 Schwarzenbach again headed to the United States, only to be repatriated from New York after a particularly bad bout of drug use, another attempted suicide and violent psychotic episodes. Within months of reaching home, she left for the Congo, in the vague hope of joining the Free French (with her marriage, she had become a French citizen and she travelled on a diplomatic passport). There she went upriver, deep into the equatorial forest, to report on Belgian and French colonialism. This discovery of yet another world brought her a rare interlude of drug-free peace and calm. On the way back to Switzerland she stopped off to see her husband, who was now a diplomat in Spanish Morocco. Schwarzenbach then went home to the chalet that she maintained in Sils, an idyllic lakeside retreat in the Engadine. There, in a freak accident in 1942, she fell off a bicycle, suffering a head injury; her body, wrecked by years of abuse, survived for only three weeks. 'Death is too incomprehensible and too inhumane … it loses its violent character only if we await it as the only means given to us finally to escape our moments of madness,' she had written.

Schwarzenbach had fallen in love with a number of women, some of them incapable of returning her affections, others unable to endure her demanding passion, and none able to save her from self-destructive urges. In addition to Erika Mann and, probably, Ella Maillart, there was Barbara Wright, the photographer with whom she first went to America; the wife of a French archaeologist with whom she stayed in Afghanistan; and one of her women doctors. There was also Anita Forrer, a Swiss neighbour, and Margot von Opel, wife of the car manufacturer. Schwarzenbach was herself on the receiving end of an obsessive passion when Carson McCullers fell in love with her in New York in 1940.

'Now I want to tell a story, beautiful and ordinary, in which one will find the words "love" and "happiness", which almost saved us, another young girl and me, from the fatality that caught up with her soon afterwards.' Thus begins the second part of Schwarzenbach's *Death in Persia*, written in Iran but fully published only posthumously. The book is a fictionalized account of Schwarzenbach's infatuation with the daughter of the Turkish ambassador to Tehran. In the novel, death pursues the narrator, who is suffering from malaria and a debilitating infection. Yalé, the daughter of a Turk and a Cherkassian, suffers from tuberculosis. They provide comfort to each other until the Turk stops their meetings and sends his daughter away; the narrator learns of her death in the midst of feverish imaginings and angelic visitations.

The French writer Roger Martin du Gard once presented a book to Schwarzenbach with the inscription 'To the inconsolable angel'. She was one of the 'bright young things' of the 1920s: fluent in several languages, a guest at the best hotels or at the homes of diplomats, and always elegantly dressed in fine Parisian couture. Her travels into the Middle East and Central Asia, Africa and America were the dream of adventurous voyagers, and her newspaper reports eloquently documented the upheaval of four continents in the inter-war years. Against this background of cultured independence, Schwarzenbach's novels and stories describe the traumas and pains of private lives. Her own life reflects the dangers faced by those who bore the heavy weight of ambition, family expectations and the temptations of a fast life. Schwarzenbach remains relatively little known – few of her writings have been translated into English, for example – but she herself has been a character in others' works. Ella Maillart made her 'Christina' in her novel *The Cruel Journey*, about their expedition to Afghanistan, which also inspired a film, *The Journey to Kafiristan* (2001).

Carson McCullers 1917–1967

L ula Carson Smith – Carson McCullers, as she would become –
was born in Columbus, a dusty mill town on the Chattahoochee
river in Georgia. 'I yearned for one particular thing: to get away from
Columbus and to make my mark on the world,' she would recall in
her uncompleted autobiography. So she did, but it was the land and
people of the American South – the pine forests and red clay soil; the
ramshackle little towns where whites and blacks lived separated by
the heritage of slavery and the Civil War; and the frustrations of their
lives, including their often thwarted yearning for sex and love – that
provided the raw material for her novels and stories. She confessed
that 'even as a grown woman I was haunted by homesickness'.

McCullers was the daughter of a jeweller and enjoyed a largely
comfortable and fulfilled existence that is not always reflected in her
writings. She displayed an early and promising interest in the piano,
but after finishing secondary school decided to go to Manhattan to
study creative writing at Columbia University and New York University. She remained in New York for the rest of her life, apart from
regular trips back to Georgia, a period in North Carolina, her travel
overseas and an extended stay in Paris, where she bought a house.

McCullers was twice married to the same man – Reeves McCullers, an emotionally insecure army officer – but their separations and
reunions, and his eventual suicide in 1953, brought her great distress.
She also had liaisons with other men, including the composer David
Diamond, a predominantly gay man with whom Reeves also fell in
love. Yet many in New York (though perhaps not in Georgia) considered McCullers lesbian in her temperament and her desires; she
sometimes dressed in men's clothes and, indeed, told one friend that,
metaphorically, she had been born a man. She experienced recurring
infatuations with other women, including Greta Garbo.

In 1940 McCullers met Annemarie Schwarzenbach, the brilliant, rich and troubled Swiss author. Hers, McCullers remembered, was 'a face that would haunt me to the end of my life, beautiful, blond, with straight short hair. There was a look of suffering on her face that I could not define ... she was bodily resplendent.' They fell deeply in love, although in her autobiography McCullers reveals only that they exchanged a kiss. When McCullers' husband asked her whether she was in love with Schwarzenbach, she replied that she did not know, and he slapped her fiercely. While the women were together in New York, Schwarzenbach tried to commit suicide – a disturbing incident for McCullers, who was much distressed to learn of the Swiss woman's death several years later. Schwarzenbach's last letter had told her, 'Carson, remember our moments of understanding, and how much I loved you', and McCullers commented: 'I don't know of a friend whom I loved more and was more grieved by her sudden death.'

McCullers' milieu included many lesbians and gay men. She lived for some time in a Brooklyn brownstone house with a remarkable assortment of largely homosexual housemates: W. H. Auden, Christopher Isherwood, Richard Wright, Aaron Copeland, Paul and Jane Bowles, and the striptease artiste Gypsy Rose Lee. She was also a frequent visitor at Yaddo, an artists' colony where she became friends with homosexuals including Tennessee Williams, the composer Colin McPhee, the literary critic Newton Arvin and the sexually ambivalent author Katherine Anne Porter.

Homosexuality appears regularly in McCullers' works, often embedded in stories of the loneliness and repressed desires of her Southern people – a strand that runs through the writing of other authors of 'Southern Gothic', from William Faulkner to Truman Capote and McCullers' fellow Georgian Flannery O'Connor, whose life was also characterized by lesbian friendships. Sensitive men, tomboy women and hints of reprobate sexual urges appear throughout

McCullers' novels. Her women, such as those in *The Member of the Wedding* (1946), refuse to be Southern belles and yearn for intimacy – sometimes with other women. One of the main characters of *The Heart is a Lonely Hunter* (1940) is Biff, a man who believes that all people belong by nature to both sexes, and who adopts such unmanly habits as wearing scent and redecorating his house. In *Reflections in a Golden Eye* (1941; it is dedicated to Schwarzenbach), Captain Weldon Pendleton is homosexual, and heterosexually impotent. He lusts after his wife's lover and has mixed, but passionate, feelings of love and hate for a comely private who spies voyeuristically on his wife. Pendleton's shooting of the soldier is a violent expression of his incapacity to act on his own erotic desires. The book earned McCullers a degree of animosity in her home town, which is close to Fort Benning, a huge army base. On one visit, she received a threatening phone call from a member of the Ku Klux Klan, who told her, 'We don't like nigger lovers or fairies' – a comment that only reinforced her anti-racist sentiments and her identification with sexual dissidents.

Perhaps her most clearly limned portrait of homosexual love (once again male) comes as a sub-plot in *Clock without Hands* (1961). Jester Clane is a 17-year-old orphan raised by his racist grandfather, a judge who takes covertly to reading the Kinsey Report on human sexuality. The young Clane develops an attraction for Sherman Pew, another orphan, who has mixed white and black parentage: Clane's desire thus constitutes racial as well as sexual transgression. Clane fears that to touch Pew would be a mortal sin, but when he has sex in a brothel he fantasizes that the prostitute is his buddy. Eventually they become close friends rather than lovers, as both youths try to unravel secrets from their past. The story leads to a tragic end, their lives mingled until the last.

In the midst of McCullers' generally dark stories of misfits and outcasts is an occasional ray of hopeful affirmation. In *The Ballad of the Sad Café* (1943), in which every character seems sexually and romantically lost or in the grip of a passion that cannot be consummated, the narrator remarks of one particularly odd partnership that 'the good people thought that if those two had found some satisfaction of the flesh between themselves, then it was a matter concerning them and God alone'.

6
ENTANGLEMENTS OF SEX
AND POLITICS

Richard Schultz 1889–1977

The life of Richard Schultz traverses the 20th century and the different phases of gay history in Germany. Born in 1889 in a small town in Mecklenburg, the son of a third-generation shoemaker, Schultz decided not to follow his father's craft but to work in what is now called the hospitality industry. He served an apprenticeship as a waiter in restaurants in Lübeck and Hamburg, and, at the age of 17, travelled to Britain, where he secured a job at the chic hotel Claridge's in London. From this point on, he led a somewhat peripatetic existence, working in hotels in Paris, the south of France, Vienna, and then back in England, before being offered a position at a hotel in Khartoum, in the Sudan (which also gave him a welcome chance to travel in Egypt). By 1914 he had a job lined up in St Petersburg, but the outbreak of war forced him to settle in Berlin, where he remained for the rest of his life. With great luck, he escaped the horrors of the First World War, despite being mobilized for service. He found employment at the grand Bristol Hotel on Unter den Linden and moved up the ranks until he was chief of staff of the service workers, a position he retained until Allied bombing destroyed the hotel in 1942.

Schultz seems to have had his first homosexual love affair – a happy relationship with a fellow waiter – by the time he moved to Berlin. Once there, he began frequenting the salon of Adolf Brand, a writer who, though married, was one of the leaders of the homosexual emancipation movement. Unlike Magnus Hirschfeld, who theorized about homosexuals as a 'third sex', Brand looked to antiquity for a model of virile comradeship. He welcomed all comers to his receptions, which provided a forum for discussion and social gatherings. Brand's drawing room was one of many meeting places for homosexuals in the fast-paced world of Weimar Berlin, albeit significantly quieter than the cabarets made famous in Christopher Isherwood's novellas, and the bars and sex-clubs that attracted homosexual clients from near and far.

Schultz's support for homosexual emancipation was discreet. He was not an intellectual and did not contribute to the burgeoning body of literature on homosexuality. Yet he met and befriended many other homosexuals, both prominent figures and the office workers, businessmen, sailors and soldiers who also joined Brand's gatherings. Schultz's friends – men and women – took part in the recreational pursuits popular at the time, such as going for holidays to the island of Rügen, where they romped naked in the Baltic sun. Through these gatherings Schultz met men with whom he had affairs, like the blond Rudi Wolf, to whom he gracefully gave his blessings when Wolf eventually fell in love with a woman. Although homosexual acts were illegal under the German penal code – and despite the grave economic and political problems that beset the country – Schultz and many others lived agreeable lives during this period.

Soon after Hitler came to power, Hirschfeld's Institute for Sexual Research was ransacked, and Nazis searched Brand's house on five occasions. The government closed homosexual clubs and forbade the publication of homosexual journals and magazines. The Nazis also rooted out homosexuals in their own midst; the best known was Ernst Röhm, chief-of-staff of the paramilitary SA. (His private life provided an additional reason for his political enemies to target him, even if homosexuality was not ultimately the motive for his murder.) The regime arrested and imprisoned thousands of men and women with same-sex inclinations, many of whom perished in concentration camps and extermination camps.

In the violently homophobic climate that characterized even the early years of Nazi rule, it was impossible for Brand's well-known gay gatherings to continue, but some of the habitués began to meet in Schultz's apartment in Charlottenburg. Right through until the end of the war, Schultz welcomed homosexual friends in his home, though he took great precautions. He consigned a bust of Antinous and several paintings featuring young men to a female neighbour, and hung a heavy curtain over his door to muffle sounds. His visitors confined their discussions to literary matters that would not compromise their security – a necessary measure at a time when Hitler's forces were rounding up homosexuals and some, including one of Schultz's close friends, were driven to suicide.

On the eve of the Second World War, Schultz was experiencing his most significant romantic relationship: a partnership with Hans Spann, a tall, blond, handsome man fifteen years his junior, whom he had met in 1938. Even after the fighting began, Schultz, Spann and their friends met regularly, enjoyed themselves at the beach and had their pictures taken by a friend who was a professional photographer. One image captures the couple elegantly dressed in suits and ties: they wear similar rings, and the salt-and-pepper-haired Schultz holds a book. Spann, almost inevitably, was sent to the front. He and Schultz continued to exchange letters, in which they spoke of their companions, their own friendship and, as far as censorship permitted, the war and their hope for its end. In 1944, however, one of Schultz's letters was returned to him with a handwritten message on the envelope that Spann had 'died for the greater Germany'.

Grieving for his friend, out of work after the destruction of the Bristol, and living through the bombardment of Berlin – where, miraculously, his own apartment escaped damage – Schultz hid several Jews in his lodgings and helped others in the war's final months. After the end of the war, Schultz joined the new Kultur-bund zur demokratischen Erneuerung Deutschlands ('League of culture for the democratic regeneration of Germany'), a club that attracted many homosexuals. He became a leading force, organizing dinners and other activities. He also hosted gay soirées at his apart-ment – his *jours fixes*, as he called them – which continued until the mid-1970s. In rooms decorated with antiques, paintings, sculptures (including the Antinous, which he recovered) and bibelots, every few weeks Schultz served a buffet dinner to some twenty visitors, who would then hear a talk on a homosexual topic. Schultz himself gave a presentation on Brand; the translator of Gide's works into German discussed the gay French writer; and others talked about James Baldwin and Jean Genet. Late in life, Schultz made friends with a young student, Hans Haug, with whom he travelled around Germany and to whom he recounted his life.

Schultz died at the age of 88, in 1977. His was an ordinary life rendered extraordinary by the circumstances in which he lived. Sur-viving Nazism and the Second World War was itself an achievement for a homosexual man like Schultz. He had managed to enjoy love and friendship during a time of great troubles, and he contributed in a quiet way to the gay culture of Berlin and to its revival after the catastrophes of the Hitler period.

Federico García Lorca 1898–1936

On 19 August 1936 a small band of men, supporters of the rebellion that would eventually bring Francisco Franco to power, burst into a house in Granada, shouting that they were looking for the *maricón* ('queer'). They 'arrested' Federico García Lorca, tortured him and dragged him away. In an Andalusian olive grove, the ringleader later bragged, he shot two bullets 'into the queer's arse' and then killed Lorca along with three other men.

The fascists had many reasons for wanting to assassinate Lorca. He was Spain's leading modernist poet, fêted in New York, Havana and Buenos Aires, as well as in Madrid. He directed an experimental theatre troupe set up by the Republican government, consorted with socialists, and had signed pro-Republican petitions. Rumours had reached Granada that he had just finished a play that focused on the sexual frustrations of the local elite. Rebels considered Lorca's family too sympathetic to workers and peasants, and too little pious in their Catholicism. Insurgents had already killed his brother-in-law, the left-wing mayor of Granada. Lorca's homosexuality – and especially his cruising for the sturdy young peasants who excited his libido – caused outrage among his enemies.

After Lorca's murder, his remains were thrown into a common grave, but he quickly became a Republican hero and martyr. Some activists and critics, as well as family members, remained uncomfortable with Lorca's sexual proclivities, however, and for decades Spanish commentators concealed both his sexual orientation and the homosexual motifs in his works. When the newly discovered *Sonnets of Dark Love*, inflected by Lorca's love for a male companion, were first published in the 1980s, the adjective *oscuro* ('dark' or 'secret') – a codeword for his sexual desires – was deleted. Only through the research of scholars such as Ian Gibson, Paul Binding and Angel Sahuquillo have readers become fully aware of Lorca's gay milieu and the many allusions to gay love secreted in his esoteric verse. Yet for Gibson, 'if he had not been a *maricón*, he would not have been the poet that he is': the 'search for erotic plenitude ... is the central theme of all of his work.'

Gibson identifies a gay network in early 20th-century Spain, which centred on Lorca and his fellow poets Luis Cernuda, Emilio Prados and the Nobel Prize-winner Vicente Aleixandre, and also extended to visiting Americans. Their professional and personal links helped to define that particularly vibrant moment in Spain's cultural history before the Falange took power.

In his early poems, Lorca hinted at 'romantic secrets', and his choice of subjects, such as Narcissus and Verlaine, speaks of a gay sensibility. An 'Ode to Walt Whitman', written in New York, swings from an almost violent denunciation of effeminate 'queers' (using a litany of homophobic synonyms current in the Hispanophone world) to an eroticized appreciation of American workers and a guarded celebration of Whitman's creed of comradeship. Stocky peasants, ambiguous angels, St Sebastian, the exotically alluring black men of Harlem, and the sexy gypsies of Andalusia all appear in Lorca's poems. Binding has even discovered coded references to oral and anal intercourse buried in his work. Lorca's plays – of which *Blood Wedding* (1932), *Yerma* (1934) and *The House of Bernarda Alba* (1936) are among the most important in the modern repertoire – often touch on issues of sex: the dilemma of a woman torn between a respectable fiancé and her true love; a household of women damned to chaste solitude; a barren wife; a spinster.

Lorca himself did not lack for sexual encounters either in Spain or overseas, sleeping with a sailor, a *mestizo* and the scion of a bourgeois family in Havana, and possibly having orgiastic encounters with African-Americans in New York. He often had the misfortune to fall in love with men unable fully to reciprocate his passion. His first great love was Salvador Dalí, a fellow student at a university college in Madrid where Lorca took up residence in 1919. The budding Andalusian poet and the Catalan painter became close friends, bound by a vision of a new culture that would break the bounds of Spanish traditionalism – linked, according to Lorca, by 'love, friendship and [enigmatically] swordplay'. Photos from a beach in Cadaqués in 1925 show the intimacy that existed between these two bright and privileged friends, and Lorca soon published a beautiful ode about his companion. To what extent theirs was a physical relationship will remain unclear. An ageing Dalí recounted that he had on several occasions refused anal intercourse with Lorca, as he found the exercise painful and was not himself gay; he characterized their love as 'tragic', because he could not entirely satisfy Lorca's desires. After a while the two drifted apart. Lorca was hurt when in 1929 Dalí collaborated with Luis Buñuel, a mutual friend with homophobic tendencies, on the film *Un Chien Andalou*, which Lorca considered an insult to him ('the Andalusian dog') and his reprobate urges. They remained in contact, however, even after Dalí married his irrepressible muse, Gala.

Lorca's second obsession was the handsome Emilio Aladrén, a sculptor and classmate of Dalí's whom Lorca's friends (and biographers) found superficial, egotistical and manipulative. Lorca was smitten, writing febrile letters to him when they were separated, and suffered when Aladrén announced his intention to marry an Englishwoman. Ill fate also beset Lorca's relationship with Eduardo Rodríguez Valdivieso, an 18-year-old whom he met at a carnival in Granada in 1932. A bored bank clerk, Valdivieso loved literature and seems to have loved Lorca, who posted touching letters from Madrid. Distance worked against the romance, and Lorca had moved on in the meantime.

The 'three Rs' was what Lorca called his final great love, Rafael Rodríguez Rapún. Though not predominantly homosexual, Rapún fell for the charming writer. The 22-year-old son of a worker, he was an engineering student and an activist in the socialist party. In 1933 he had volunteered to be a secretary-accountant for La Barraca, Lorca's theatre company. Handsome, athletic, engaging and intelligent, he seemed the poet's ideal, and remained a faithful friend. Rapún was so devastated by Lorca's murder that he volunteered as a soldier for the Republicans; exactly a year after Lorca's death, Rapún fell to Francoist gunners.

Lorca wrote his last completed work, the *Sonnets of Dark Love* (1936), for Rapún. Aleixandre called it 'a prodigy of passion, enthusiasm, happiness, torment, a pure and glowing monument to love'. Lorca here proclaimed his love, yearned for letters, rejoiced in a telephone conversation, mused about sending Rapún the gift of a dove, wrote that 'the beloved sleeps on the poet's breast', and described a night (so the coded words suggest) of ardent lovemaking.

Lorca also wrote a gay play, *The Public* (1929–30; published posthumously), only part of which survives. He informed a friend that the theme was '*frankly* homosexual'. The experimental and virtually unperformable work calls for the liberation of all sorts of love, challenging the verities of bourgeois beliefs as well as theatrical conventions.

Only a couple of generations after Lorca's death, gay life flourishes in Spain, from the bars of Barcelona to the beaches of the Balearic islands. Pedro Almodóvar's films dramatized the sexual liberation of the post-Franco *movida*. Under a socialist government, Spain – land of the Inquisition, bullfights and Franco – became, in 2005, one of the first countries to legalize gay marriage and adoption.

Newton Arvin 1900–1963

G ay men in mid-20th-century America found many opportunities for intimacy and pleasure, but they also faced the possibility of harassment and arrest, even when they tried to remain discreet. One such man who fell foul of persecution was Newton Arvin.

Born in Indiana to a middle-class family, Arvin studied English at Harvard. Soon after graduation, he found a job at Smith College, a small, elite women's institution located in rural Northampton, Massachusetts. Arvin may have been part of the 'lost generation' but, unlike those who fled overseas, he remained immune to Europe's temptations and in 1922 settled down to what promised to be a quiet life in a leafy college town. At regular intervals he produced well-received books, such as works on Nathaniel Hawthorne, Walt Whitman and Herman Melville, as well as articles for newspapers and magazines. He earned a reputation as one of America's leading literary critics and scholars, and moved up the ranks to a professorship and election to the American Institute of Arts and Letters. In academic New England his leftist political views, which he occasionally voiced in political debates, provoked little of the opposition that they might have sparked elsewhere.

The local community knew of and accepted the close friendships and 'Boston marriages' that existed between women on the Smith College staff, though male homosexuals found less of a welcome. While Arvin did have several affairs with male colleagues, he avoided associating with those who were obviously homosexual. Like many at that time, he married, having started a relationship with a former student in the 1930s; after a couple of years of happiness the couple drifted apart, then became antagonistic and finally divorced in 1940. Arvin's inability to accept his sexuality frequently cast him into severe depression, and more than once he attempted suicide. Therapy in private clinics and public hospitals, including electroshock treatment, failed to provide either a 'cure' or to help him accept his desires.

Arvin nevertheless found a congenial refuge where he enjoyed academic stimulation and easier contact with other sexual dissidents. This was Yaddo, a 55-room mansion set in 400 acres in Saratoga Springs, New York. It had been built by Spencer and Katrina Trask, who had made a fortune on the stock market. After the deaths of their children, the Trasks turned their property into a 'residence and retreat' for writers and scholars, welcoming some of the most celebrated names in American cultural life. From the late 1920s onwards, Arvin benefited from regular sojourns. Sexuality posed no problem for the administrators and fellows at Yaddo: among those with whom Arvin mixed were a number of famous homosexual figures, including the writer Carson McCullers, who became a close friend.

It was at Yaddo that the 46-year-old Arvin met the 21-year-old wonder boy of American writing, Truman Capote. The two fell in love, enjoying a happy sexual and emotional relationship, though Capote was far more flamboyant than Arvin. Capote began to spend every other weekend at Smith. A feature on Yaddo in *Life* magazine, which pictured the strikingly handsome Capote sprawled seductively on a couch next to a photo of Arvin making his bed, caused minor embarrassment to the professor. Their affair gradually metamorphosed into a life-long friendship sustained by letters and mutual interests. Arvin resumed a quieter life but, now in his fifties, became bolder in his sexual explorations. He had several affairs with young lecturers at Smith, episodically ventured into the saunas and bars of New York, and began cruising for sexual partners at the bus station and public toilets of Springfield, a small city near his college. This was dangerous behaviour at a time when homosexual acts remained illegal and police entrapment was common. Even the occasional *soirées* at which Arvin and his friends passed around their collection of physique pictorial magazines and beefcake photographs were risky.

In 1960 a Smith alumna (the sister of the conservative political commentator William F. Buckley) published a pamphlet denouncing 'liberals' at her old college. In the meantime, the American Postmaster-General had begun a campaign to crack down on 'smut': American law made the sending or receiving of 'obscene' materials by post illegal. Concerned about radicalism at Smith, and probably having tapped Arvin's mail, police raided his house and those of seven other men in Northampton, including several fellow Smith lecturers. They found compromising photographs and mail-order picture magazines, as well as Arvin's diary, which recounted his sexual adventures. Although the raid was illegal, since the police lacked a warrant, they arrested Arvin. Under pressure, he revealed the names of two other homosexual men, whom police also arrested. The 60-year-old professor's world was shattered as he was taken to jail. Pleading guilty to the transport of obscene materials and to being a 'lewd and lascivious person' (another offence on the statute books), he received a one-year suspended sentence, a hefty fine and a long probation.

The arrests of Arvin and the other lecturers threw the college into turmoil. Smith decided to grant Arvin early retirement, on pay, though it rescinded the contracts for his untenured colleagues. Yaddo, after much debate, did not renew his membership on their board. Many distinguished academics and personal friends (including Capote) sent Arvin messages of support and money. After voluntarily spending several months in a mental hospital, he returned to Northampton with embarrassment and some discomfort, and began to rebuild his life by writing a book on the poet Longfellow. Just after the book was published, in 1963, Arvin died of pancreatic cancer.

The law courts later overturned the convictions of Arvin's 'accomplices' (one of them a former lover), but his life provides ample illustration of the ways in which social opprobrium, misguided medical treatments and the law threatened a homosexual, even a reclusive scholar, with self-destructive mental agitation, public shame and arrest.

In his will Capote established a prize for literary criticism in Arvin's memory. In 2002 Smith College set up the Newton Arvin Prize in American Studies, and a Fund for the Study of Civil Liberties and Freedom of Expression in honour of Arvin's colleagues who had suffered dismissal.

Lilly Wust 1913–2006
and Felice Schragenheim 1922–1944

In the early 1990s a Viennese feminist and scholar, Erica Fischer, began reading the contents of two trunks of letters, diaries and photographs belonging to an elderly woman living alone in a small flat in Berlin, Lilly Wust. The book that results from her research, *Aimée and Jaguar*, brought to light the extraordinary story of a lesbian love affair between a model German woman of the Third Reich and an outlawed Jew. The book led to an exhibition, and inspired a television documentary and a film. 'I gave my story to the world,' said Wust, and her papers now rest in the archives of Berlin's Jewish Museum.

In 1942 Lilly Wust was, to all appearances, an upstanding German citizen. She came from a middle-class Berlin background. She was married to a soldier, then stationed outside the capital, who was vocally supportive of the Nazis, even if he was not a member of the National Socialist Workers' Party. By giving birth to four Aryan children Wust earned a motherhood medal from Hitler's government. She had kept her fine figure and sported an alluring head of reddish hair around her pretty face. She lived a comfortable life looking after her young family. Yet all was not as it seemed. Günther Wust kept a mistress, with whom he would soon live, and Lilly enjoyed dalliances with several male lovers. The arrival of a young woman in her household introduced her to still other pleasures.

Inge Wolf, an assistant in a bookshop, landed on Lilly's doorstep to work as a domestic help, sent there as part of her national service. The two became friends, and Inge gradually introduced Lilly to her circle of women friends. Among them was Felice Schragenheim, a feisty, quick-witted and elegantly attractive young woman turned out in tailored clothes, the daughter of two dentists who had died in her childhood. Felice enchanted Lilly with her sparkle and her kindness, visiting her in hospital, large bunches of roses in her hand, when Lilly underwent minor surgery. Soon Felice seduced her, and the two fell madly in love (to the slight consternation of Inge, who had been romantically linked to Felice). Felice visited Lilly more and more regularly, making friends with her children and presenting her to her other friends. Sometimes Felice disappeared for hours or even days for purposes that she did not disclose to Lilly; she did disclose, however – partly in response to a passing anti-Semitic comment from Lilly – that she was Jewish.

German anti-Semitism was entering its most virulent and murderous phase when the two women met. Jewish citizens were barred from their professions and forbidden to own telephones, take public transport, buy newspapers or sit on park benches other than those designated for their use. Their identity papers were marked with a 'J', and they were forced to wear a yellow star. Their property was confiscated, and ultimately most would be rounded up and deported to extermination camps.

Felice had earlier made plans to escape from Germany: she had relatives in America, England and Palestine, and Felice herself had obtained an entry permit to Australia. But the start of the war had made it impossible for her to get passage out. When she met Lilly, she was leading a clandestine and very dangerous existence, seeking refuge with friends, trying to safeguard her possessions, and perhaps working (it seems) for the Jewish underground during those unexplained absences. Yet the horrors of life for a Jew in Hitler's Germany did not overwhelm the happiness that Lilly and Felice – or Aimée and Jaguar, as they called each other – shared for almost two years. They made do on the increasingly reduced rations of wartime, they danced and went for walks, they socialized with other lesbians and heterosexual friends, and they played with what they now called 'our' children. Lilly secured a divorce from her husband, and the two women, on what they knew as their 'wedding day', exchanged rings. When they were apart, even for a day, they wrote each other intensely passionate letters. On 21 August 1944 they took an excursion to the beach at the Havel river; photographs taken with a timer show them relaxing in prim bathing costumes and kissing each other on the lips.

When they returned from the idyllic outing, they found two Gestapo agents waiting in Lilly's apartment. They arrested Felice and carried her off to a Jewish detention centre, while Lilly was subjected to lengthy interrogation. She managed to visit Felice in the detention centre, taking her parcels of food and clothing before Felice was sent to the concentration camp at Theresienstadt. Desperate, Lilly followed her by train, using an illicit travel document, but the attempt to see her was unsuccessful. She did succeed in getting packages and letters to her, and even dared to write of her love, knowing that her letters might be read by Nazi officials: 'Dearest, we must have hope, my sweet! … Without you I would never have known what love is, what love is capable of. How happy we were, how happy! Do you remember how I rushed to meet you each time? Do you remember how, when we were first together, I always traced your mouth with my finger? … Oh, I must love you, and only you, for eternity.'

Fate did not prove kind, and the letters from Felice stopped coming. After the liberation of Berlin, Lilly learned that Felice had been marched, along with thousands of others, to the Bergen-Belsen camp, where she no doubt perished.

Lilly Wust lived for another six decades. Soon after the war, she tried to commit suicide. She had a one-year marriage with a brutish man, in whose shop she worked. Living in hermit-like near-poverty, she then took jobs as a cleaner. In honour of Felice, she frequented the tiny Jewish community in Berlin, and one of her sons migrated to Israel. Obsessively preserving her memories of Felice, every year, on 21 August, she opened her trunks to read the letters and poems that they had written to each other.

VISIONS OF MALE BEAUTY

Eugène Jansson 1862–1915

Gymnasts and swimmers feature in many of Eugène Jansson's paintings, their presence revealing much about his personal life, the possibilities for homoerotic sociability in Scandinavia, and the potency of the fit body in the homosexual imagination.

Jansson was born in Stockholm, where he lived for the rest of his life. His background was petty bourgeois, but the death of his father, a concierge in the postal department, reduced the family's circumstances. Jansson and his mother and brother moved to a working-class district on the heights of Stockholm, a location that afforded magnificent views of the city, stretching over the water to the sky. Jansson, who had studied at the Royal Academy of Fine Arts and had already won critical attention for his landscapes, began to paint brilliantly lyrical blue canvases of the Stockholm night, 'nocturnes' as he called them. Occasionally, factories or workers' housing sit in the expanses, an indication of Jansson's socialist politics (though such plebeian and modernist motifs did not endear him to collectors).

Around 1904, after a trip to Italy, Jansson changed themes. As a child, Jansson had suffered a bout of scarlet fever and other maladies that left him with partial deafness and enduring kidney problems; he had taken up physical exercise to restore his health and had become interested in athletics. Now gymnasts started to appear in his paintings, entirely naked men wrestling, hefting barbells or exercising on athletic apparatuses in elegantly minimalist wood-floored, whitewashed and sun-drenched rooms. Some of the images are rather grotesque: contorted gymnasts, hanging from rings, look like pieces of meat on butchers' hooks. Others are more inviting, such as a 1907 picture of a nude athlete in a cruciform pose, framed by a door, perhaps beckoning a visitor into the room or forcing someone to brush past his body in order to enter. The model was in fact a long-term, intimate friend of Jansson, and the picture seemed to illustrate a comment made by a fellow artist in his elegy after Jansson's death: 'You searched for the beauty of the human body, pictured in all its vigour and the force of its youth.'

Jansson set some of his works in the Swedish navy swimming baths in Stockholm. Again the men are naked, artfully lounging around the pool or gracefully diving into the water. Each figure is a study of a comely, slender sailor, unembarrassed at showing his buttocks or genitals, and happy to share the masculine camaraderie of the pool and to gaze on the prowess of others, hovering between water and sky in their dives. In one painting, Jansson has depicted himself among the nude swimmers, rather incongruously attired in a white suit, blue cummerbund, yellow tie and jaunty hat decorated in blue and yellow (the Swedish national colours). He was an accomplished swimmer, and he enjoyed frequenting the young sailors and swimmers, apparently giving them gifts or money in return for their companionship. Here he has literally painted himself into their company as visitor, patron and – though he faces out of the canvas, away from the swimmers – as voyeur.

Jansson's athletes and swimmers radiate a kind of innocence, a comfort in their nakedness. They belong to the naturist fashions of the early 20th century, which preached the gospel of 'a healthy mind in a healthy body', and remind us of the Olympic Games that took place in Stockholm in 1912. They personify the health that Jansson did not enjoy, and perhaps the freedom that the introverted artist, who was obliged to care for a psychologically troubled mother, could never experience. They fit into a long history of homoerotic images of swimmers, and look forward to the California pool paintings of David Hockney.

Homosexual acts remained illegal in Sweden until 1944. Jansson's brother, who was also homosexual, burned all of the artist's papers after his death. As is all too often the case with homosexual figures of the past, the documentation of his private life was thus destroyed. Jansson's art is little known outside Scandinavia, and his works portraying athletes and swimmers proved unsettling to the general public during his lifetime, though they were the ones for which he wished to be remembered. Today they give us a glimpse of idealized Nordic beauty, of the role of physical fitness (either as pastime or fantasy) for gay men, and of the significance of gymnasiums, swimming pools and fitness clubs as venues for discreet or overt sexual fraternization.

Magnus Enckell 1870–1925

The Finnish painter Magnus Enckell was born into a Swedish-speaking family in a provincial town of eastern Finland, the sixth child of a Lutheran minister. He studied in Helsinki, then at the Académie Julian in Paris, where he became the leader of a small group of expatriate Finnish artists who embraced Symbolism. While there, he saw Vaslav Nijinsky dance in *L'Après-midi d'un faune* – the inspiration, according to the art historian Juha-Heikki Tihinen, for several paintings of fauns. The Ballets Russes impresario Sergei Diaghilev helped Enckell to arrange a display of Finnish art in the French capital. After returning to Helsinki from a stay in Italy, he helped found the Septem group and was a major figure in Finnish culture, even if he never fully subscribed to the nationalistic themes that dominated his generation as the country struggled for independence (realized only in 1917). Photographs show a handsome, dapper gentleman. He had a son, though he never married the mother.

Although Enckell is still little known outside his native country, his compatriots placed him in the pantheon of great national artists. Not until 1994 did a commentator refer in print to the artist's homosexuality, which nevertheless seems to have been an open secret during his lifetime. A decade later, the biographer Harri Kalha published a volume that addressed the question of Enckell's private life for the first time.

Coming from the far north of Europe, Enckell was one of those men with homosexual inclinations for whom the Mediterranean was both destination and inspiration. He lived in Italy from the mid-1890s until 1905, when he returned to Helsinki with a new artistic style and with richer colours that marked a change from his earlier sombre palette. He also came back with a man named Giovanni, who worked as his model, driver and manservant (photographs show a robust Italian posing nude in Enckell's studio).

Enckell painted many variations on the theme of the male nude. A dark-haired youth emerges naked from his bedcovers in *The Awakening* (1893), Enckell's most famous painting. Elsewhere a young blond sits meditatively on a rock by the water, radiating sunshine, while in another work a youth not yet tanned by the summer rests his head pensively in his hand as he gazes into the distance. In *Wings* (1923), two boys stand together, the one in front looking beatifically upwards, his arm silhouetted against a burst of cloud and sky, while his friend glances modestly downwards. In a nod to mythology, a slender youth balancing a lyre on his thigh, a cloth discreetly covering his private parts, perches on the edge of a pond on which six mysterious black swans swim. Another naked boy, his back and buttocks revealed as he wades in a pool, wrestles with a massive white swan. A mustachioed faun stares mischievously from one canvas. A handsome Narcissus bends across a boulder to stare at his reflection in the water. In one of the loveliest pictures, *The Faun* (1914), a beautiful boy whose carmine lips and cheeks match the tunic thrown across his loins reposes on the forest floor, his smooth marble-like flesh capturing the rays of morning sun as he raises his hand to his forehead as if roused from a long sleep.

Enckell's pictorial world is an Arcadia of statuesque ephebes who disport themselves in glades and rivers, evoking sylvan innocence (though it conceals, or perhaps reveals, ardent desire), budding manhood and intimated passion. Some Finnish critics viewed his works with discomfort, criticizing those paintings suffused with a Mediterranean, mythological spirit as foreign and decadent. Homosexuals, on the other hand, no doubt found in him a kindred spirit. In the secret of his notebooks, Enckell confessed his kinship with antiquity. In a poem on 'Antinous' he declared, 'I also am of your family / I know you well', swearing a vow to honour the sacred memory of the beauty, love and sacrifice of Hadrian's companion.

Enckell's images of bathing boys recall Thomas Eakins' *The Swimming Hole* and other softly erotic *mises en scène* of young men by the water, including those by Verner Thomé, a fellow Finn and member of the artistic group Septem. They bring to mind a culture of easy nudity at the seaside, and the magic of the brief Nordic summer. There is, to be sure, a streak of melancholy – one naked boy crouches on the ground holding a human skull – but also an effort to capture an ideal of beauty in a northern setting.

Homosexual acts remained criminal in law and unacceptable in Finnish society, but the sensitive and shy artist found ways to embody his desires in his pictures and, with Giovanni, to find personal happiness.

Donald Friend 1915–1989

Donald Friend was a peripatetic artist and novelist whose paintings and drawings illustrate his sexual and romantic liaisons. Recorded in his voluminous diaries, these encounters took place all over the world, from Australia to Nigeria, from Britain to Italy, and from Sri Lanka to Bali.

Friend was born in Sydney, the son of a wealthy family of graziers, and spent his childhood either on their vast sheep station or at their city apartment. His earliest meaningful sexual adventure was with a half-Thai man who worked on the family estate. 'He was ... my first friend,' Friend remembered, 'and I suppose, though my interest had lain in that direction since childhood (Christ knows what was the original cause) [it] had much to do with that interest in orientals and orientalism which spread to include the whole coloured races of the world and has always been the strongest factor and influence in everything I've done.' When they were discovered in bed, Friend ran away to Cairns, in far north Queensland, where he took up with Malay, Melanesian and Aboriginal inhabitants of the then ramshackle pearl-lugging port. The tropical cosmopolitanism made a change from outback Australia and from Sydney, which in the inter-war years was still a staid British outpost. The luxuriance of the environment and the appeal of the men inspired a life-long journey.

In the early 1930s Friend moved back to Sydney and studied at art school. In 1936 he took the decision – as was *de rigueur* for Australian gentlemen and artists – to travel to London. While he was there, a Nigerian acquaintance and bed-partner, who also modelled for Friend's first mature oil painting, suggested that he should go to Africa. So it was that Friend spent several happy years in the country of the Yoruba people, working in a vague capacity for the local ruler and continuing to draw, paint and write.

With the start of the Second World War, Friend returned to Australia and enlisted in the army. After a stint as an artillery gunner, early in 1945 he became an official army artist. He was sent to the island of Borneo, which provided further opportunities for art (he painted harrowing images of the ravages of warfare) and sexual adventure. The experience sharpened his critical view of colonialism and reinforced his yearning for overseas places. His travels continued after the war: back to Sydney, then on to the Torres Strait, an abandoned mining town in rural New South Wales, Italy in 1949, and once again to England.

In 1957 Friend halted for five years in Sri Lanka. Here he found the landscapes, and the type of young men, that he loved. His work from this period, which borrows some motifs from Ceylonese temple art, is especially accomplished. After a five-year stint in Australia once again, in 1967 the footloose Friend moved on to Bali, an island of legendary beauty that since the 1920s had attracted a coterie of homosexuals, such as the artist Walter Spies and the composer Colin McPhee. 'The island itself for years had been a favourite part of my imagination's geography,' reminisced Friend, adding that 'a Westerner could live like a king in Bali in 1967, and I did … My 25 houseboys liked working for me … They called me Tuan Rakasa, which means Lord Devil, but I was a benevolent devil.' He had a final homecoming to Australia in 1980 and spent his last years in Sydney.

Critics acknowledged Friend as a fine artist – Robert Hughes judged him the best draughtsman among Australians – and his work found eager collectors and exhibitors. His constant theme, though by no means the sole one, was young men, especially the 'exotic' youths he encountered while travelling. They appear in unadorned portraits, or are shown slumbering in island heat, playing indigenous musical instruments, or posed against landscapes of the

Australian outback or Asian villages. Friend's paintings are never pornographic, but his young men – who were generally his lovers, houseboys or neighbours – do carry a seductive charge. Friend was open about his homosexuality – hardly a welcome subject everywhere, particularly since homosexual acts were still illegal in Australia. Artistic talent, wealth, discretion and his frequent absences overseas kept him from trouble, however, even though the last perhaps made his work less appreciated during his lifetime than it might otherwise have been.

Friend was also a fine (and still undervalued) writer in a number of genres. His memoir *Donald Friend in Bali* (1972) offers a colourful account of life in the East Indies. His novels often include mordantly humorous stories about expatriates in remote corners of the world. Friend's great skill at satire is especially evident in several illustrated albums, especially one boisterous volume entitled *Sundry notes & papers: being the recently discovered notes and documents of the Natural & Instinctive Bestiality Research Expedition, collected and collated under the title Bumbooziana.* It is a wild sexual romp – in this case cheerfully pornographic – in the form of an illustrated adventure tale. The exploits of a 'Beast of Basra' who displays formidable phallic prowess, a German scholar who specializes in toilet graffiti, a Polynesian prince with tattooed genitals who is all the rage in Mayfair, and a discourse on Little Red Riding Hood as a transvestite exhibitionist lesbian with a grandmother fetish are only a few of the book's delights.

Since Friend's death, a four-volume edition of his diaries and a one-volume abridgement have been published. They deserve a place among the classics of both Australian and gay literature. Friend was a deft literary craftsman, and his diaries chart the evolution of artistic milieux in Australia and Britain, and the colonial and post-colonial situations of the countries in which he lived, as well as the development of his own work. Not surprisingly, they also detail his sexual adventures. Friend treats these in a witty, reflective and self-critical fashion, showing the opportunities but also the hazards that awaited the European gay man abroad, in places where the homosexual living was easy, but where romantic entanglements could make for some hard choices. He writes, too, about his long-lasting sexual partnership, and then enduring friendship, with an Italian who shared his life in Ischia, London and Sydney.

'Goodbye world of lovely colours and amicable nudes,' was how Friend signed off his diaries. His life had been lived in the company of artists, writers, expatriates and friendly 'natives', full of globetrotting pleasures and serious dedication to art and literature.

Alair Gomes 1921–1992

A lair Gomes was a Brazilian photographer whose main subjects – to judge from the 170,000 negatives he left behind – were the young men who went to the beach of Ipanema in Rio de Janeiro. Gomes shot them from the windows of his sixth-floor flat, or invited them into his apartment for sexual encounters and photographic sessions.

Gomes' photographs constitute a remarkable compendium. He noted that pictures of male nudes usually fell into three categories – pornography, 'artistic' studies, or images in which potent masculinity is somehow subverted – but rightly felt that his own works did not fit into any of these genres. He drew inspiration from many and varied sources: classical culture (illustrations of statuary decorated the walls of his apartment); the work of Henri Cartier-Bresson, of whom he spoke admiringly; religious iconography, which informs his 'triptychs' and friezes of nudes; and film and music. Gomes' masterwork is a series of 1,767 photographs of men entitled *Symphony of Erotic Icons*, arranged in distinct 'movements' of allegro, andantino, andante, adagio and finale. He insisted that his visitors might only see the pictures if they agreed to view the entire sequence in order, and that the images should not be otherwise displayed.

Gomes photographed the carnival in Rio, and shot urban scenes during his trips to the United States and Europe, but it is his images of men that command most attention. The long hairstyles worn by his subjects in the 1960s, and the bell-bottomed trousers that appear occasionally in the American photos, are the only hints of a specific time. As for place, the men inhabit a setting that could be Carmel (which he did photograph), Sitges or Bondi as easily as Rio. Shadowed on the pavement, they cross the street, sometimes carrying surfboards; they exercise on gym equipment on the beach or lounge in the sand, wearing only small swimming costumes. The indoor portraits show them lying naked on a bed, the camera focused on their genitals, buttocks or chests. Gomes' subjects are uniformly masculine and beautiful. His pictures highlight their virile attributes of muscles and body hair: indeed, few other photographers take such an interest in the hirsute landscapes of chests, buttocks and legs. Somewhat oddly in a country that has so many people of mixed ethnic heritage, Gomes' men almost always have stereotypically European features and skin colour.

Gomes admitted that he was an obsessive photographer, and remarked of his men that 'when they see me photograph them obsessively, they understand this as a glorification of their beauty'. The 'erotic homage' (his words) that the corpus of his photographs represents has something of the ethnographic or even zoological: countless specimens of spectacular bodies, the images emphasizing the animality of the taut, lithe, feline young men; bodies caught in innocent play, but also sometimes curled into vulnerable curves. There is, too, a dialogue between exhibitionist and voyeur. In one picture a young man holds a mirror above his naked, hairy body, in which is reflected the bespectacled, weedy photographer with his camera, crouched between the boy's legs, arms encircling the youth's thighs.

Gomes came from a middle-class background and had graduated in civil engineering. He worked for the Brazilian railways for a while, but also established a literary review. After a religious crisis in his twenties, he returned to university to study science and philosophy, and won a fellowship for travel in the United States, where he spent a year at Yale University. Having returned to Brazil, from 1962 he taught philosophy of science at the Federal University of Rio and contemporary art at a school of visual arts, regularly participating in international academic conferences and publishing papers in art criticism and the philosophy of science. For a decade from the age of 32, he kept a detailed 'erotic diary' that recorded his sexual liaisons, and painted and drew nudes. Only in his forties did Gomes begin taking the photographs that would become his passion.

There is a complicity between subject and object in Gomes' work, but a complicity within limits. One wonders what emoluments Gomes might have provided to his young men. What did they make of the ageing photographer, who must have been a familiar figure in Ipanema, wandering the beach or taking a succession of men into his flat? What were the circumstances under which one man Gomes had invited home murdered him, at the age of 71?

Bhupen Khakhar 1934–2003

By the last decades of the 20th century, overtly homoerotic art was common in the Western world. What was surprising was to see this art coming from India, especially when it portrayed mature men rather than the sleek, buffed boys omnipresent in Europe and America. Such themes, nonetheless, formed the dominant subject of the Indian painter Bhupen Khakhar.

Born in 1934, at a time when India was still under the rule of the British Raj, Khakhar came from a middle-class Gujarati-speaking background – his father was a successful cloth merchant and his mother the daughter of a schoolteacher – and spent his early life in Bombay. He took degrees in economics and finance at the University of Bombay. To the distress of his family, Khakhar then moved to Baroda, the centre of a nascent artistic movement and a fine-arts university, where he took a diploma in art criticism. He would nevertheless spend his professional life as a chartered accountant, painting oils or watercolours before or after his day at the office. With little formal training in art, he became famous enough to enjoy one-man exhibitions at the Tate Gallery in London and the Centre Pompidou in Paris.

Khakhar's artistic influences ranged from Jain temple maps, Mughal miniatures and the popular kitsch oleographs and posters sold in bazaars to the paintings of *le douanier* Rousseau and Fernand Léger; they also encompassed 14th-century Italian artists such as Ambrogio Lorenzetti, whose frescoes he discovered on a trip to Europe in the 1970s. Khakhar's own work, which is often described as naïve, shows his interest in narration and his choice of figurative art over abstraction. Having first experimented with collages, he moved on to bright, geometric renditions of Indian daily life, depicting such subjects as a barber, a watchmaker, a teashop and his parents.

The artist knew early on that he was homosexual, though he was troubled by his desires. 'I was very much ashamed of my sexuality. I never wanted it to be known I was gay,' he remembered. Despite having had a number of liaisons in early adulthood, only his experience of the relative tolerance of homosexuality in England in 1979, and the death of his mother the following year, gave Khakhar the confidence to express his sexuality more openly. A 1981 painting, *You Can't Please All* – which features a naked man on a balcony watching life below – represents a symbolic coming out: 'I am also here taking off my clothes before the world.' Khakhar's coming out in life and art constituted a courageous gesture: under the old colonial-era law code, homosexual relations remained illegal in India until after his death, and opposition to homosexual expression is still widespread.

Glimmers of homosexuality appear in earlier works, but it was at the beginning of the 1980s that Khakhar began openly to portray same-sex sexual desire. *Two Men in Benares* (1982) features a dark-headed younger man and his white-haired partner, possibly the artist, standing naked and embracing; around them, in an arrangement Khakhar often used, small auxiliary scenes depict landscapes, a man receiving a massage and various enigmatic figures. *My Dear Friend* (1983) pictures two men conversing in bed while two others voyeuristically gaze at them, it seems, through the roof. *In a Boat* (1986) shows a vessel floating on a dark body of water, a rocky landscape in the distance. What appears to be an orgy is about to take place on board: two naked men begin an embrace, two others almost divested of their clothing look on expectantly, and yet another man offers a glass to a muscular partner, who flirtatiously sticks out his tongue. Perhaps Khakhar's most remarkable homoerotic work is *Yayati* (1987), named after a legendary king. Arranged across the top of the canvas are Khakhar's characteristic vignettes of small landscapes and a domestic scene, but the painting is dominated by two greenish-grey men with erect penises set against a lurid pink-and-white background. Over one recumbent figure hovers a winged angel; the two figures' arms and feet touch, evoking a visitation of desire and its satisfaction, or perhaps a dream of fulfilment.

Khakhar's art communicates a kind of magical realism, tinged with considerable humour. One of his best-known works is *An Old Man from Vasad Who Had Five Penises Suffered from Runny Nose* (1995). There is tender lyricism as well, as illustrated by the two men in *How Many Hands Do I Need to Declare My Love to You?* (1995). Their multiple arms, string of beads and garland transform the couple into soaring Hindu gods.

Despite his concerns, the homoerotic content of Khakhar's paintings did not compromise his reputation – in fact, the ageing artist earned honours at home and overseas. Producing portraits of such figures as Salman Rushdie, he became one of India's best-known artists. The straightforwardness with which his works present sexual themes continues to surprise, but the masted ships, domed shrines, and bakers and tailors of the marketplace all provide a recognizably Indian backdrop, distinguishing his paintings from the vernacular homoerotic art of the West. By his own admission, he focused on tenderness and warmth, on ordinary, nondescript men, and on the quiet enactment of sexual desires. (Western-style gyms, gay bars and placard-wielding activism were in any case unknown in Khakhar's India.)

Although Khakhar never abandoned his observation of other aspects of daily life, the sexual panoramas gained him new fame in gay circles. These homoerotic works by an Indian painter are not some Orientalist fantasy dreamed up by a European traveller, but the expression of same-sex eroticism embedded within the indigenous culture of his homeland. In the gallery of Khakhar's paintings, a man savouring *jalebi* sweets, a sage celebrating a religious festival, a group gathered for a tea party on a terrace and two men having sex blend easily into the infinitely varied canvas of Indian society.

8
LOVE IN THE LEVANT

Abu Nuwas   *c.* 757–*c.* 814

There is a long tradition of homoeroticism in classical Arabic and Persian writing. Indeed, one type of poetry, which exalts the beauty of youths, is sometimes interpreted as a metaphor for the mystical love that exists between man and God. One of the earliest and most famous practitioners of this genre, and, according to some, the greatest of all Muslim poets, was Abu Nuwas.

Abu Nuwas – actually a nickname that means something like 'the man with flowing locks' – was born in the mid-8th century, most likely in Ahwaz, which is situated in modern-day Iran. His mother was a weaver, and his father, whom he never knew, was a soldier. Mother and child moved to Basra, where the handsome young Abu Nuwas attended Koranic school and, under the influence of his uncle, began to write poetry. He then moved to Baghdad, where Harun al-Rashid (immortalized in *One Thousand and One Nights*) held court. The pious caliph did not take to the poet, however, and twice had him imprisoned for his dissolute life, satirical works and involvement in court politics. Abu Nuwas's alliance with a disgraced vizier's family also forced him briefly into exile in Egypt, during which time his only son died.

Apart from that one unwelcome absence, Abu Nuwas spent the remainder of his life in Baghdad, one of the great centres of Arabic civilization. He got on well with Harun's successor and son, al-Amin, a former student who (according to the Orientalist Vincent-Mansour

Monteil) shared Abu Nuwas's taste for youths, wine and hunting. Four years of libertine life in the pleasure quarters of Baghdad – where Christians, Zoroastrians and Jews sold wine, in principle forbidden to Muslims – followed al-Amin's accession to the caliphate and Abu Nuwas's return from exile. Abu Nuwas gained a reputation as a fine poet, a drinker and a lover of ephebes (notwithstanding occasional dalliances with courtesans), though he also reputedly completed the pilgrimage to Mecca. The last two years of Abu Nuwas's life, after the assassination of his protector, were more difficult. Sources diverge on whether he died at home, in prison or in the house of a cabaret-owner.

Abu Nuwas is best known for his erotic and bacchic poetry, in which he expresses his enjoyment of wine and the delights of the youths he called 'gazelles' (the word is also translated as 'fawns'), many of whom were servants or slaves. Abu Nuwas wrote lyrically about long evenings in the tavern, far from the rigorous demands of mosque worship. One poem enjoins a waiter to refill the cup of a cute lad so that he will loosen his trousers and allow his drinking companion to take him into his arms. In another Abu Nuwas confesses that he has given up girls and war for young men and aged wine. The poet flirts, is infatuated, seduces and falls in love; his verses linger on the beauty of a pale shoulder, a pretty face, well-shaped legs or a gentle voice. Away from the cabaret, the school also provides fetching youths; and in the bathhouse, he says, that which trousers hide is deliciously revealed. His overtures meet with success. Even when passion is not reciprocated, in the next cabaret or around the corner there is always another beckoning youth – a new conquest for him to pursue.

Abu Nuwas had many successors, and works touching on affections between men, extending from pure intimate friendships to the varieties of sexual intercourse, became an important part of medieval Arabic and Persian literature. Ahmad al-Tifashi, born towards the end of the 12th century in present-day Tunisia, devoted five out of twelve chapters of one of his treatises – available in English as *The Delight of Hearts* – to a miscellany on homosexuality, including poems, jokes and gossipy anecdotes. His descriptions of same-sex encounters run the gamut of experiences, ages and emotions. They include the attraction of adult men for each other ('beardophiles'), as well as the lust of older men for youths. Taken at face value, they portray an unbridled and unabashed homosexual culture.

In his treatise al-Tifashi reproduces more than a dozen poems by Abu Nuwas and repeats several anecdotes about him. In one story, Abu Nuwas passes through the city of Homs, where a resident, hoping to converse with the famous poet, takes his son to find him at his inn. They ask the first man they see there to direct them to Abu Nuwas, and the stranger promises the information in return for a kiss from the handsome boy (the man, of course, turns out to be Abu Nuwas himself). In another anecdote, Abu Nuwas says that his great dream would be to find a young man to bed without committing a sin. Another partner, however, counsels him that he will receive no favours in heaven if he does not favour those whom he loves on earth. Al-Tifashi's stories – which may or may not have a basis in fact – also record that Abu Nuwas had a sexual relationship with his teacher, and that he composed his first poem, on the theme of a handsome boy, in a verse-making contest with a Bedouin who had recited an ode to camels.

The 13th-century Anatolian Rumi and the 14th-century Persian Hafiz count among later Muslim versifiers who extolled the pleasures of wine and youths, although, as with Abu Nuwas, some commentators insist that the works about sexual intercourse should be seen as symbolizing ecstatic union between the human and the divine. Their poems nevertheless inspired many Western homosexuals, including those who travelled to Arabic countries in search of the joys they promised. A procession of visiting writers – from André Gide and

Jean Genet to Paul Bowles and Joe Orton – popularized the idea of North Africa as a destination where seductive young men, for love or money, eagerly offered companionship and sex in the seductive setting of the kasbah, amid a haze of hashish and the eroticism of the exotic.

The law codes of almost all states where Islam is the major religion now deem homosexual acts to be criminal, punishable in some countries by long terms of imprisonment, public flogging and even execution. Homosexuality nevertheless exists throughout the Arabic and Islamic world (as it does almost everywhere), even if relatively few who engage in same-sex relations consider themselves homosexual in a Western sense and most men, whatever their erotic and romantic inclinations, marry and beget children. A new tradition of homosexual representation is now emerging gradually in Arabic countries and within the Muslim diaspora – for instance, in the novels of the Moroccan who writes under the name of Rachid O., and in the 2009 Tunisian film *Le Fil* ('The String'). The works of Abu Nuwas remain testimony to an earlier, celebratory tradition of Middle Eastern eroticism.

Constantine Cavafy 1863–1933

In the late 19th and early 20th centuries, the Mediterranean port of Alexandria hosted a variegated population of Egyptian Arabs, Jews, British (virtual rulers of Egypt, even if the country was not officially a British colony), Frenchmen, and a large community of Greeks. Sited at the crossroads of three continents, it was a city of elegant cafés and busy markets. Lawrence Durrell's *The Alexandria Quartet* captures its atmosphere well. Alexandria blended its Hellenistic heritage with modern commerce and the dynamics of imperialism. The stock exchange handled vast supplies of Egyptian cotton, which were dispatched to European factories from its crowded port. Luxury and squalor, adventure and mystery mixed in a city where Orthodox cathedrals and mosques stood near each other on French-style boulevards.

Alexandria was Constantine Cavafy's city: it appeared, in its ancient and contemporary incarnations, in his poetry, and was also the theatre of his erotic pursuits. Cavafy was born in Alexandria to a family of Greeks who had moved there from Constantinople. His mother was the daughter of a diamond merchant, while his father worked as the head of an import–export business established in England with one of his brothers in the 1840s. A few years after Cavafy's birth, the family returned to England, where the boy spent his adolescence, becoming fluent in English and conversant in English literature. After his father's death, the company began to struggle and was finally liquidated in 1879. The family returned to Alexandria, then moved to Constantinople, where Cavafy spent three years in the 1880s. Returning permanently to Alexandria in 1885, he worked briefly on a newspaper, then as an assistant to a stockbroker brother. At the age of 29, Cavafy secured employment with the Irrigation

Service of the Ministry of Public Works, a job he kept, rising to the position of assistant director, for thirty years.

In the meantime, Cavafy had begun writing poetry. He was a meticulous stylist; using language that blended literary and demotic Greek, he worked and reworked his poems, rarely allowing publication, but gradually gaining a high reputation among those who knew his writings. They included E. M. Forster, whom he met during the First World War when Forster served as a volunteer in the British medical service in Alexandria. The two became friends: Forster wrote about Cavafy in his books on Alexandria and helped arrange publication of some of his poems in England.

Cavafy's two themes, sometimes intertwined, were history and eroticism. In the first lines of a poem not published until decades after Cavafy's death in 1933, two naked swimmers emerge from the water on a perfect Mediterranean summer's day; the lovely scene then merges into a disquisition on a 14th-century Neoplatonist defender of Hellenic education. The period of history that most interested Cavafy was the transition between paganism and Christianity, between the Hellenistic and Byzantine worlds – life as it was lived on the eastern margins of the old Greek civilization. His eroticism was homosexual.

Biographers know relatively little about Cavafy's own romantic and sexual life. It seems that he had a couple of meaningful short-lived affairs, as well as casual encounters. His sexual initiation may have come when he was living in Constantinople, but it is clear that he wrestled with his sexual orientation, and only began showing, and occasionally publishing, his erotic poems when he was in his forties.

Most of Cavafy's poems about love and sex are memories of encounters, whose details have sometimes faded with the passage of years. Sitting alone, he recalls chance meetings, hears the half-forgotten voices of partners, dreams of the caresses of his lovers. As 'the body's memory awakens', he remembers, with renewed yearning or a sensation of serene comfort, the beautiful young men with whom he had sex.

Cavafy's lovers, and the lovers of the historical characters who haunt his poems, are handsome, well-built men in their twenties, with grey or sapphire eyes, jet hair and pale foreheads – men often of modest condition whose brazen beauty is revealed only when they throw off tattered clothing. A man seemingly fashioned by Eros himself beckons from a café. Meetings take place in the twilight of busy streets or late at night in tavernas. Two men exchange looks outside a tobacco shop and begin their lovemaking in a carriage. Another couple connects on a jetty. Just at closing time, a passer-by fabricates a wish to buy handkerchiefs, to make contact with a shop assistant whom he spies through the lighted window. In the small hours of the morning, a wine-shop forms the backdrop for another encounter, two young men rushing to satisfy their desires behind a screen while the waiter dozes. Sometimes a pair takes refuge in a sordid little hotel room. The encounters are fortuitous, but they are also facilitated by money given to an impoverished youth – perhaps the son of a sailor, or a blacksmith's apprentice – in the city's bars and restaurants.

Behind debauchery, there lies innocence. A village youth dreams of the pleasures of the metropolis; a city boy waits anxiously for his beloved, late for a rendezvous; a man tries to resolve unrequited passion, or relives the affection of a lover conjured up by a portrait; a shocked newspaper reader learns that an old flame has been murdered on the waterfront.

In evocative language and crystalline narratives, the poet resurrects these men from his memory; they appear as the 'shades of love' before his lamplight. The pleasures may have been illicit, desire at times shadowed with shame, or unions may have been sundered after a few moments. For Cavafy, the yearnings are innate, not degenerate, and 'needless the repentance'. Those who dare to unbridle their impulses – and Cavafy bemoans the ones, possibly including himself, who do not dare enough and who must live with the regret of being so close so many times – will experience ecstasies that, like youth and place, can only be transitory, but that can also become the stuff of both poetry and memory.

Cavafy's poems have great power and depth. They are well known in translation – 'Waiting for the Barbarians' (1898) and 'Ithaka' (1910), for instance, stand as two of the greatest modern poems in any literature – and his erotic verses have been illustrated by David Hockney, Alekos Fassianos and other artists. A rather mannered movie, made in 1996, openly considered his homosexuality, a subject that many early commentators thought taboo, since Cavafy is viewed as the most important modern Greek poet. Today's visitors to dating websites and frenetic clubs might find an ageing recluse's recollections of furtive encounters in the backstreets of a Levantine city somewhat dated. Yet the essence of desire and its satisfaction, placed in the seductive setting of the ancient and modern *polis*, has no finer or more intoxicating distillation than the verses of the Alexandrian poet.

T. E. Lawrence 1888–1935

To many in Britain and beyond, Lawrence of Arabia was a great hero of the early 20th century. He seemed the very model of an Edwardian scholar–gentleman, with his cosmopolitan interest in the romantic past and 'exotic' overseas places. He was born in Wales, to a baronet father and a mother who had been a governess; the couple lived as husband and wife, although they never married. Lawrence was educated at Jesus College, Oxford; like many undergraduates he travelled to the Continent during the long vacation, but also ventured farther afield, visiting Crusader castles in Lebanon and Syria, then part of the Ottoman Empire. Reading widely during his university years and afterwards, he mastered a number of languages, and would later publish a translation of Homer's *Odyssey*. After graduation, Lawrence spent four years as a field archaeologist, working in Turkey, Syria, Egypt and Palestine, particularly on Assyrian and Hittite sites at Carchemish.

However, it was for his military and literary activities rather than his archaeological work that Lawrence became famous. In 1914 he was commissioned in the British armed forces and posted to an office job in Cairo, but soon became involved in the Arab Revolt. Arab nationalists, supported by the British government for strategic reasons during the First World War, began to mount a campaign against Ottoman domination. Lawrence allied himself with Emir Faisal and took part in Arab operations that conquered Aqaba and Jordan. His exploits were widely recorded, and Lawrence returned home from the war a lieutenant colonel and a celebrity.

Lawrence became a government advisor, first at the Foreign Office, and then at the Colonial Office. In 1917 he took up a fellowship at All Soul's College, Oxford. This gave him the opportunity to write his memoirs of the Arab campaign: a huge, sprawling tome called *Seven Pillars of Wisdom*, which was published in 1926 and abridged one year later as *Revolt in the Desert*. Despite his efforts as a delegate at the Paris Peace Conference in 1919, Lawrence's hopes for an independent Arab state had been dashed. The British and French divided up the old Ottoman Empire into protectorates that they ruled, effectively as colonies, under League of Nations mandates. Not until after the Second World War would the Arab lands become independent states, except for Palestine, partitioned to create the Jewish state of Israel.

After the Great War, Lawrence continued in military life, amid his other activities. In 1922 he enlisted in the Royal Air Force under a pseudonym, then was forced to transfer to the Royal Tank Corps when his identity became known. After successful petitioning he was allowed back, and served in India for a couple of years. He left the military in 1935, shortly before his death in a motorcycle accident.

Behind Lawrence's heroic, if enigmatic, public persona lurked several homosexual secrets – or rather half-secrets, since he intimated his sexual proclivities and experiences in his writings. The first pages of *Seven Pillars of Wisdom* reveal Lawrence's erotic interest in young Arabs and the sexual tensions of his desert life with them. He explicitly mentions their sexual play and his empathy with their frolicking. In 1911 he met Selim Ahmed, a 14-year-old known as Dahoum ('dark'), well built and handsome. Lawrence took to the youth and sculpted his likeness (nude) in limestone for the roof of his house. His diaries began to include discreet references to the young man as their relationship grew stronger. Lawrence finally took Dahoum on a visit to England, where he introduced him (and another Arab boy who had come along) to his mother and brother; one of Lawrence's friends was so impressed with Dahoum's beauty that he commissioned a portrait. Dahoum died, probably from typhus, during the war. Lawrence dedicated *Seven Pillars of Wisdom* 'To S.A.', and told the poet Robert Graves that Dahoum was the only person he would ever love. The book contains a poem that links his love with his struggle for Arab freedom: 'I loved you, so I drew these tides of men into my hands / and wrote my will across the sky in stars / To earn you Freedom, the seven-pillared worthy house, / that your eyes might be shining for me / When we came.'

Another 'secret' revealed in *Seven Pillars* was the fact that Lawrence had been raped during the war. The details remain unclear, and Lawrence's account leaves questions unanswered. Disguised as an Arab peasant, Lawrence had been reconnoitring the railway crossroads at the Syrian city of Dara'a for a possible attack when he was captured by Turks. The bey had Lawrence's clothes stripped off and tried to fondle him; Lawrence kicked back. Lawrence was then slapped, cut with a knife, beaten with a whip, and repeatedly raped. (He later confessed in his recollections that he had experienced some sort of sexual pleasure during the incident.) The Turks bandaged his wounds, and Lawrence managed to escape. Lawrence's most recent biographer, Michael Asher, comments that 'there are no witnesses, no relevant diary entries, and no corroborating accounts' of the incident, and that Lawrence was not reported missing to authorities over the two days that he was absent. Details vary in the different versions of the event that Lawrence recorded, and Asher casts some doubt on the veracity of his memory. Whether every point is true to life, however, it is certain that the experience and recollection of whatever occurred at Dara'a had a lasting impact on Lawrence. Back in London after the war, in 1922, Lawrence met a rough Scotsman named John Bruce, with whom he served in the military. Swearing him to secrecy, Lawrence hired Bruce to whip him, inventing a complex and far-fetched tale about his being obliged to receive corporal punishment as part of a promise to a vague relative, the 'Old Master', to whom he owed a financial and moral debt. In the carefully crafted scenario he invented for the first beating, Lawrence showed Bruce a letter purporting to come from the 'Old Master', specifying twelve strokes to his buttocks. Bruce, and perhaps other men, continued to flagellate Lawrence regularly until his death.

An explanation of Lawrence's masochism, and any relation it may bear to the incident in Dara'a, is best left to psychologists, but it is worth remembering that Lawrence's experience in the Levant was much coloured by his romantic and sexual sensations: an erotic charge felt among Middle Eastern youth; affection for Dahoum (which may or may not have extended to a sexual relationship); and the rape (no matter the exact details). The last was a rare and traumatic experience. As for the sexual thrill and the romantic obsession, Lawrence, like many other homosexual men – Gide and Forster among them – found in the Arabic world the seductiveness of attractive men and the pleasures of erotic friendship.

Yannis Tsarouchis 1910–1989

M en are omnipresent in Yannis Tsarouchis's art. Late in life he illustrated a collection of poems by Constantine Cavafy – a fellow Greek with whom he clearly felt both a cultural and a sexual affiliation – with simple line drawings of muscular youths and winged ephebes. Many of the men who appear in other works are soldiers or sailors. A young conscript prepares his belongings for his departure from home, a sailor sits quietly at a café table, reading and smoking; others pose in the sun, fit and statuesque, the glaring white of their uniforms contrasting with their black hair and swarthy skin. Soldiers in khaki dance the *zeibekiko*, their hard bodies animated by the gentle movements of arms and legs.

The erotic suggestions – Tsarouchis portrays Eros as a virile young man, not as a cheeky cherub – burst with barely contained desire, and sometimes hint at its satisfaction. One soldier divests himself of his clothes, while another sits on a rock and washes himself. In a painting of 1957, *The Forgotten Guard*, three sailors inhabit the cool Neoclassical décor that Tsarouchis favoured, their gazes a triangle of masculine intimacy. A man sits at a table, contemplating his two companions, one of whom, painted from behind, stands naked except for his leather military belt, shoulder strap, shoes and spats, facing another nude comrade. The extraordinary *Seated Sailor and Reclining Nude* (1948) depicts a seaman, smart in his white and blue uniform, seated on the bed of a naked, hairy-chested companion, who reclines on rumpled bedclothes. The painting was taken down from an exhibition after police declared it an insult to the Greek navy and threatened to ransack the art show. (Perhaps as a commentary, decades later Tsarouchis painted a work called *Military Policeman Arresting the Spirit*, in which the spirit was represented by his signature motif of a nude winged youth.)

Besides his homoerotic subjects, Tsarouchis also painted land-scapes, still lifes, pictures of women (almost always in traditional folk costume, though his men wear uniforms or are undressed), and allegories of the seasons. While a catalogue of 1975 points out (in italics for emphasis) that his *'real theme ... is the masculine humanity of petty-bourgeois and semi-proletarian town-dwellers'*, much later scholarship avoids the subject of homosexuality in his life and his art, and an autobiographical novel that he completed remains unpublished. The commentary to a collection of his prints and lithographs, issued just after the artist's death, speaks of 'love as lust and memory, an intention or promise, as desire and defer-ment', and declares that 'the love which Tsarouchis's figures exude is a pagan, idolatrous and platonically idealistic love', typified in his 'renaissance-type guilt-free restoration of beauty'. The author declines to say that this is homosexual lust and love. Not until 2010, in a catalogue published by the Benaki Museum in Athens, did the art-historical literature pay due attention to Tsarouchis's homosexuality. Here, at last, was a frank discussion of how the artist accepted his orientation, despite the disapproval of his family and of Greek society, and his own estimation that he was a pioneer in overtly homoerotic art.

Tsarouchis was born in 1910 in the port city of Piraeus and educated at the School of Fine Arts in Athens. He began painting at an early age, but earned his living mainly as a designer of theatre sets and costumes, working for La Scala, Covent Garden, and the Théâtre National Populaire in Paris, and with Franco Zeffirelli. In 1935 Tsarouchis went to Paris for the first time, where his ideas, already influenced by the Fayum portraits, Byzantine icons, Coptic weaving and Greek popular art, were further fertilized by exposure to the Old Masters and Matisse. His own style continued to reject the trends of the avant-garde in favour of figurative art. He held his first solo exhibition in 1938, after his return to Athens.

During the Second World War, Tsarouchis served in the Greek army on the Albanian front. Afterwards, he settled into a happy and successful period, painting, working in the theatre and increasingly gaining an international reputation. In 1967 he went into self-imposed exile during the military dictatorship in Greece, living near Paris. In 1980 he returned to Athens, where he died nine years later.

Tsarouchis's men resonantly strike the gay spirit. Works of the 1970s feature androgynous, long-haired hippies, reflecting the fashion of the times. But most of his images are of masculine soldiers and sailors, objects of fascination and fantasy. Tsarouchis's variation on the theme of machismo is to invoke a gentle, joyful and sometimes melancholy innocence that kindles thoughts of youthful idols rather than the aggression of real military life. Groups of sailors disrobe on the beach or commune in the café, posing seductively for each other and for the viewer. The peasants, fishermen and artisans-turned-sailors seem ready to offer, or bargain, their bodies for pleasure, unconcerned about troublesome questions of sexual identity or social conventions.

The stylized, minimal backgrounds of Tsarouchis's erotic paintings evoke sun and sea, strong coffee and dark red wine. His art is deeply Mediterranean, his pictures occasionally evoking classical ancestors: a painting of the eternally youthful and forever sleeping beauty of Endymion; a shapely young man beside a bust of Hermes; a drawing of Orestes and Pylades as two nudes in a modern bedchamber. The title of one work is descriptive of the connection between ancient and modern: *Youth Wearing Pyjamas Posing as a Statue from Olympia*. Hunky men sporting wings (occasionally highly coloured like those of butterflies) seem to be visitors from a world of antique gods or erotic Christian angels. 'Love, Love, Love' reads the inscription on one such work, an acclamation of the god's vocation and the artist's longing.

Tsarouchis said that he was attracted to both the Occident and the Orient, the West of modernity and the Levantine East, where, he opined, vestiges of a more happily primitive society survived. Like Wilhelm von Gloeden and Pier Paolo Pasolini, he found in the *ragazzi di vita* the inheritors of the ancient world and the preservers of pagan morals. Perhaps the universality of Tsarouchis's vision of homosexual desire, combined with the particularly evocative backdrop of the Mediterranean, explains the power of his works.

Ali al-Jabri 1942–2002

Naming gay men in the modern Arab world is difficult. Few men speak openly about their same-sex attractions; laws and the conventions of society condemn homosexuality; sex is not a matter for public show; and gay men run real risks if they pursue their desires in Cairo, Tehran or the other cities of the Middle East. Ali al-Jabri, partly protected by his privileged background, was something of an exception. His life and death – he was killed in his apartment in Amman by his Egyptian lover in 2002 – show the possibilities for homosexual expression in this world, but warn that limits can sometimes be trespassed with fatal consequences.

Al-Jabri boasted an extraordinary lineage, but the family's past and his discomfort with their expectations weighed heavily on him. He was born in 1942 in Jerusalem. His father had graduated from a university in Istanbul, and his mother (a cousin of her husband) had studied at the elite Vassar College in the United States. They both came from a grand, landed and wealthy family from Aleppo in Syria. Al-Jabri's maternal grandfather was first secretary to the Ottoman Sultan Mehmet V, then became chamberlain to the future Saudi King Faisal during the Arab Revolt (1916–18); much later, in 1958, he switched his support from Arab monarchs to the socialist Gamal Abdel Nasser and won appointment as prime minister of the United Arab Republic, the short-lived union of Egypt and Syria. A great uncle of al-Jabri initially contested French expansionism in Syria after the First World War, then became prime minister of the French protectorate. Al-Jabri's uncle served as prime minister of Jordan (he was murdered after his crackdown on Palestinians in 1970), and his father held several ministerial portfolios in Damascus, though he spent much of his professional life working as a contractor in Kuwait.

Al-Jabri's route through life was no less extraordinary than his pedigree, taking him across the Arabic world and far beyond. He was sent to Victoria College in Alexandria (and briefly to boarding school in Switzerland), but after the *coup d'état* against King Farouk in 1952 he was dispatched to England, where he finished his secondary education at Rugby. He continued his studies at Stanford University in the United States, but in the heady atmosphere of sex and drugs of the mid-1960s the tall, handsome, elegantly dressed Levantine dropped out, prompting his father to fly to California to bring him under control. Having returned to England, he finished a degree at the University of Bristol, then spent a period in London in the 1970s, working as a low-level bureaucrat at the Jordanian embassy, painting and living a bohemian existence. He spent the last decades of his life mostly in Cairo, with occasional periods in Amman, and largely lived off handouts from his aunt, who was the widow of King Hussein's prime minister. Sporadic artistic commissions, including ones from Queen Noor of Jordan, rounded out the budget.

Al-Jabri's homosexuality, according to his friend and biographer Amal Ghandour, was an open secret. His liaisons ranged from unrequited affairs to long-term intimacies and casual encounters. For quick rendezvous, al-Jabri ventured into Cairo's huge cemetery-cum-shantytown. His diary records fragmentary impressions: 'Hustle, Hustle, Hustle … one o'clock … A taxi to the City of The Dead in search of pals and dope but a wrong stairway got me straying into a gang of miscreants … followed me threaten menace … wrench my wrist, grab watch and demand bread … Thank God I was not too far deep and got away … smack into two soldiers hungrily waiting for it … on a darkened plain by a tin statue of defunct poet staring into oblivion … more money changed hands, though this time more equally…' . Such misadventures did not dissuade al-Jabri from other lustful peregrinations. Again he wrote in his diary that 'they want money, I want love! – or is it me who hunts for the dark gutter's silver lining finding only the fascination of the unobtainable? Tastes, the bitter keenness, solitary marathons in the midnight streets … hideout haunts, the City of the Dead, among tombs, domes, sand piles, crumbling mortar … the sweet music of Muslim mortality made miraculously into living flesh by the music of the living among the early shadows of morn'.

Many of al-Jabri's paintings picture the distinctive architecture of Middle Eastern cities, focus on the austere details of stone buildings or are quiet still lifes, while a series on *The Arab Revolt* caricatures modern Arabic society and politics, of which he was highly critical. There are portraits of his grandfather and of the singer Oum Khalthoum. There are also more suggestively sensual works: a bare-chested youth framed by a Cairo cityscape in *Into the Night*; a statuesque, bearded man silhouetted against the beautiful Shajarat al-Durr mausoleum; an inviting-looking soldier; a mustachioed charmer; a smiling ancient statue, in a painting called *The Fatal Seduction of the Time of the Pharaohs*; a shapely nude man.

Al-Jabri's art, with its necessary discretion and delicacy, offers a vision of the erotic Arab that so entranced travellers like Lawrence of Arabia, whose *Seven Pillars of Wisdom* fascinated al-Jabri with its evocation of the author's friendship with the young Dahoum. Al-Jabri himself eulogized 'Sultry skin of every chocolate to café shade, ideal bodies of a smooth mercurial voluptuousness built for high speed action as for the steamy languor of the hammams'. But, like others who had a penchant for risky encounters with rough young men – one thinks of the Italian filmmaker and novelist Pier Paolo Pasolini and the Franco-Algerian poet Jean Sénac – al-Jabri met his fate in a paroxysm of lust and murder.

The difficulty of living as a homosexual in Middle Eastern countries was vividly illustrated in Alaa al-Aswany's popular novel *The Yacoubian Building* (2002), in which the cultured homosexual editor meets a violent end at the hands of his lover. In a notorious real-life incident that took place in 2001, fifty-two Egyptian gay men party-ing aboard a disco boat in the Nile were arrested and charged with 'habitual debauchery'; twenty-one were given the maximum sentence of three years in prison. The Saudi and Iranian regimes have put gay men and lesbians to death, and according to Amnesty International two dozen homosexual men and youths were killed in post-'liberation' Baghdad. Al-Jabri himself was murdered, in unclear circumstances, in his apartment in Amman, Jordan, in December 2002. Nonetheless, such tragedies do not seem to have extinguished a lively homosexual life in the countries where al-Jabri lived and painted.

9
JAPONISME

Ihara Saikaku 1642–1693

Ihara Saikaku is a famed Japanese author of erotic literature. Born into a prosperous merchant family in Osaka, he went on to train as a poet, becoming a lay monk after the death of his young wife in 1675. A thousand-verse poem brought him recognition as a writer, after which he turned to prose fiction. *The Life of an Amorous Man*, circulated in 1682, recounts the adventures of a gentleman who had sex with 3,742 women and 725 young men over the course of sixty years. Saikaku followed up this volume five years later with a collection of stories about sex between men, called *The Great Mirror of Male Love*.

Saikaku's stories cover a spectrum of homosexual life *à la japonaise*. There is wild lovemaking and unrequited love, and men who cruise along the byways and in the pleasure quarters of Kyoto and Edo (modern Tokyo). Merriment with boys forms one of the attractions of the 'floating world' of sensual delights. Men enjoy casual encounters or buy sex for a few coins (sometimes griping about rising prices). Others swear undying love to companions, take their own lives to avoid disappointment, or pay visits to the graves of departed lovers. Boys play tricks on suitors and wrap them around their fingers. Young men flirt and sleep together, but two 60-year-old men have been bound in a union since adolescence. Speakers (sometimes in a decidedly misogynist accent) vaunt the superiority of boy love, and even a male doll looks for a male lover. One character confesses that 'in my 27 years as a devotee of male love I have loved all sorts of boys, and when I wrote down their names from memory the list came to 1,000' – testimony, at least, to a prodigious power of recall.

Some of Saikaku's tales are on an operatic scale. In one, Korin, the handsome, kindly son of a masterless samurai, is introduced into the house of a lord. 'The boy's hair gleamed like the feathers of a raven perched silently on a tree' (in Paul Gordon Schalow's translation), 'and his eyes were lovely as lotus flowers.' The lord quickly beds him. Korin refuses to return his affections, but the lord's attachment only grows stronger when Korin slays a goblin. The youth, on the other hand, has fallen for Sohachi, the son of a military officer, and sneaks out of his host's bedroom in order to consummate his desire. 'In their passion, Korin gave himself to the man without even undoing his square-knotted sash. They pledged to love each other in this life and the next.' A spy informs on him, however, and the infuriated lord forces Korin to confess, hacking off the arms with which he embraced Sohachi and slashing off his head. Sohachi, in revenge, kills the man who revealed their affair. After assuring the safety of Korin's mother, he goes to Korin's grave, sets up a signboard recounting their love, and commits ritual suicide, using the sword to cut the marks of Korin's family crest into his stomach. Villagers decorate the site in honour of the lovers.

Japanese culture exhibited a tolerant, even celebratory, attitude towards intimate relations between men long before the time of Saikaku. The saintly Kūkai (Kōbō Daishi) (774–835), a poet, scholar and the founder of a major branch of Buddhism, is widely thought to have had intense romantic attachments to other men at his monastery on Mount Kōya. According to legend, he introduced homosexual behaviour to Japan after a pilgrimage to China. In one episode from the most famous of all Japanese works, the 11th-century *Tales of Genji*, the hero cannot make love to a woman he desires, so finds satisfaction with her brother instead. Another medieval classic, Kenkō Yoshida's

Essays in Idleness, speaks of the beauty of young men and of their companionships with scholars and priests. The most famous author of *haiku*, Matsuo Bashō, reminisced about his fondness for young men. A book published in the same year as Saikaku's *Great Mirror*, by Hanbei Yoshida, provides advice to young men about hairstyles, cosmetics and other ways of making themselves attractive. In 1713 what is perhaps the world's first anthology of homosexual erotic literature was published, and by one count six hundred works dealing with same-sex relations appeared during the Tokugawa period (1600–1868).

The terms *nanshoku* ('male colours') or *wakashudō* ('the way of [loving] boys') represent the tradition of erotic liaisons between an adult man (the *nenja*, who in principle took the active sexual role) and an adolescent – a practice particularly common in the monastic and samurai worlds. The age difference might have varied in practice but, according to convention, when a young man reached around 18 years of age he donned different robes and had his pate shaved. Having thus entered adulthood, he ceased to be the younger partner and began to find *wakashu* of his own. 'No youth, even one who is happy without a lover, should refuse a man who expresses a sincere interest in him,' counselled one writer, and even most shoguns openly engaged in such liaisons.

Although hierarchical and asymmetric, these relationships – as the historian Gregory Pflugfelder has pointed out – involved more than just the breathless lovemaking depicted in literature and art. A Confucian metaphor often employed by the Japanese was of brotherhood: the younger partner should regard the senior one as his benevolent mentor, who passes on values and skills. Some couples swore oaths to each other, exchanged tokens of their affections, and occasionally engaged in self-mutilation – scarifying themselves, or cutting off a finger-tip – to prove their devotion. Most partnerships lasted for a limited time, but the fleeting nature of the young men's charms, destined to fade as the youths grew older, and the sense that lust and love between two people would change just like the seasons fit into the mainstream Buddhist notion of the transitory nature of beauty and pleasure.

Pflugfelder emphasizes that romantic and sexual engagements were more a question of accepted behaviour and pleasure than of identity. Men and youths contracted varied bonds, and most (there were a few declared 'women-haters', *onnagirai*) married and fathered children. Same-sex love was not a free-for-all: although homosexual acts incurred no social disapproval, the authorities took pains to uphold propriety, issuing regulations to control male prostitution and the behaviour of 'kabuki boys' (apprentice actors who sometimes sold their sexual services) and the travelling actor–prostitutes known as 'fly-boys'. Ironically, the prohibition against women appearing on stage, enacted in 1629, meant that female roles were played by specialized male actors (*onnagata*) who, along with shop workers, incense-peddlers, pages, priests' attendants and sandal-bearers, were generally considered to be available for sexual encounters.

Tokugawa Japan was not a homosexual paradise, but few historical societies (with the exception of ancient Greece) seem to have been so welcoming of same-sex practices. One denizen of the pleasure quarters of Kyoto sighed in Saikaku's book: 'We were fortunate enough to be born in a place where boys are available for us to do with as we please. As connoisseurs of boy love, we cannot help but pity the rich men of distant provinces who have nothing half as fine on which to spend their money.' It is no surprise that the first European visitors to Japan in the 16th century, entranced by the country's aesthetic attractions, expressed shock at such mores.

Nobuko Yoshiya 1896–1973

A new genre of literature emerged in late 19th-century Japan: 'girls' fiction' (*shōjo shōsetsu*), sentimental writings destined for girls between the age of puberty and marriage. One of the most celebrated novelists was Nobuko Yoshiya, whose works, like her life, reveal her lesbianism.

Yoshiya was born in Niigata prefecture, into a family with samurai ancestry. Since her father was a civil servant, she moved around frequently during her childhood. She began writing in her teens, specializing in stories and serialized novels that first appeared in periodicals. By the 1930s she was the highest-paid writer in Japan, earning three times more than the prime minister (her success allowed her to build eight houses and to keep six racehorses). She was also a prolific writer: already by the end of that decade, Yoshiya had seen the publication of a twelve-volume anthology of her work. As a war correspondent, she filed reports from Japanese-occupied Shanghai and Manchuria, and various countries of South-East Asia, in the late 1930s and early 1940s.

Yoshiya's first major work, entitled *Flower Tales*, comprised fifty-two stories and appeared between 1916 and 1924. Many were set in girls' higher schools and told of intimate but doomed friendships between young women. The topic coincided with several social developments of the Taishō era. This was the time of the 'modern girl, modern boy' in Japan – a quest for modernity, and Western ideas and fashions, before the advent of authoritarianism and militarism in the 1930s. Schooling played a large role in the life of the 'new woman' in the early 20th century. There was also growing interest in sexology in this period.

Borrowing from the new Western concept of homosexuality – a word that they translated as *dōsei ai* – sexologists wrote positively about friendships between young women and between young men. They were generally less approving of physical relations between those of the same sex, however, even if some thought that hugging and kissing did no harm and might prepare girls for married life. Passionate infatuations with schoolmates or teachers were part of a global phenomenon: called 'spoons' or 'raves' in Britain, and 'smashing' in America, they formed the subject of the world's first lesbian-themed film, the German *Mädchen in Uniform* ('Girls in Uniform'; 1931). Havelock Ellis's essay on 'The School-Friendships of Girls' (1901) appeared in translation in a Japanese women's magazine in 1914, the same year that another magazine reproduced sections of Edward Carpenter's *The Intermediate Sex* (1906) (both periodicals had lesbian editors).

Young women's crushes, such as those described by Yoshiya, were termed *haikara* (from the English 'high collar', or stylish) or denoted by the Western letter 'S' (from the English 'sister'). They sometimes led to scandals or tragedies, as occurred in 1911 when two 20-year-old women from Yoshiya's home province, lovers who were graduates of a Tokyo school, committed suicide by tying themselves together with a pink sash, weighting their kimono sleeves with stones and throwing themselves into the sea; they left a farewell note elegantly signed 'Two Pine Needles'. The case attracted attention because of the young ladies' elite background, and newspapers reported over three hundred other incidents of women who died in copycat joint suicides during the inter-war years.

Flower Tales thus appeared in a context of great social change and widening knowledge about same-sex romance. Michiko Suzuki, a professor of Japanese language and literature, provides an insight into Yoshiya's work for the non-Japanese reader by explaining that, while chaste affections are presented positively, the mood usually turns melancholic or tragic: 'Love is often unrequited, or even when it is reciprocated, the relationship is terminated due to a change of heart, separation, disease, or death.' Yoshiya's girls do not grow up into the 'good wives, wise mothers' that society expected, and remain nostalgic for the intimate friendships of a lost youth. This melancholy mood reflected a typical Japanese appreciation of what is transitory, be it the beauty of springtime cherry blossoms or a passing love.

Suzuki has discovered lesbian themes scattered throughout Yoshiya's work. In 'Yellow Rose', for instance, a teacher tells a favoured student about her admiration for Sappho: 'a person who gave her passionate devotion to a beautiful friend of the same sex and was betrayed'. Yoshiya's novel *Two Virgins in the Attic*, published in 1922, concerns a romance between two women in a boarding house. It was based on Yoshiya's own affair with a woman at the Tokyo YWCA – a 'proving ground' for lesbian relationships, according to the anthropologist Jennifer Robertson. For Suzuki, the work 'challenged the conventions of girls' fiction by celebrating a post-higher girls' school love relationship'; it ends confidently, the women leaving their rooms to start a life together as a couple. Suzuki further remarks that Yoshiya's writing style, with its ample sprinkling of ellipses and dashes, and its use of language that was traditionally both male and female, regularly transgresses gender norms.

From 1925 Yoshiya edited a short-lived journal called *Black Rose*, which published feminist works criticizing patriarchy and sexism. The inaugural issue carried as a frontispiece a picture of 'Sappho under the sea', and included the first instalment of Yoshiya's 'A Tale of a Certain Foolish Person'. Suzuki provides a synopsis: Akiko, a 22-year-old teacher, falls in love with Kazuko, her 19-year-old student, who reciprocates her affection. Although troubled by her sexuality, Akiko affirms her identity: 'It cannot be denied that mutual male–female love is the primary true way of humanity. But there must also be a secondary path; is this not a path that should be allowed for the small number who walk the way of same-sex love?' Kazuko's father, who is already arranging her marriage, blames the teacher for making his daughter lovesick. Kazuko graduates, and a disconsolate Akiko resolves to leave town. The story ends shockingly when Kazuko is found raped and murdered by a man. Akiko faints at the news, hearing a voice calling out, 'thou foolish one'.

The titles of other stories – 'Husbands Are Useless', for instance, or 'Female Friendship' – intimate women-centred themes, although Yoshiya wrote historical novels and much non-fiction as well. In 1935 a silent film was made of her story 'Pheasant's Eyes', which tells of a relationship between an adolescent girl and her sister-in-law. She also collaborated with the Takarazuka Revue, an all-female musical theatre troupe.

Yoshiya's partner for almost fifty years was Chiyo Monma, a mathematics teacher she had met in 1923, when Monma was 23 and Yoshiya 27 years of age. They had a passionate courtship – the letters they exchanged when Monma was teaching for a year in Shimonoseki are filled, Robertson says, with steamy sexual content – and began living together in 1926. Monma looked after the couple's house, business affairs and entertainment. To ensure that Monma would be her heir, Yoshiya legally adopted her. Yoshiya's diary reveals her affection: 'Chiyo, on your birthday, I give thanks to fate which gave this person to me.' After Yoshiya died – Monma holding her hand – Monma told a journalist: 'Even in her old age, Ms Yoshiya remained in pursuit of the sweet fragrance of her girlhood dreams. Perhaps that is what attracted me.' Yoshiya provided a suitable epitaph for herself: 'There is nothing shameful about loving someone, nor about being loved by someone.' The house that the two women shared in Kamakura is now the Yoshiya Nobuko Memorial Museum.

William Plomer 1903–1973

William Plomer's novel *Sado* (1931) tells the story of Vincent Lucas, a young Englishman and aspiring painter, who journeys to Japan. On the ship, he makes friends with the captain and a radio officer, whose conversations begin to teach him about this strange new world. Once he arrives, Lucas meets an English woman, Iris Komatsu, the wife of a Japanese man, and the Komatsus offer him their garden house to use as a studio. Lucas also meets Sado Masaji, a handsome and warm, if somewhat melancholy, country boy who has come to the city to study. Iris Komatsu disapproves of him, although the young man is an acquaintance of her husband. Iris gradually falls for Lucas. He, however, draws closer to Sado, who moves in with him. Sado poses for him, and they enjoy long talks, travel together and become intimate – the author just hinting at a sexual consummation of their friendship as they disappear together into the woods during a picnic. A European woman friend of Lucas's visits and tells him that it is time for him to return to England; Lucas reluctantly agrees. He realizes that, despite his love for Japan and for Sado, he can never make the country his home. He and a forlorn Sado sadly shout 'Sayonara' to each other as the ship pulls away from the dock.

Virginia Woolf, whose Hogarth Press published *Sado*, confessed that she did not really care for the novel, and Stephen Spender judged, rather unfairly, that it did not confront what he called 'real values – food, fucking, money and religion'. Some of Plomer's acquaintances felt that he was too timid in his portrayal of the erotic friendship between Lucas and Sado, but E. M. Forster, a long-time friend of Plomer in the Bloomsbury set, thought highly of it. The book remains a carefully drawn picture of Japanese life, a thoughtful meditation on the attractions, but also the difficulties, of homoerotic intimacies across borders, and a reflection of Plomer's own experiences in Japan, where he had lived and taught from 1926 to 1929.

Born in the Transvaal, in South Africa, to English parents (his father was a colonial official), Plomer was educated at a school in Johannesburg and at Rugby in England. He returned to South Africa to work on a sheep farm in the Cape, and then, from 1922 to 1925, in a trading store on a Zulu reserve in Natal. His first novel, *Turbott Wolfe* (1926), for which he drew on his experiences, tells the story of an interracial marriage; it shocked many readers in South Africa, where racial segregation was the norm.

Along with two others, in 1926 Plomer set up the bilingual literary and political journal *Voorslag*, to be a liberal and anti-racist voice in South Africa. One of his collaborators was the Afrikaner journalist Laurens van der Post, who had defended two Japanese journalists against a racist coffee-shop owner in Pretoria. By way of thanks, he was offered a trip to Japan and invited Plomer to join him.

Just like Lucas in his novel, Plomer made friends with the captain, Katsue Mori. Mori was the descendant of a samurai family and a former national *kendō* (fencing) champion; he was an attractive, well-built man, but Plomer's interest was in the captain's insight into Japanese culture and politics. Mori provided a warm reception for the visitors, and would keep up a correspondence with Plomer for the rest of his life. As the tour of Japan came to an end and Van der Post prepared for departure, Plomer decided to remain.

Plomer found a job teaching at an English-language school before transferring to an elite institution that prepared students for entry into the Imperial University. He was a successful and popular teacher, and the institution's ambience encouraged extra-curricular contacts between teachers and students, one of whom became his companion and factotum. It is possible that Plomer, who was still probably bisexual, had brief affairs with a couple of other pupils. On a field trip to a mountain resort, he drew particularly close to Morito Fukuzawa, a farmer's son who became his housemate. Fukuzawa introduced Plomer to the classics of Japanese literature, and together they hosted sake parties for friends. Throughout his life and writings Plomer was discreet about his sexual and romantic life, but it seems that he was in love with Fukuzawa: 'We understood each other, we were used to each other, we were fond of each other … We had lived on terms of close friendship under the same roof, and had travelled about the country together, understanding one another perhaps as nearly as the barriers of tradition, race, love and education would allow.'

Plomer decided he could not stay forever in Japan, and in 1929 returned to England. There he continued to publish novels, poetry and works of non-fiction (including a biography of Cecil Rhodes), and worked as reader for a publisher, where he discovered such new talents as Ian Fleming, of James Bond fame. He also wrote several librettos for Benjamin Britten, including *Curlew Beach*, which is based loosely on the plot of a Japanese Nōh play. He spent the last decades of his life in a relationship with Charles Erdmann, a German refugee whom he had met during the Second World War.

Despite repeated invitations to visit and teach there, Plomer never again set foot in Japan, but the country remained a strong and happy memory. 'Japan was my university,' Plomer recollected. In Japan – so different from the country of his birth – he said that he was 'able to do what I had always wanted to do and never could in Africa, that is to say, to live at ease with people of an extra-European race and culture'. The experience 'helped me to understand that Europe was not everything, and to see Europe from a distance through Asian eyes'. Recalling Mori, Fukuzawa and his life in Japan, he concluded: 'Civilisation has many dialects but speaks one language, and its Japanese voice will always be present to my ear, like the pure and liquid notes of the bamboo flute [*shakuhachi*] in those tropical evenings on the Indian Ocean [during the journey to Japan] when I heard it for the first time, speaking of things far more important than war, trade, and empires – of unworldliness, lucidity, and love'.

Other homosexuals followed in Plomer's wake to Japan, including such writers and teachers as James Kirkup, John Haylock and Donald Keene. Donald Richie's *Japan Journals* record his own adventures and those of many visitors who were fascinated by Japanese culture and appreciative of the Japanese perspectives on sex and love.

Yukio Mishima 1925–1970

In his 1949 novel *Confessions of a Mask*, Yukio Mishima writes autobiographically about youthful sexual desires and fantasies. His 4-year-old self is fascinated by a swarthy man removing nightsoil. The smell of sweat from a passing parade of soldiers arouses 'a sensuous craving'. Dressing up as a child, he is interested in princes, and is 'all the fonder of princes murdered or princes fated for death. I was completely in love with any youth who was killed.' He fantasizes about men at the seashore and at the baths, and about the figures painted on Greek vases. Guido Reni's painting of St Sebastian – the beautiful martyr pierced with arrows – becomes a personal icon. As an adolescent, he falls in love with a rustic student, obsessed by his strong muscles and the tufts of abundant hair in his armpits. He befriends a girl, but realizes that he feels no sexual passion for her; and a visit to a brothel proves his heterosexual impotence. *Confessions of a Mask* – not translated into English until 1958 because publishers found it too shocking – made Mishima a literary celebrity in Japan at the age of 25.

Mishima was the son of a government official and the grandson of a colonial governor, and was raised in Tokyo largely by a tyrannical grandmother of samurai descent who kept him isolated even from his own mother. He studied at the Peers' School, a commoner in an academy for noblemen, where he graduated top of the class and received a gold watch from the emperor. By that time he was already a published poet, although his father, who thought writing effeminate and degenerate, occasionally tore up his manuscripts. Against the background of the Second World War – the grand designs of Japanese military leaders had come undone, the Americans had devastated Tokyo and atom bombs had destroyed Hiroshima and

Nagasaki – Mishima continued his studies at Tokyo's Imperial University and soon after the Japanese surrender took a law degree. He then entered the prestigious civil service, but resigned after a year to pursue a writing career.

Mishima's other major book with a homosexual theme, published in Japanese in the late 1950s and one of the most important homosexual novels of the 20th century in any language, was *Forbidden Colors*. In this story of an ageing writer and a young man, the focus shifts from the individual 'coming out' of *Confessions of a Mask* to a community of men. 'They are all my comrades,' realizes the hero: 'they are a fellowship welded by the same emotion – by their private parts, let us say. What a bond!' Shunsuké, a womanizer and misogynist, seeks revenge on women; Pygmalion-like, he trains the godly Yūichi, a student sure of his own homosexual inclinations, to do the work. The novel, written in an almost documentary style, covers gay cruising in the toilets and grasslands of Ueno Park, nightlife in a Ginza bar called Rudon's (modelled on a real place, called the Brunswick), bisexuality, liaisons between older and younger men (and between Japanese and foreigners), long-lasting partnerships and casual encounters, male prostitution, gay parties at rural retreats, and yearning reciprocated and rejected. It explores the spectrum of same-sex affections – lust, patronage, dreams of 'marriage' – through the troubled relationship between Shunsuké and Yūichi, which reflects that between Socrates and Alcibiades. Disquisitions on beauty, love and desire are infused with Zen sentiments, and the book alludes to sources as diverse as Winckelmann, Pater and medieval Japanese texts. Sex between men assumes the shape of a metaphysical, aesthetic and existential choice, with intimate friendships representing the 'reconciliation of spirit and nature'.

Mishima published forty novels, eighteen plays, twenty volumes of stories and many essays. He starred in movies about a leather-jacketed gangster and a samurai assassin, and in 1966 made a horrifyingly exquisite film, *The Rite of Love and Death*, about a nationalist officer who commits ritual suicide – foreshadowing his own *seppuku* four years later. He went on world tours, sometimes accompanied by his wife, the daughter of an artist, and gave interviews in fluent English. Expatriates in Japan, such as Donald Richie, remembered him as elegantly courteous, charismatic, a dandy who used translators, photographers and editors to promote himself.

Mishima had been a pale, small and sickly young man, but from the early 1950s he re-created his body through weightlifting, bodybuilding and *kendō* (fencing), happily displaying his taut torso to photographers. He also frequented the gay bars of Tokyo, ostensibly doing research for *Forbidden Colors*. Occasionally there were liaisons; after Mishima's death, his children sued one lover whose memoir about his affair with Mishima had included letters from the famous author without permission.

Although he had previously shown little interest in politics, towards the end of his life Mishima became increasingly immersed in Shinto mysticism, ultra-nationalism and emperor-worship – a reaction against modernism, Japan's subjection to American overlordship, and the leftism that he feared would extinguish samurai virtues. In 1967 he enlisted in the Ground Self-Defence Force, and the following year swore a blood oath 'in the spirit of the true men of Yamato to rise up with sword in hand against any threat to the culture and historical continuity of our Fatherland'. He organized a private militia, the Shield Society, which was fully equipped with uniforms and trained at boot camps.

In 1970 Mishima posed for a series of photographs called 'Death of a Man', for the magazine *Blood and Roses*, and worked on a novel of almost three thousand pages. After a last night spent writing the novel's final words, he and a band of would-be warriors infiltrated an army building and tied up the commandant. Mishima emerged onto the roof to harangue soldiers and spectators who had gathered below, but fell silent after only a few minutes in the face of jeers. It was clear that his attempt to provoke a coup would come to nought. He climbed back inside, unbuttoned his tunic and slit his stomach with his sword. A disciple chosen to administer the *coup de grâce* – a young man, probably a lover, with whom he had taken a suicide oath – twice failed in his task, and another cadet was obliged to decapitate Mishima.

Mishima's gruesome, comic-opera demise hardly left a joyful testament. For his friend Donald Richie, 'His may have been a political statement, an aesthetic statement, but it was also a despairing personal statement.' Mishima's gesture seems grandiose, but in a pathetic way. Psychologists may muse on its relation to his childhood, success, sexuality, the disappointment he felt at not winning a coveted Nobel Prize, or his regret at not having fought in the Second World War. Was it an act of misguided heroism or of ultimate exhibitionism, the destruction of his perfected body and his career at their zenith?

Western audiences greeted Mishima's unsettling works with acclaim. For homosexuals his life and work had a particular resonance: some recognized the sadomasochistic tendencies, but many others looked to the chronicles of sexual awakening, his stripping away of masks, the avowal of homosexual desires, the encounters, the references to Wilde and Huysmans, Antinous and Endymion, the cult of the strong male body. In the mid-20th century, he was the best-known voice of homoerotic passion from outside the West, and his romantic and tragic scenarios remain a testimony to his genius.

Tamotsu Yato 1928–1973

Two photographs of the author Yukio Mishima appear in Tamotsu Yato's album *Young Samurai: Bodybuilders of Japan*, published in 1967. In one image, Mishima, dressed only in a loincloth and holding a sword, sits tautly on a tatami mat in a Japanese room, in front of a scroll showing a painting of a large bird of prey. Mishima also contributed the introduction to the book, somewhat disingenuously saying that the pictures of him provided an imperfect exception to the panoply of impeccably toned and muscled bodies. Mishima lauds bodybuilding, evoking classical Greece and ancient Japanese mythology and bemoaning the lack of a modern tradition of physique development in Japan. He credits bodybuilding to American influence, and intimates that such exercise could rejuvenate and revivify Japan.

Yato's bodybuilders are all cast in the American mould: they have overly muscular, oiled bodies and strike the poses characteristic of the 'physique pictorial' magazines that were popular with American homosexuals looking for snapshots of naked men in the 1950s. Captions give the names, ages, professions, sporting affiliations, height and weight of the musclemen. Almost none of the men in the pictures are shown against recognizably Japanese landscapes, but several are photographed inside a stadium – a reminder that Tokyo hosted the Olympics in 1964.

Several years after the appearance of *Taidō* ('The Way of the Body') – as the book was titled in Japanese – Yato published *Naked Festival* (1968; *Hadaka Matsuri*, 1969), again introduced by Mishima. Yato here directed his camera at the bodies of young men, who generally wore only a *fundoshi* (cotton loincloth) but were sometimes naked, as they participated in the rural festivals (*matsuri*) that marked harvest-time and the arrival of the new year in Japan. Traditionally the festivals included moments of ritual purification and Shinto observance, but they were also joyous village fêtes, in which young men processed in streets, carrying torches and *mikoshi* (ornate portable shrines), competed for ritual balls or talismans tossed by the priests, or ran through the snow and plunged themselves into freezing water – rites of passage and displays of virility emboldened by copious quantities of sake. The festivals had no erotic intent; as one of the ethnographic essays in Yato's book points out, nakedness carried no shame in old Japanese culture, and the *fundoshi* did not so much hide the men's private parts as protect them with a symbolic garment.

The bodies of *Naked Festival* are not the barbell-sculpted forms of *Young Samurai*, but the sleek, toned young proletarians or salary-men of provincial Japan, sweatily climbing over each other to grapple for prizes, massed together with entwined arms in a spirit of camaraderie, or stoically shivering in the winter sea. The anthropological essays underline the cultural significance of the *matsuri*, and Mishima's text laments the decline of such venerable celebrations, owing to Westernization and its puritanical attitudes towards even 'sacred nakedness'. 'Here we find none of those pitiable Japanese who commute in crowded subways to air-conditioned offices ... Blue-collar workers from huge factories, bank tellers, construction workers – they have bravely cast aside all clothing in favor of the ancient loincloth, they have reclaimed their right to be living males.' For both Mishima and Yato, these gatherings were something primal, proudly primitive: a festival of virility and joy. To viewers, *Naked Festival* represents a documentary record, a photographic exercise, and a celebration of beautiful Japanese youth. Indeed, the author Donald Richie has suggested that the young men's 'erotics are emphasized'. Echoing Mishima's view of the desires exhibited here, he adds that 'Yato goes through an adult erotics to return to something like an adolescent innocence.'

Yato's third and final book was *Otoko* (1972) – the word means 'man', but can also signify 'lover' – which he dedicated to the memory of Mishima. In this volume he compiled eighty-one photographs of fifty-one men, most around 20 years of age. Though they are fit and handsome, they are not bodybuilders or festival-goers, but young men posing for photographs solely because of their beauty. They are either nude or wear just a *fundoshi* or a *yukata* (light cotton robe). All are Japanese, as are the props: a warrior's helmet, a parasol, a screen painting, *noren* curtains, a *katana* sword, a tea service. Yato's work here constitutes a vision of Japan, its culture and its arcadian landscape. But Western references appear too: one young man holds a Wildean lily; another lies supine like a mock bloodied St Sebastian, pierced in the groin by an arrow. These pictures are also more explicitly erotic than in Yato's previous books: one boy rummages in his *fundoshi*; bodies enfold; a head is cradled in a lap; a face moves down a belly; a youth presents himself on a bed. The homosexual sensibility glimpsed in *Young Samurai* and *Naked Festival* is now more open: one wonders what Yato might have attempted in the next volume he was planning.

Yato was born in Nishinomiya, near Osaka, in 1928. He worked as a dancer until an automobile accident made it impossible for him to continue his career. In one of Tokyo's homosexual haunts, in the early 1960s, he met an American expatriate publisher, Meredith Weatherby, who was also a translator and friend of Mishima. They became lovers, and Yato served as Weatherby's factotum. Weatherby encouraged his photography and was credited as 'producer' of his three books. After they broke up in the early 1970s, alcohol and tobacco aggravated Yato's heart condition, which led to his death in 1973.

10
DIVERSE CALLINGS

John Henry Newman 1801–1890

On 19 September 2010, Pope Benedict XVI beatified the English cleric John Henry Newman, for his holy life, works of faith and the requisite performance of a posthumous miracle. This makes the 'Blessed' Newman an object for prayer and veneration, and places him on the path to full canonization in the Roman Catholic Church. The pontiff paid tribute to Newman's 'long life devoted to the priestly ministry, and especially to preaching, teaching, and writing'.

In his homily, the pope said little about Newman's personal life and did not mention his friendship with Ambrose St John. One of Newman's most recent biographers, John Cornwell, quotes some of Newman's comments about the fellow Oxford-educated scholar, convert to Catholicism and priest who for many years lived with Newman and other clerics at an oratory in Birmingham: 'As far as the world was concerned I was his first and last', and 'From the very first he loved me with an intensity of love, which was unaccountable.' He was 'Ruth to my Naomi'. When St John died, Newman confessed: 'I have ever thought no bereavement was equal to that of a husband's or wife's, but I feel it difficult to believe that any can be greater, in any one's sorrow, greater than mine.' In accordance with his 'imperative will' and 'command' (his words), Newman was buried in St John's grave after his death.

Contemporaries remarked on a certain gender ambivalence, even effeminacy, displayed by the young Newman. One described his community of Oratorians as inhabited by 'old women of both sexes'. Cornwell notes that the 'unaccountable' special friendship with St John caused some in the Church hierarchy to remonstrate. Newman replied, beautifully, of his friendship: 'I can do nothing to undo it, unless I actually did cease to love him as well as I do.'

In a review of Cornwell's biography, the philosopher Sir Anthony Kenny comments that the question of whether Newman was gay is anachronistic: 'Nineteenth-century Anglicans and Catholics did not classify themselves in accordance with forms of sexual orientation'. For celibate priests, any sexual act would have been a grave sin, and sexual emotions represented temptations. He continues: 'I do not know whether those who wish to set up Newman as a gay icon believe that he was homosexually active, but any suggestion that he was is absurd.' He suggests that the Christian prohibition of homosexuality promoted a different sort of intimacy between men and the effusive expression that it engendered.

Newman's life spanned almost the full 19th century. Born the son of a prosperous banker in London (though his father later went bankrupt), he was educated at Trinity College, Oxford, but a breakdown during his examinations meant that he graduated in 1821 with only lower second-class honours. He nevertheless won election to a fellowship at Oriel College. Newman was ordained as an Anglican priest in 1825, and then became the curate of an Oxford church. From this point on he gained a reputation as one of the city's best preachers.

His closest companion at the time, also a fellow at Oriel, was Richard Hurrell Froude, the son of an archdeacon. Cornwell notes: 'Newman wrote that the attachment developed into "the closest and most affectionate friendship"'. (Froude's journal contains enigmatic hints of his own sexual guilt, especially about feelings for one male pupil.) The two travelled happily through the Mediterranean in 1832. Froude's death from tuberculosis four years later left Newman greatly distressed. He memorialized this early friendship in a poem called 'David and Jonathan', which was headed with the biblical epigram about love 'passing the love of women': 'Brothers in heart, they hope to gain / An undivided joy'.

In 1833 Newman became involved with the Oxford Movement, a group of churchmen who saw the Church of England as but one branch of the universal Catholic Church, and who wanted to move it away from Protestant 'Low Church' liturgical practice towards a celebration of the 'beauty of holiness'. Under Newman's direction, the Tractarians (as they came to be known) published a series of religious pamphlets. In one of these essays, written in 1841, Newman argued that the Thirty-Nine Articles, which historically had provided the basis for Anglican Protestant doctrine, did not constitute a wholesale refutation of Catholicism – a viewpoint for which he earned a rebuke.

Newman soon began to withdraw from Anglicanism. He set up a small community of like-minded priests, including St John. In 1843 he resigned his Anglican appointment, and two years later was received into the Catholic Church and ordained a priest in Rome. He then moved to Birmingham and set up an oratory in Edgbaston. In the early 1850s, for a period of four years, he was the rector of the Catholic University of Ireland (the future University College Dublin); one of his most enduring and eloquent works is *The Idea of a University* (1852). In 1878 his old college at Oxford, which only in the previous decade had begun to admit Catholics to read for degrees, elected him an honorary fellow.

Newman wrote brilliantly on many aspects of religion and epistemology, and was also a fine poet. His collected works, including letters and diaries, stretch to dozens of volumes. His *Apologia Pro Vita Sua* (1864) is considered one of the classics of autobiography. Newman was not afraid to take a stand on issues, such as the role of the laity and papal infallibility, that sometimes put him at odds with the Vatican. He denied being a liberal, although ultramontane opponents considered him as such. On the other hand, his writings show no opposition to progressive ideas like evolution, which others considered anathema. In 1879 the relatively modern Pope Leo XIII elevated Newman to a cardinalship, making him a prince of the Roman Catholic Church.

Strands of homosociality and homoeroticism weave through 19th-century Anglo-Catholicism and Roman Catholicism, from celebrations of spiritual friendship to emotional verses about choir-boys. The poet Gerard Manley Hopkins, for instance, fell in love with an adolescent named Digby Dolben. It was Newman who received Hopkins into the Catholic Church when he converted from Anglicanism (he later became a Jesuit priest). The priesthood, whether Catholic or Anglican, offered a career for the religiously inclined that provided shelter, a learned profession and the comfort of camaraderie with other men. Despite its damnation of homosexuality, Christianity offered the consolations of model friendships between saints, the affection of Christ for his followers, and the sometimes sexually charged imagery of heroes and martyrs of the faith. The precise nature of the relationships between priests is unknowable, but the significance of affective attachments for men like Newman is undeniable. The church's obsession with sex perhaps helps explain why the idea of erotic feelings within the clergy creates such discomfort.

It is generally admitted nowadays that many Catholic priests – at least in the desires of the mind, if not the sins of the body – are homosexually inclined. Thousands of cases of sexual abuse by priests and teachers in Catholic schools have come to light in recent years, involving young people of both sexes; they have shown that, within the context of enforced celibacy, a much darker type of sexuality exists. In the same year as Newman's beatification, and after the deaths of 25 million people from AIDS since 1981, Pope Benedict guardedly conceded that, in restricted circumstances, the use of condoms – the major preventive of HIV infection, but until then completely banned by the Church – might be permitted for Catholics.

Rosa Bonheur 1822–1899

R osa Bonheur's intimate ties to two other women did not involve trauma, scandal or shame. Although her manly dress sometimes caused raised eyebrows – a provocation that she seems to have enjoyed – Bonheur did not really shock those around her, as did some lesbians and gay men of her time, either intentionally or unwittingly. She lived her life largely outside public circles of sexual nonconformists. A critic has to look hard to find evidence of women-oriented attachments in her artwork.

Bonheur was born in Bordeaux in 1822 to a moderately successful painter father and a mother who hailed from a well-to-do merchant background. Seven years later the family moved to Paris, where they established themselves with some difficulty and lived in genteel poverty. After a brief and unhappy apprenticeship as a dressmaker, Bonheur began to study art with her father (her brothers and sister would also become artists). By the age of 14 she was copying paintings and taking classes at the Louvre. In particular, she took an interest in the research on flora and fauna carried out at the Museum of Natural History, where her father was employed. She began showing her paintings at the annual Paris Salon in 1841, at just 19 years of age, gradually winning critical acclaim for her landscapes and studies of animals. She scored a triumph in 1848, winning the salon's gold medal, and was commissioned by the state to produce a work showing ploughing in the Nivernais region. The result was a grand, realistic painting – now in the Musée d'Orsay, Paris – that demonstrated her keen ability to portray farm animals. The bucolic vision of peasant life doubtlessly reassured Parisians during a turbulent political period.

To perfect her technique as an *animalière*, Bonheur examined butchered animals at slaughterhouses, having secured permission

XII A man and a youth drink wine by a stream – the type of scene celebrated in Abu Nuwas's poetry. Glazed dish, Iran, *c.* 1200.

XIII John Everett Millais, *John Newman*, 1881. The priesthood offered camaraderie and close friendship between men: Cardinal Newman would compare the grief of his dearest friend's death to losing a husband or wife.

XIV Édouard-Louis Dubufe, *Rosa Bonheur with Bull*, 1857. Bonheur studied animals in the field and in the slaughterhouse for her art; she told friends, 'In the way of males, I like only the bulls I paint'.

xv Frieda Belinfante, Dutch musician, conductor and Resistance fighter in the Second World War, disguised in male attire; photographed in 1943.

XVI Simon Nkoli, South African gay rights and anti-apartheid campaigner, *c.* 1990. He viewed both causes as a single struggle for emancipation.

XVII Japanese entertainment district, early 19th-century silk painting. Ihara Saikaku's stories were set amid a 'floating world' of sensual delights.

H. H. THE MAHARAJA OF CHHATARPUR

XVIII Postcard of the Maharaja of Chhatarpur, *c.* 1920. He met
E. M. Forster in 1912–13, but it was another gay writer, his secretary
J. R. Ackerley, who portrayed the Maharaja in *Hindoo Holiday* (1932).

XIX Claude McKay and Baroness Elsa von Freytag-Loringhoven in Harlem. Photographic print created by the latter, *c.* 1922. McKay became a seminal figure in the Harlem Renaissance of the interwar years.

xx Traditional Chinese opera singer Shi Pei Pu dressed as a mandarin
for a role in 'The Spring Lounge', 1962. Beyond the stage, Shi was
involved in a long-running relationship with a French diplomat and spy.

from the Paris police to wear men's clothes in that unusual – and, for most women, disagreeable – environment. But she also journeyed to the countryside to study living creatures, and in Paris itself frequented the horse market near La Salpêtrière. Her visits there inspired a massive painting now in the Metropolitan Museum of Art, New York: *The Horse Fair* (1853), which is arguably the most significant work by a woman painter in mid-19th-century France. It dramatically pictures a dozen white, brown and black horses; handlers struggle to control them as they nervously push, rear up and run across the dust, against a backdrop of plane trees and the cupola of the Salpêtrière hospital.

Bonheur felt a mystical personal connection with animals – which did not prevent her from either eating meat or being a good hunter – and they became her passion. Even in Paris, she filled the family apartment with pets, including a sheep; and once she was successful enough to own country estates, her menagerie encompassed horses, goats, sheep, moose, an otter and several lions (photographs show her fondly petting a lioness in her garden). When a colleague painted her portrait, she asked him to replace the table on which her arm was resting with the head of a bull. Bonheur became *the* painter of realistic animals in mid-19th-century France, and horses remained a speciality. After seeing one of Buffalo Bill's 'Wild West' shows at the 1889 Paris Exposition, she enlarged her repertoire to include Native Americans and their horses as well.

Bonheur earned fame and made a great deal of money. She enjoyed the patronage of Emperor Napoleon III, whose consort personally decorated her with the Légion d'honneur – the first time it had been awarded to a woman artist – and her works sold well, particularly in Britain and the United States. Her style, however, evolved little, and she took almost no notice of new artistic currents, so that by the last years of her life the French public and art market had lost much of their interest in her work, considering her a painter of technically proficient but rather spiritless beasts and nostalgic rural scenes. Of her early success, *Ploughing at Nivernais*, Cézanne paid a backhanded compliment in calling it 'horribly like the real thing'.

As a child, Bonheur had met Nathalie Micas, the daughter of another painter. After the deaths of her parents, she moved in with the Micas family, and on his deathbed Nathalie's father enjoined the two young women to look after each other. Over the years they grew closer, at some point becoming partners, and they remained with each other until Micas' death in 1889. When Bonheur earned enough to rent an apartment, Micas moved in (initially bringing her mother along). In time she bought a chateau outside Fontaine-bleau, where the three women continued to live together, and built a villa near Nice. Whether she and Micas had a sexual relationship is unknown; Bonheur once told friends that she was not the mar-rying type, and commented that 'in the way of males, I like only the bulls I paint'.

Occasionally the male attire in which Bonheur wandered around city and countryside surprised her neighbours. She wrote wittily to her sister about the good people of Nice: 'They wonder to what sex I belong. The ladies especially lose themselves in conjecture about "that little old man who looks so lively". The men seem to conclude, "Oh, he is some aged singer from St Peter's at Rome who has turned to painting in his declining years to console himself for some misfortune."'

Micas did the underpainting on Bonheur's works, kept house and tended to the animals. She was also an inventor, although her prize design – a brake for railway engines – failed to attract inves-tors. The two regularly travelled around the French provinces and to Britain. They received well-known guests who admired Bonheur's art, such as the emperor of Brazil. After Micas died, Bonheur wrote: 'Her loss broke my heart, and it was a long time before I found any relief in my work from this bitter ache ... She alone knew me, and

I, her only friend, knew what she was worth.' Micas was buried in Père Lachaise cemetery in Paris.

Shortly afterwards Bonheur met a young American painter, Anna Elizabeth Klumpke; nine years later they met up once again, when Klumpke painted Bonheur's portrait. The two women grew very close during the sitting: indeed, Klumpke installed herself in Bonheur's house almost immediately. Bonheur announced that they had decided to 'associate our lives' and told Klumpke: 'This will be a divine marriage of two souls.' They lived together for the last decade of Bonheur's life, and Bonheur made Klumpke her sole heir. Bonheur's will instructed that she was to be interred in the same vault as her beloved Micas, in Paris. When Klumpke died in 1942, her ashes were also entombed alongside.

This 'woman-centred woman' was the most important female artist of her day, and one of Europe's greatest painters of animals. She was decorated by the governments of France, Spain, Belgium and Mexico, and given membership to numerous artistic societies (as well as the French Society for the Protection of Animals). Bonheur challenged stereotypes about women in her profession. She was not an artistic or political radical, but in her own way she was a feminist: 'I have no patience with women who ask permission to think,' she once wrote. Whatever the exact contours of her intimate partnerships, they represented significant emotional unions between women.

Hubert Lyautey 1854–1934

Military forces portray themselves as embodying the best of virtues, particularly those that are defined as traditionally masculine: fitness, discipline, loyalty, valour and comradeship. Those censorious of same-sex desire have often considered homosexuals bereft of these virtues; historically, they have feared that the presence of homosexuals in the armed forces might not only sap soldierly spirit, but also endanger the fatherland. As a consequence homosexual men and lesbians have been excluded from the armed forces in many countries, or allowed to sign up only if (as in the American case) they followed a path of self-denial embodied by the phrase 'don't ask, don't tell'. Scholarly studies and veterans' memoirs have shown, however, that many gay men and women have served with distinction, and that a subculture of homosexual contacts thrives, generally furtively, in barracks and on the battlefield. A French officer provides insight into this homoerotic culture.

Hubert Lyautey was born in Lorraine into a prominent family (his mother had aristocratic forebears) and graduated from France's elite military academy. He developed a love for North Africa after being posted to Algeria as a young lieutenant, and was entranced by what he saw as the merit of France's colonization, the beauty of the desert and the nobility of Arab warriors and nomads. A later posting took him to Tonkin, in present-day Vietnam, where his role was to advance the French conquest of Indochina. From 1897 he held command over a vast region of another new French possession, Madagascar, where his success brought him promotion to the rank of brigadier general.

When France established a protectorate over Morocco in 1912, Lyautey became the colonial pro-consul there, serving until 1925 (except for a brief stint as minister of war in 1916). Although he left that position with some bitterness, having been marginalized by another commander (the future head of the Vichy regime, Philippe Pétain) during the Rif War, Lyautey remained the most prominent colonial statesman in France. He rose to the rank of marshal, the highest in the army, won election to the Académie Française and organized a grand international Colonial Exposition in Paris in 1931. On his death three years later, he was honoured with a state funeral and buried, according to his wishes, in Morocco. His remains were transferred to Les Invalides in Paris and entombed near Napoleon's after Morocco regained independence.

Lyautey's penchant for handsome young officers was well known. His wife, whom he married when he was 45 years old, joked with his fellow officers that she had managed to cuckold them. A French minister, Georges Clemenceau, remarked crudely that Lyautey 'always had balls between his legs … even when they weren't his own'. Lyautey's old foe Pétain, in the eulogy he delivered as minister of war in 1934, spoke more guardedly about his 'romantic obsession', 'turbulent soul' and 'sometimes troubling caprices'.

The historian Christian Gury has argued that Lyautey was the model for the homosexual aesthete Baron Charlus in Marcel Proust's *À la recherche du temps perdu* ('In Search of Lost Time'; 1913–27). The always dapper Lyautey was indeed a welcome guest at aristocratic and literary salons in Paris. He furnished his Lorraine chateau with a Moroccan room, and displayed trophies and souvenirs in what would now be seen as a very 'camp' style.

In his writings – he was a prolific author and a fine stylist – Lyautey enthused about classical statues he had seen in the museums of France and Italy, such as a youth who represented 'a triumphal evocation of voluptuous and strong beauty'. Descriptions of Arab and African men reveal an appreciation of their seductiveness (he seems to have found the Vietnamese less alluring, however). He clearly enjoyed the homosocial camaraderie of military camps and garrisons, and in particular extolled the martial attraction of the youthful French soldiers with whom he liked to surround himself. He recounted, in veiled language, visits to his chambers by favourite subalterns. One was a 'sub-lieutenant ... who pleases me so much ... [and] who came from ten p.m. to two a.m. to warm up my old thirty-year-old self with his hot and rich sap. What a young, vigorous and generous nature!' Lyautey elsewhere maintained that 'before ending the day, after the heavy quotidian tasks, nothing equals this happy bath of fertile and creative sap'.

Douglas Porch, a military historian, suggests that Lyautey's homosexuality offended some fellow officers, 'which is one of the reasons why he sought the company of writers, artists and left-of-center politicians ... It also helps to explain why ... he was so enthusiastic about colonial service.' The colonial forces provided an outlet for many who did not 'fit in' at home, and Lyautey was far from the only French officer with homosexual tendencies. Another was Pierre Loti, a navy captain who served in Polynesia, Africa and Asia; like Lyautey, he was a flamboyant aesthete and a prolific author of novels, some of which had homosexual themes. A British example was Sir Hector Macdonald, a Scottish ranker and hero of the Anglo-Boer War, who rose to become military commander of Ceylon. Summoned for court martial on accusations of sexual misbehaviour with young men, Macdonald shot himself. Lord Kitchener and Lord Baden-Powell (the author of *Scouting for Boys* and founder of the Boy Scouts movement), both military heroes with probable homosexual inclinations, escaped Macdonald's fate.

The army and navy have often excited the fantasies of homosexuals, and many (Oscar Wilde among them) have found that impecunious military men make ready casual partners. Sailors' rugged masculinity has been a perennial theme in erotic art and literature. *Billy Budd*, for instance – a novella left unfinished at Herman Melville's death in

1891 – deals with an officer's sadistic obsession with a young rating, and its tragic consequences. It was transformed into an opera by Benjamin Britten in 1951 and recreated as a film (set in a French Foreign Legion camp) in Claire Denis's *Beau Travail* (1999). Jean Genet's lusty novel *Querelle de Brest* (1953) also centres on the image of the sexually potent sailor, as does the work of such artists as Jean Cocteau, Charles Demuth and Yannis Tsarouchis.

Frieda Belinfante 1904–1995

Frieda Belinfante was a Dutch musician, a pioneering woman conductor and a Resistance fighter in the Second World War. She was born in Amsterdam into a musical family: both of her parents were musicians, and her two sisters and brother also played instruments. She began to study the cello with her father, and gave her first public performance with him when she was still a child.

As a teenager, Belinfante was a promising young performer. She was also an active lesbian, beginning a seven-year affair with Henriëtte Bosmans at the age of 18. Bosmans, herself the daughter of musicians, was on the way to becoming a celebrated pianist and soloist with the Concertgebouw. Together with Belinfante and a flautist named Johan Feltkamp, they formed a chamber trio; in 1930 Belinfante married Feltkamp, but their union lasted only for six years, and Belinfante remained predominantly lesbian.

During the 1930s Belinfante's musical career progressed. She played for several years with a Haarlem orchestra, but she also began to conduct – a rare and daring move into a career that was (and is) almost completely dominated by men. She took charge of two choirs: one from the University of Amsterdam, and a children's choir. In 1938 Belinfante established a chamber orchestra, Het Klein Orkest, with whom she conducted works from both the classical and modernist repertoires. The following year she beat a dozen men to win a Swiss prize for conducting, and secured an invitation as guest conductor of the Orchestre de la Suisse Romande, although the outbreak of the Second World War made it impossible for her to take up the engagement.

Belinfante's father was Jewish, and her mother Christian, although the entire family was secular in outlook. After Germany's invasion of the Netherlands, in May 1940, Belinfante was obliged to register with a Nazi-sponsored cultural organization. She refused and disbanded her orchestra. Before long she had joined an underground Resistance group, composed of about one hundred cultural figures, that forged identity cards for Jews. One of her fellow members was her friend Willem Arondeus, a painter, poet and author; Arondeus was gay, and had lived openly with his younger boyfriend for several years. Belinfante sold her valuable cello to the owner of the Heineken brewery in order to fund the group's operations. She, Arondeus and the others hatched a plan to destroy the registry in Amsterdam that contained copies of all Dutch identity cards; its destruction would mean that the fake cards and passports that the Resistance were making could not be proved false. Arondeus and several others overpowered the guards and set fire to the building in March 1943. The group was betrayed, however. Arondeus and two other gay men were among those arrested, and a total of twelve – including Arondeus – were executed. Belinfante, now in grave danger, managed to escape to Switzerland, disguised in men's clothing.

She remained a refugee there for the rest of the war. She returned home in 1945, but was disillusioned with Dutch life and in 1947 migrated to the United States. Having settled in California, she spent the next few years teaching music at UCLA, playing in Hollywood studio orchestras and giving private tuition. In 1954 she founded the Orange County Philharmonic Orchestra and became its conductor – the first permanent female conductor of a full-scale orchestra. It continued to give performances until 1962, when it dissolved on account of administrative and artistic disputes.

Belinfante passed the last decades of her life quietly, giving private music lessons, and died in retirement in New Mexico, where she had moved in the early 1990s. The year before her death, she gave an interview about her Resistance activities and musical career, which provided the basis for a documentary film, *But I Was a Girl* (1999).

Klaus Müller – her interviewer, and the film's assistant director – suggests that Belinfante's lesbianism contributed to her earlier lack of recognition as a musician and as an active member of the Resistance.

Ronnie Kray 1933–1995

Not all homosexuals have followed the straight and narrow. The criminalization of homosexual acts has meant that many over the ages have faced police and judges for their sexual behaviour, sometimes suffering dire penalties. But some homosexuals have also perpetrated 'ordinary' crimes: there are homosexual fraudsters, thieves, brigands and serial killers. Others have taken to a life of crime as a career choice, though perhaps only a psychologist could diagnose whether their sexual proclivities had any bearing on their professions.

One homosexual outlaw of a violent sort was Ronald ('Ronnie') Kray. Born in 1933 in Hoxton, east London, of Irish, Jewish and Romany descent, Ronald and his identical twin, Reginald ('Reggie'), were the sons of a scrap-gold trader who himself sometimes appeared on police wanted lists. They were pure products of the rough-and-tumble working-class world of London's East End, growing up in Bethnal Green and attending school in Brick Lane. The handsome young men both excelled as boxers – a traditional pursuit in their milieu – and fought professionally for a time. In 1952 they were called up for National Service with the Royal Fusiliers but deserted repeatedly, eventually finishing in jail awaiting court martial. Once they had been dishonourably discharged, two years later, they and their elder brother Charlie became involved in petty crime, soon working their way up to more serious exploits, including protection rackets, arson, hold-ups and gambling. By the late 1950s the twins and their brother, who had surrounded themselves with a circle of motley villains known as the 'Firm', were well known in the London underworld. During the swinging sixties they operated a club in fashionable Knightsbridge, where they rubbed shoulders with international celebrities such as Judy Garland.

In 1960 Ronnie Kray earned an eighteen-month sentence in connection with a protection racket. In 1966, in the midst of a gangland war with another mob, Kray shot and killed a man in a Whitechapel pub who had allegedly referred to him as a 'fat poof'. In 1968 the Kray brothers' period of untouchability came to an end. On 8 May both twins were finally arrested (Ronnie was supposedly in bed with a young blond man when he was apprehended by police) and sent to jail for murder the following year. Ronnie died in Broadmoor secure mental hospital in 1995, having suffered from paranoid schizophrenia for many years. While in prison, he took up art as a hobby, and eight of his paintings, which were discovered in an attic in Suffolk, sold for £16,500 in 2008.

A police report from the 1950s – found in a Durham police station in 2010 – describes Ronnie as a man 5 feet 7 inches (170 centimetres) in height, 'with a fresh complexion, brown eyes and dark brown hair'; it also noted that 'Ronald Kray has been the leader of a ruthless and terrible gang for a number of years ... he has strong homosexual tendencies and an uncontrollable temper and has been able to generate terror not only in the lesser minions of his gang, but also in the close and trusted members.' The journalist and biographer John Pearson later wrote that Kray 'liked boys, preferably with long lashes and a certain melting look around the eyes. He particularly enjoyed them if they had no experience of men before. He liked teaching them and often gave them a fiver to take their girl-friends out on condition they slept with him the following night ... He never seems to have forced anyone into bed against his will and, as he proudly insisted, was free from colour prejudice, having tried Scandinavians, Latins, Anglo-Saxons, Arabs, Negroes, Chinese and a Tahitian.'

Laurie O'Leary, a childhood friend, remembered that Ronnie Kray considered bringing back to London an Arab boy he had fallen for on holiday in Tangier. Others recalled that he liked to show off his handsome young companions in smart London restaurants. O'Leary added that Kray seemed to be at ease with his sexuality, having already fallen in love with a boy when he was a teenager. Kray himself said he felt no shame in being homosexual: 'There is nothing necessarily weak about a homosexual man – and I believe he does no wrong … I hate people who pick on homosexuals.'

Reginald Kray, who was bisexual, and the other members of the Krays' gang, seem to have accepted Ronnie's sexual interests with equanimity (perhaps by necessity). O'Leary clarifies: 'Even if they objected, Ron just smiled at them and told them they didn't know what they were missing.' Kray's father and elder brother did object, although his mother proved tolerant.

In 1964 the tabloid *Daily Mail* printed an article about a relationship between an outlaw and a Tory peer, without naming either man. Baron Boothby – a Scotsman educated at Eton and Magdalen College, Oxford, and a member of parliament before his elevation to a life peerage – sued the newspaper for libel. Boothby was known to be a philanderer, even earning the nickname 'the Palladium' ('because he was twice nightly') while at university. He had an affair with the wife of Prime Minister Harold Macmillan, married twice, and also enjoyed the company of boys. It seems that he had met Kray through an East End cat burglar who had been a sexual partner. According to some reports, Kray provided Boothby with a number of young men. Boothby settled his case against the *Mail* out of court and received a payment of £40,000 in damages. In 2009, however, the *Mail* revealed that newly found letters proved that Boothby and Kray shared rent boys and claimed that they contained information 'too base to be revealed in detail'.

The scandal involved another friend of Boothby, allegedly known also to Ronnie Kray. Tom Driberg was a well-known and long-serving Labour member of parliament who had had several brushes with the law for 'indecent assault' and other homosexual offences. (Indeed,

Winston Churchill is once supposed to have quipped: 'Tom Driberg is the sort of person who gives sodomy a bad name.')

The life stories of an East End gangster and two Oxonian parliamentarians could hardly have been more different, but their erotic interests drew them – and a cosmopolitan assortment of partners – into a network that existed on the fringes of legality (at the time, homosexual acts were criminal under British law). Driberg escaped prosecution largely because of his status and contacts, as did Boothby, while Kray's conviction for murder – partly provoked by a homophobic comment – was a reward for a life of violent crime that had nevertheless made him and his brother into outlaw celebrities.

Yves Saint Laurent 1936–2008

Many people in Anglo-Celtic countries have supposed that men who work in certain professions – interior decoration, floristry, window-dressing, hairdressing and fashion design among them – are gay. Although not all men in these fields are homosexual, of course, there may be a grain of truth to the idea that, at least until recent decades, men with homosexual inclinations often gravitated towards jobs where the type of machismo (real or affected) associated with typically 'manly' posts was not a prerequisite. Whether or not statistics bear this out, it is certain that some of the most acclaimed practitioners in the worlds of art and design have been gay.

A famed example is Yves Saint Laurent. He was born in 1936 in Oran, Algeria (then a French colonial outpost), where his father was a businessman. Saint Laurent moved to Paris after he had finished secondary school. When he was only 17 years old, his talent was spotted and he became an assistant to Christian Dior – a discreet homosexual who, shortly after the Second World War, had risen to the heights of renown as the inventor of the 'New Look' of womens-wear. Saint Laurent assumed control of Dior's fashion house when his mentor died, at the age of 52, in 1957. Three years later the French army called up Saint Laurent for military service, where, in a complicated turn of events, he suffered a mental breakdown. He was then dismissed by the Dior company in 1960.

Two years later, Saint Laurent established his own fashion business. His designs quickly catapulted him to fame, fortune and celebrity. His creation of the Rive Gauche line in 1966 – meant to exemplify the casual chic of Paris's bohemian Left Bank – and his expansion into menswear in 1974, then into perfumery and accessories, made YSL a household name among shoppers. The status of the brand remained strong when Saint Laurent retired in 2002.

Two decades previously, in 1983, he had been honoured with the first solo exhibition devoted to a clothing designer at the Metropolitan Museum of Art, New York, and in 2007 – the year before his death – the French government made him a *grand officier* in the Légion d'honneur, one of the country's highest state awards.

In 1958 Saint Laurent met Pierre Bergé, a 28-year-old business-man who began to take over the running of his fashion business. The two were lovers and remained so for many years; soon before Saint Laurent's death the men entered into one of the new French civil partnerships. Throughout their almost fifty-year relationship, they worked together as business partners. They also shared an apartment in Paris, a grand house – the Maison Majorelle, known for its exqui-site gardens – in Marrakesh, and six other residences filled with an enormous collection of art and furnishings. Bergé has been a major supporter of French gay endeavours, such as the magazine *Têtu* and the AIDS groups Act-Up and Sidaction. He and Saint Laurent also lent their support to François Mitterrand, who won election as president of France in 1981 and whose government removed residual discriminatory laws against homosexuals from the French penal code.

By no means have all gay designers and their partners been as open about their sexuality, or as politically active, as Saint Laurent and Bergé. One whose legacy is very much associated with gay rights, however, is Rudi Gernreich. Born in Vienna in 1922, he fled Austria when the Nazis took power and settled in the United States. By the 1960s he had become a prominent designer, favoured by such clients as Jacqueline Kennedy. Gernreich's long-term partner was Harry Hay, with whom he founded the most important early homophile organization in America, the Mattachine Society. Gernreich was listed in its membership rolls only as 'R', but provided considerable financial backing to the association.

Some homosexual designers are more open than others about their sexual preferences. The Italian Gianni Versace, who was assassinated

YVES SAINT LAURENT

in Miami by a serial killer at the age of 51, had a long relationship with a former model who now operates his own fashion company. In Britain two dressmakers to the queen – who were knighted for their services – were also known to be homosexual. These were Sir Norman Hartnell and Sir Hardy Amies. Always discreet, Amies had a partner for forty-three years. Of his friend and rival Hartnell, Amies once remarked wryly: 'It's quite simple. He was a silly old queen, and I'm a clever old queen.'

Did these designers' sexuality have anything to do with their profession? The British 'fashion knights' were moderately conservative, but several of the others gained fame for daring designs that broke with tradition. Gernreich, who experimented with vinyl and plastic clothing and the 'futuristic' look, gained notoriety for his topless bikini – an unparalleled assertion of sexuality. Saint Laurent designed women's outfits that crossed gender lines, such as his smoking jacket, pinstripe suits and pantsuits for women. Versace's clothing for men, with its dramatic colours and styles, marked a departure from gentlemen's traditional haute couture. Saint Laurent himself posed nude in an advertisement for his Pour Homme fragrance in 1971. Contemporary designers like Tom Ford, John Galliano, Jean-Paul Gaultier and Marc Jacobs have continued these gender-bending innovations, at the same time as being openly gay in their own lives.

II
RADICALS AND ACTIVISTS

Magnus Hirschfeld 1868–1935

People became more interested in sex in the 19th century – sex, that is to say, as a subject for research, medical investigation and public debate. In particular there was an increasing focus on 'unnatural' sex: behaviour that from the 1870s would be called 'homosexuality'. Scientists and social scientists – Ambroise Tardieu, Richard von Krafft-Ebing, Havelock Ellis, Paolo Mantegazza and Sigmund Freud among them – tried to discover the cause of homosexuality, its signs and symptoms and, for some, its 'cure'. Others, such as Heinrich Hössli, Karl Heinrich Ulrichs, Edward Carpenter and John Addington Symonds, took a more legal, historical and philosophical approach, defending the same-sex desires that they shared.

Among these men Magnus Hirschfeld is pre-eminent. He combined scholarship with political activism, earning an international reputation and suffering several homophobic attacks. Hirschfeld was born into a non-practising Jewish family in Pomerania, on the Baltic Sea. After a happy childhood, he led a peripatetic student life – like many young Germans at the time – attending courses in Breslau, Strasbourg and Munich before taking a degree in medicine in Berlin, in 1892. In 1896 he set up as a doctor in the German capital.

The same year, under a pen name, Hirschfeld published a 35-page pamphlet called *Sappho und Sokrates*, the first of his many writings on the theme of homosexuality. In 1897, along with a publisher, a railway official, a philologist, a barrister and an Austrian aristocrat, he set up the Scientific-Humanitarian Committee – the single most important organization in the homosexual emancipation movement at the time, and for half a century afterwards. The committee's specific goal was the repeal of Paragraph 175 of the German legal code, which criminalized homosexual activity. Its strategy was public education, lobbying and petitions to the Reichstag. Despite these enormous efforts, the campaign proved unsuccessful, and it was not until 1994 that the newly unified Germany repealed the original Paragraph 175. That delay should not obscure the pioneering work done by Hirschfeld's committee.

Hirschfeld continued to contribute to the field of sexology. In 1899 he founded and edited the *Jahrbuch für sexuelle Zwischenstufen* ('Yearbook on Sexually Intermediate Subjects'), which treated a wide range of topics related to sexuality – particularly non-conformist sexuality – including history, ethnography, medicine, law and culture. These yearbooks represented the first concerted effort to study homosexuality in all its variations.

In 1919 Hirschfeld established the Institute for Sexual Research in an elegant mansion in central Berlin, which also housed his office (and apartment), consulting rooms and a lecture hall. In hundreds of talks each year, speakers presented the latest research on sexuality, and thousands came to seek treatment for sexual problems or for reassurance about their sexual feelings. Four years later, Hirschfeld set up the World League for Sexual Reform with two fellow physicians, the British sexologist Havelock Ellis and Norman Haire, an Australian working in London. At international conferences in London, Copenhagen, Vienna and Brno, delegates from around the world discussed the need for law reform on the basis of their scientific studies of contraception, abortion, homosexuality and other areas.

Hirschfeld published his research in countless articles and lengthy books. His hypothesis explaining homosexuality was that human beings at embryo stage are of indistinct sexual orientation; at the point of endocrine development, however, some become a 'third sex', meaning that in later life they feel desires not for the opposite sex, but for their own. This theory, although shared by many, aroused the hostility of other sexual researchers.

One group who had initially supported his initiatives, led by Benedict Friedländer and Adolf Brand, broke away in 1903 to found a journal that focused on conceptions of a virile intergenerational homosexuality, based on the Greek model. Such rivalries served only to stoke Hirschfeld's energies: he published a thousand-page book on homosexuality, a three-volume work on sexual pathology, and a four-volume one on post-First World War mores, as well as the first major study of transvestism. For good measure, he also appeared in one of the first films about homosexuality, *Anders als die Andern* ('Different from the Others'), which had a short run in 1919 and 1920 before it was banned by the government.

Hirschfeld spread his ideas on sexual reform by crisscrossing Europe to attend meetings, give lectures and make contacts. In 1930 he embarked on a 500-day journey around the world. The American sector, in which he gave thirty-six lectures in fourteen weeks, proved an enormous success, and he garnered acclaim also in Japan, China, India and Egypt, consecrating his position as the world's premier sexologist. The Asian journey was particularly significant: as he continued with his punishing schedule of lectures, he also came into contact with the continent's sexual cultures. The trip sharpened his political ideas, too, encouraging his support for Indian independence and women's emancipation, and his suspicion about Zionism.

As well as provoking the rivalry of fellow scholars and colleagues, and a certain amount of criticism for his methods – giving lectures illustrated by real patients, lending his name to a dubious patented aphrodisiac, engaging unashamedly in self-promotion – Hirschfeld also attracted the hatred of the German right wing. Thugs appeared at his lectures to heckle, and in one attack in Munich, in October 1920, they threw stones and spat on him; he was knocked unconscious and seriously hurt. As the Nazis gained in influence, Hirschfeld's institute became a symbol of all that was decadent in Weimar Germany. His Jewish background and support for the socialist party made his situation still worse. When he landed back in Europe after his world tour, in 1932, associates warned that it would be unsafe to return to Germany. He took refuge in Paris; while there, he learnt from a cinema newsreel that, shortly after Hitler had gained power, the Nazis had pillaged his institute and burned most of its 20,000 books. His German citizenship revoked, Hirschfeld was still living in exile when he died, in Nice, in May 1935.

Although discreet, Hirschfeld was homosexual. His long-term partner was Karl Giese, whom he met around 1919, when Giese was in his early twenties and Hirschfeld over fifty. As Hirschfeld's most trusted collaborator, Giese became the archivist of the institute, where he also lodged. But during his world tour Hirschfeld met another young man, a Hong Kong Chinese medical student living in Shanghai. They immediately became intimate, and Li Shiu Tong accompanied Hirschfeld on the remainder of his tour and followed him to Europe. Giese and Li rushed to Nice (both were training as doctors elsewhere) when they heard of Hirschfeld's death, and Giese delivered the eulogy at his funeral. Hirschfeld's will stated that his possessions were to be divided between the two men. Giese never benefited from his inheritance, committing suicide in Brno in 1938 after the Nazi invasion of Czechoslovakia. Li returned to Hong Kong in 1958, before emigrating to Vancouver, where he died at the age of 83.

Hirschfeld's influence was enormous. As well as providing a focal point for sexological research, his institute was one of the centres of gay life in inter-war Berlin. His work paved the way for the famous Kinsey Institute, established in Indiana in 1947; even if his theories about homosexuality were later discredited, Hirschfeld's use of interviews and surveys established a methodology for later researchers. His agitation for law reform was taken up elsewhere, and gay movements might well have borrowed his declaration 'Not you, not nature, but the law is wrong' as a slogan. His achievements in the fields of research and activism are commemorated by the Magnus Hirschfeld Society, and by a plaque on the site of his institute in Berlin.

Del Martin 1921–2008

The years after the Second World War saw the foundation of homosexual emancipation movements in several countries: COC in the Netherlands in 1945; the Danish F-1948 three years later; the Mattachine Society in the United States in 1950; and Arcadie in France in 1954. These groups provided spaces where gay men and lesbians could socialize, offered education about homosexuality and promoted changes in discriminatory laws. Most argued for the integration of homosexuals into society, and often were at pains to present gay men and women as upstanding citizens and respectable members of the community – just like heterosexuals, except for their erotic preferences.

The associations included women members but were largely dominated by men. One of the first groups aimed specifically at lesbians was set up by Del Martin, her partner, Phyllis Lyon, and six other women in San Francisco in 1955. The Daughters of Bilitis, as it soon became known, was named after a lesbian-themed poem published in 1894 by Pierre Louÿs, which purported to be the work of a (fictional) contemporary of Sappho. Martin and the others chose the obscure name in order to keep the organization's aims a secret.

Martin and Lyon had met in 1949, when they were both working on the same trade journal in Seattle, and they had been lovers since 1952. Dorothy Louise Taliaferro Martin was born in San Francisco and studied journalism at San Francisco State College and the University of California at Berkeley, where Lyon, who was originally from Oklahoma, had also been a student. In a joint interview with the American National Public Radio in 1992 – which acknowledged the two women as the 'mothers of the gay rights movement' – Martin said that she became aware of her feelings for women when she was 10 or 12 years old. As a young woman she married, thinking that perhaps her proclivities had been a passing phase, but the marriage came to an end when she fell in love with the woman next door. (She retained her husband's name, however.) When Martin and Lyon met in Seattle, neither had any real idea of what 'lesbian' meant in terms of a social identity. As she explained to her interviewer, at that time there were no role models for lesbians or lesbian couples: most of the books they found, discouragingly, portrayed lesbians as sick, and only in Radclyffe Hall's *The Well of Loneliness* did she find some comfort. When Martin announced to Lyon, at a meal in the Seattle press club, that she was a lesbian, even Lyon appeared somewhat bewildered.

By 1955 the two women were living together. They recalled how, to a degree, they began to conform to the butch–femme stereotypes common at the time: Lyon jokingly reminisced that Martin was already butch, so 'I didn't have much of an option,' to which Martin fondly replied that she was a 'sissy butch'. More seriously, alluding to the need to create an identity and a life in the 1950s, Martin declared: 'We've had to invent our lives as we go along.'

For its first year the Daughters of Bilitis remained a very small circle of acquaintances but, after Martin and Lyon began organizing public forums, taking out advertisements and publishing a newsletter, it grew. Its first national convention, in 1960, attracted two hundred participants. Chapters were formed around the United States and as far away as Australia. Lyon and Martin, in turn, edited the Daughters of Bilitis magazine, called *The Ladder*, which was sent to a confidential list of subscribers who paid one dollar a year. Among the articles it contained were pieces on the civil rights of lesbians, at a time when police were regularly raiding bars frequented by homosexuals. Martin and Lyon did feel that women's concerns were somewhat different from those of men: rather than worrying about criminal charges resulting from anti-sodomy legislation, lesbians focused more on rights relating to their children, keeping their households together,

DEL MARTIN

and general discrimination against women in the workplace and in public life. In the United States of the 1950s – the time of the Cold War, Joseph McCarthy's witch-hunts against subversives and the conformism of the Eisenhower presidency – such concerns as Martin and Lyon raised were new and challenging.

By the late 1960s the numbers in the Daughters of Bilitis had declined: more radical groups and ideas (including lesbian separatism) beckoned, and the women's movement, exemplified by the National Organization of Women, gained ground. That network was often uncomfortable with lesbian issues, and with lesbians themselves, however: it was only after a struggle that Martin was elected as the first openly gay woman on NOW's board of directors.

In 1970 the Daughters of Bilitis disbanded; *The Ladder*, which had been run independently since the break-up, ceased publication two years later. Nonetheless, Martin and Lyon continued to be active in a variety of organizations: the Council on Religion and Homosexuality; the Alice B. Toklas Democratic Club; the American Civil Liberties Union; and, late in life, Old Lesbians Organizing for Change. Both women were delegates to a White House conference on ageing held in 1995.

Despite their commitment to political activism, Lyon found the time to complete a doctorate in education and Martin took a Doctor of Arts degree from the Institute for Advanced Study of Human Sexuality in San Francisco. In 1972 Martin and Lyon published *Lesbian/Woman*, followed the next year by a short guide to *Lesbian Love and Liberation*. In 1976 Martin published one of the first books on domestic violence, *Battered Lives*.

In 2004, when San Francisco made gay marriage legal, Martin and Lyon wed. Within a few months, however, the California supreme court voided all of the gay marriages. Four years later, when gay unions were again allowed in California, the mayor of San Francisco suggested that theirs should be the first ceremony he performed.

Martin died after a fall just over two months later, with Lyon at her bedside. They had been together for fifty-five years. The mayor ordered flags to be flown at half-mast in her honour, and Lyon was quoted in *The New York Times* as saying, 'I am devastated, but I take some solace in knowing we were able to enjoy the ultimate rite of love and commitment before she passed.'

In *Lesbian Love and Liberation*, Martin and Lyon wrote: 'Happiness is personal. Some women find it with other women. It's really as simple as that.' Happiness as a lesbian came from 'knowing it, accepting it, and finding a compatible and loving woman, or women, who share your same values'. The words provide a good summation of their views on life.

Harvey Milk 1930–1978

W hen Harvey Milk moved to San Francisco in 1972, it was the
most liberal and sexually vibrant city in the United States.
It had a long frontier tradition of welcoming migrants from all walks
of life: miners who arrived during the gold rushes; Chinese, Irish and
Italian settlers; Beat Generation poets and bohemians. More recently,
San Francisco's Haight-Ashbury district had been the home of hippie
culture in the 1960s; and the university in Berkeley, across the bay,
was a rallying point for student demonstrations, the anti-war movement and the activities of the New Left. San Francisco was also the
centre for a gay community that had become increasingly public over
previous years. Castro Street was its high street, and acted as a mecca
for visitors and refugees from small-town America and further afield.
The place, and its atmosphere, would be memorably chronicled in
Armistead Maupin's best-selling *Tales of the City*.

Milk's life was a very American story. He was born in the New
York suburb of Long Island, into a middle-class family of Lithuanian
Jewish migrants who had done well. Having taken a degree in
mathematics at Albany State College in 1951, he entered the armed
forces during the Korean War, serving aboard a submarine and at
a naval base in San Diego, California, and eventually rising to the
rank of lieutenant. After demobilization, he became a teacher at a
secondary school.

In 1956 Milk began an affair with a man he had met at the beach.
They moved, briefly, to Dallas, but returned to New York, where
Milk found employment first with an insurance firm and then with
a Wall Street investment company. After six years the relationship
ended, and Milk began another, this time with a man who played
an active part in the homophile Mattachine Society. More lovers,

changes of job and relocations followed (in matters of sex and work, Milk was something of a drifter), but at the beginning of the 1970s he and his current partner, Scott Smith, ended up in San Francisco.

In good entrepreneurial American fashion, Milk opened a camera shop in Castro Street. He was becoming increasingly aware of politics, on both a local and a national level, from the arrests of gay men in his home city to the Watergate Scandal unfolding in Washington. In 1973 he decided to stand for election as a city supervisor. Despite Milk's charisma, powerful rhetoric and support for policies that proved popular in the Castro – such as the decriminalization of homosexual acts and the legalization of cannabis – his bid was unsuccessful. Working at grass-roots level, Milk had nevertheless begun to build a coalition of gays, unionists, small business people, the retired, and others who felt disenfranchised by San Francisco's political elite and their electoral machines. After supporting the winning candidate, the Democrat George Moscone, in the 1976 mayoral elections, Milk was appointed to a position on a city advisory body – a first for an openly gay man.

The same year, Milk tried to gain election to the California State Assembly but failed by a small margin. His homosexuality no doubt contributed to his defeat, at a time when gay rights were becoming an increasingly volatile issue in American politics. In a series of anti-gay campaigns, John Briggs introduced a legislative act to ban gays from teaching positions in California schools, and Anita Bryant, a Christian fundamentalist (and a star of television adverts for orange juice), led national calls for the defence of traditional 'family values'.

Milk actively combated both, but also turned his attentions back to San Francisco. His public profile, the growing gay population of the Castro Street neighbourhood, and recent voting reform that saw supervisors elected by particular wards rather than on a city-wide basis all played roles in Milk's election to the board of supervisors in 1977. He was now one of the few openly gay people to hold public office in the United States, and his stance on particular issues made him, in a very conservative country, a radical. Supporters hailed his election as the successful mobilization of a local community and as a great victory for progressive politics and gay emancipation.

In his speeches Milk called for gay men and women to 'come out' and to defend their human rights. Likening the gay struggle to the civil rights movement in America, he enjoined gays not to agree docilely to sit at the back of the bus. 'Gay people, we will not win their [*sic*] rights by staying quietly in our closet,' he told one audience: 'We are coming out to fight the lies, the myths, the distortions!' While Briggs and Bryant implied that gays were child molesters, Milk warned about the dangers that homophobic campaigns posed for all minority groups, lambasting the time and money spent on 'morals' issues at the expense of other pressing concerns. But his vision encompassed more than just gay rights. He talked about the need to tackle poverty, the lack of education, transportation problems, the plight of the aged, and other concerns relevant to San Francisco. As well as proposing a by-law banning discrimination against gays and lesbians in San Francisco (a measure the council passed overwhelmingly, with just one supervisor, Dan White, voting against it) and campaigning against homophobia across the country, Milk was also responsible for a 'pooper-scooper' ordinance requiring San Franciscans to clean up after their dogs. The city, he promised, could be a beacon in America: 'a place for the individual and individual rights', a metropolis where 'we sit on the front stoop and talk to our neighbors once again, enjoying the type of summer day where the smell of garlic travels slightly faster than the speed of sound'.

Milk's personal life was sometimes difficult, and lovers and friends occasionally tired of his unrelenting political activity. After Milk's election his young lover, Jack Lira, who had been suffering from depression, hanged himself. But Milk basked in his new role and in the adulation of the supporters whose efforts he had galvanized.

With his outspoken political views, Milk had made many public enemies; he even managed to ruffle the feathers of more conservative gays and lesbians. Not surprisingly, he was regarded as a major enemy – indeed, as little less than evil – by those on the right. Dan White, one of his colleagues on the city council, also frequently quarrelled with Milk, disapproving of many of his views. In November 1978 White resigned from his post on the pretext that his salary was insufficient. Just over two weeks later, he burst into City Hall and shot and killed Moscone and Milk.

The assassination turned Milk into a martyr. Crowds, angry and grieving, streamed into the streets of San Francisco to pay tribute to the murdered leaders. Milk's reputation grew, especially following the publication of Randy Shilts' biography of the 'mayor of Castro Street', and thirty years after his death a film was made of his life story. In 2009 Barack Obama posthumously awarded him the highest civilian honour in the United States, the Presidential Medal of Freedom.

Guy Hocquenghem 1946–1988

Sexual liberation was one of the themes that characterized the new social movements exploding on the streets of Paris in May 1968. Guy Hocquenghem, who was a student at the time, eagerly participated in the demonstrations, sit-ins and public debates. Three years later, he joined the newly founded and dramatically named Homosexual Front for Revolutionary Action (FHAR) and, through his publications, television appearances and political activism, the handsome and articulate Hocquenghem became perhaps the best-known gay man of his generation in France.

Hocquenghem was an intellectual in the French style. A child of the post-war baby boom, he came from a prosperous middle-class background and studied at the elite École Normale Supérieure, which enrolled only three dozen students a year. He flirted with Communism – even though his homosexuality made him unwelcome within the staid French Communist Party – and with Trotskyism and Maoism. During the 1970s Hocquenghem began to appropriate many of the fashionable ideas of the day, such as Gilles Deleuze and Félix Guattari's 'anti-Oedipal' psychology, and to apply them to an analysis of sexual desire. During this period he taught philosophy at the University of Vincennes, wrote for the newspaper *Libération*, set up by Jean-Paul Sartre, and in 1979 collaborated with the director Lionel Soukaz on an amateurish documentary film about homosexuality called *Race d'Ep!*

Hocquenghem published extensively and in a variety of genres, producing philosophical–sociological treatises, travelogues and novels. His public comments were often confrontational: his first writings on AIDS denied the severity of the disease, for instance, and he infamously said that, even if some homosexuals did succumb to the illness, it meant that not every man would die quietly and boringly as an old man in bed. Such views made him a media celebrity and an *enfant terrible* of the gay intelligentsia.

Hocquenghem and the FHAR represented a revolutionary stage in the history of French homosexual activism. The FHAR's manifesto was intentionally inflammatory:

> Down with the moneyed society of the hetero-cops!
> Down with sexuality reduced to the procreating family!
> With active–passive roles!
> Let's stop hiding in the shadows!
> We want self-defence groups who will use force to oppose the
>   sexual racism of the hetero-cops.
> We want a homosexual front that will have as its mission to
>   mount an assault on and destroy fascist sexual normality.

Hocquenghem's writings of the early 1970s tried to provide an intellectual basis for such slogans and for the rebellious campaign that they accompanied. He argued that homosexuality is but one part of a natural polymorphous desire – a desire that is stifled by social norms, the demands for procreation, and fears surrounding sexuality, especially taboos related to the eroticism of the anus. Society is marked by an 'anti-homosexual paranoia' and, historically, by 'the constitution of homosexuality as a separate category going along with its repression'. For Hocquenghem, the expression of homosexual desire is in itself revolutionary, since it challenges the whole canon of social norms and can be the point of departure for a new personal and social experience of sexuality in general. He thus sees protean sexual experiences – a happy promiscuity – not only as a right, but also as emancipation on various levels. Through an open and celebratory sexual life, as he wrote in *Le Désir homosexuel* ('Homosexual Desire'; 1972), a gay man rejects society's demonization of sodomy and its fixation on the anal taboo. Engaging in wild sex helps break down the boundaries of sexual normativity. As he writes at the book's outset, 'The problem is not so much homosexual desire as the fear of homosexuality', so both the individual and society must stop fearing the *pédés*. Homosexual desire – only one manifestation, after all, of the multiple sexual desires that any person is capable of feeling – must be released by an assault on masculinist and patriarchal codes entrenched in capitalist society. In setting out such views, Hocquenghem's theoretical work constituted both a deconstruction of society's concept of homosexuality and a manifesto for action in the widest sense.

Hocquenghem's positions often shocked even other gay commentators, although critics generally appreciated his fictional writing, which displays a great breadth of knowledge, skill and interests. His novel *L'Amour en relief* ('Love in Relief'; 1982) tells the story of a blind Arab boy and his amatory adventures in Paris, New York and Los Angeles. The subject of *Les voyages et aventures extraordinaires du frère Angelo* ('The Voyages and Extraordinary Adventures of Brother Angelo'; 1988) is an Italian Renaissance friar, who ends up evangelizing to Native Americans. In *Eve* (1987), the hero, Adam, is the son of a lesbian who was implanted with an ovule created by Nazi eugenicists; ranging across Europe, South America, the Caribbean and Africa, the plot encompasses imprisonment, murders, AIDS, homosexual and heterosexual couplings, incest, and a series of revelations about the origins of Adam and Eve, his relative and sometime lover. Hocquenghem's other works are no less provocative. *Co-ire, album systématique de l'enfance* ('Co-anger: Systematic Album of Childhood'; 1976), for example, looks at the construction of childhood sexuality, while *Le gay voyage* (1980) recounts the author's sexual peregrinations around the world. In two other works, he condemned the racism he discerned at the heart of French society and castigated those who abandoned the demands and hopes of 1968 in favour of comfortable bourgeois security.

Hocquenghem's life and writing belong to a radical phase in the history of homosexuality. He and his fellow activists in the FHAR laid claim to being sexual, political and social revolutionaries, snubbing their noses at respectability, flaunting their sexuality and sexual conquests, and firing shots at established society. Their sentiments were shared by militant liberationists elsewhere who drew a direct line between the personal and the political; they saw (to quote the title of one American essay) 'cock-sucking as an act of revolution'.

The moment did not last. Revolution did not occur, and the militant groups such as the FHAR fragmented in doctrinal and personal disputes. In countries like France, rather than being marginalized, homosexuals were increasingly absorbed into the mainstream. Moreover, the arrival of AIDS changed the real and theoretical situations that most homosexuals confronted. Nonetheless, Hocquenghem's committed activism, his tonic willingness to challenge taboos, and his intellectual and literary approach to questions surrounding homosexuality made him one of the most important figures of the gay world in the 1970s and 1980s. His death from AIDS also linked him to the phenomenon that would dominate the next stage in the history of homosexuality.

Simon Tseko Nkoli 1957–1998

Some African politicians have claimed that homosexuality is an import, brought in by Westerners, and that same-sex sexual encounters did not take place before the colonial era. Anthropologists, however, have shown that homosexual behaviour of many different types – 'boy-wives', intergenerational sexual relations, situational homosexuality in mining camps, and so on – has a long history in Africa, though the subject remains taboo.

One notable African who was publicly active in an emergent gay movement was Simon Tseko Nkoli. He was born in Soweto, a black township in South Africa; his stepfather worked as a chef, and his mother as a domestic worker and shop assistant. Nkoli became aware of politics at an early age, once hiding his parents (who were considered illegal squatters) from police. He came out to them in his late teens and had his first homosexual affair, with a white man. His mother reacted badly and sent him to traditional African healers – some of whom decided that he had been bewitched and prescribed numerous cures – and a Christian pastor told him he was damned. He was also sent to see a psychologist, a man who happened to be gay himself. He told Nkoli and his partner that they were normal and suggested that they move in together, opening a bottle of champagne for all to share. Nkoli's mother eventually changed her attitude, while his stepfather had taken Nkoli's sexuality in his stride from the first.

Nkoli became involved in anti-apartheid politics as a student, joining the Congress of South African Students (though he almost lost his position as the Transvaal regional secretary when he came out) and the United Democratic Front. He also became involved in the largely white Gay Association of South Africa (GASA), which was established in 1982; disappointed with its lack of engagement with apartheid, however, he formed the Saturday Group, the first black gay organization in the country.

For Nkoli, the anti-apartheid and gay movements were both part of a quest for emancipation: as far as he was concerned, 'my baptism in the struggles of the township helped me understand the need for a militant gay rights movement'. Before the arrival of apartheid reform, he had written: 'If you are black in South Africa, the inhuman laws of apartheid closet you. If you are gay in South Africa, the homophobic customs and laws of this society closet you. If you are black and gay in South Africa, well, then it really is all the same closet.'

Having already been detained for political activism in 1976, Nkoli was arrested again for his anti-apartheid protests in 1984 – a crime for which he faced the death penalty. He was kept in detention for sixteen months and finally arraigned before the court in 1986 to take part in the Delmas Treason Trial. Interrogators brought up the fact that he was a 'moffie' (a homosexual), torturing him and threatening him with rape. When another accused was found to be having an affair with a fellow prisoner, Nkoli came out to his cellmates, saying, 'I seem to have been coming out of closets all the time.' Several of them, outraged, demanded a separate trial (they were unsuccessful), but others in the prison were more encouraging. In the outside world Nkoli's case prompted expressions of support and solidarity from around the world.

Nkoli was freed in 1988 and returned to anti-apartheid activism. He also recognized new challenges in the fight for gay rights, founding the Gay and Lesbian Organization of the Witwatersrand (GLOW) and helping to set up the National Coalition for Gay and Lesbian Equality. Having learned, and publicly disclosed, that he was HIV-positive, he established the AIDS Township Project and several men's health initiatives.

The leaders of the African National Congress (ANC), of which Nkoli was a member, were not initially supportive of gay rights, but

Nkoli's actions played a major part in encouraging them to change their stance. Thabo Mbeki, the future president of South Africa, understood the need for gay rights to be recognized, stating that 'the ANC is very firmly committed to removing all forms of discrimination and oppression in a liberated South Africa. That commitment must surely extend to the protection of gay rights.' Marc Epprecht, an expert on sexuality in Africa, notes that the 1991 trial of Winnie Mandela for assault and kidnapping – in which she claimed she had been trying to save black youths from white homosexuals – nevertheless showed that the issue of homosexuality remained controversial.

Nkoli was warmly received by Nelson Mandela in 1994, and the same year the ANC manifesto included a commitment to include sexual orientation within the country's new anti-discrimination legislation. The Bill of Rights of the South African Constitution, finally adopted in 1996, states: 'The state may not unfairly discriminate directly or indirectly against anyone on one or more grounds, including race, gender, sex, pregnancy, marital status, ethnic or social origin, colour, sexual orientation, age, disability, religion, conscience, belief, culture, language and birth.' South Africa was thus the first country in the world to outlaw anti-gay discrimination constitutionally. The last anti-homosexual laws were removed from the statute book in 1998, the year of Nkoli's death. In 2006 the South African parliament legalized marriage equality.

Among the many memorials to Nkoli are the streets in Johannesburg and Amsterdam that bear his name, and a documentary film about his life and political activism. Called *Simon & I* (2002), it was directed by Beverley Ditsie, a fellow founding member of GLOW.

Gay activism of the sort Nkoli pioneered is not widespread in Africa; and even in South Africa not all communities are welcoming to openly gay and lesbian people. The former president of Zimbabwe, Robert Mugabe, characterized homosexuals as 'worse than dogs and pigs', and a former president of Namibia, Sam Nujoma, publicly declared that 'homosexuals must be condemned and rejected in our society'. Homosexual acts are a criminal offence in well over twenty countries in Africa. Almost 24 million Africans, most of them heterosexual, are HIV-positive; they frequently lack treatment because of the cost of supplying medication, the absence of government initiatives, and the taboos that still attach to public discussion of sexual activities.

12

INTERNATIONAL LIVES IN THE
MODERN ERA

Maharaja of Chhatarpur 1866–1932

His Highness Maharaja Sir Vishwanath Singh Bahadur was the hereditary ruler of the princely state of Chhatarpur, now part of Madhya Pradesh in central India. He came to the throne in 1867, when he was just one year old, but did not actually rule until he reached adulthood and had received a British education. According to the elaborate protocol of colonial India, the maharaja was entitled to an eleven-gun salute and a return visit after he called on the viceroy. The maharaja married in 1884, but his wife died before she had children; his second wife gave birth to a son. E. M. Forster had met Chhatarpur on his first trip to India, in 1912–13, when he worked as an amanuensis for the maharaja of Dewas Senior, and it seems that Chhatarpur decided that he, too, would benefit from the services of an English secretary. Forster proposed J. R. Ackerley, a recent Cambridge graduate who was destined to become literary editor of the BBC's magazine *The Listener*, as well as a popular author and well-known homosexual.

Ackerley wrote a memoir about his time in India. Called *Hindoo Holiday*, it was published to acclaim in 1932, and contains a vivid portrait of the maharaja and his court. Ackerley describes him as physically unprepossessing (saying that he looked like a Pekinese dog), but intellectually curious and personally endearing. Ackerley also discovered that the maharaja shared his homosexual proclivities, which he directed towards favourites in his retinue and, in a strictly homosocial way, towards Ackerley himself: 'He wanted some one to love him … He wanted a friend. He wanted understanding, and sympathy, and philosophic comfort.' He had a weakness for male beauty, surrounding himself with comely subalterns and searching out new acquaintances. 'We were on our way to the village of Chetla,' Ackerley recorded on one occasion, 'where a fair was being held, and where also, His Highness told me, there was a very beautiful boy.'

The maharaja displayed a keen, if undisciplined, interest in the West, quizzing Ackerley on Darwin, Huxley and Spencer, on Roman history, Christianity and motor cars, and declaring that he envisaged his realm as ancient Greece. He even entertained fantasies about building a Greek villa ('like the Parthenon') and having his subjects don togas. The maharaja's sexual tastes were also Greek. When Ackerley exclaimed that one of his young companions was a 'bronze Ganymede', the maharaja laughingly asked, 'But where is the eagle?', clearly seeing himself as Zeus swooping down on a fetching cupbearer. According to Ackerley's biographer, Peter Parker, the publishers of *Hindoo Holiday* insisted on the excision of certain passages saying that the maharaja had been sodomized by a virile (if not altogether enthusiastic) valet, and that he had watched while the young man had sex with his wife. Indeed, the valet may have fathered the heir to the throne.

In Ackerley's published account, which mischievously renames Chhatarpur as 'Chhokrapur', or 'city of boys', the maharaja happily chats about the beauty of his young servants with the Englishman, who is far from immune to their charms. Among the ruler's extensive retinue were the 'gods': male adolescents who danced, played music and put on plays. They seemed at times to perform other services as well.

Ackerley noted that, although some of the retainers quietly mocked the maharaja's proclivities, they were not above developing intimate connections with one another. Even those who were married were sometimes not averse to dalliances, and it is likely that men whose sexual urges were primarily homosexual nevertheless wished to marry and to father children (and that their families expected them to do so). Ackerley, too, entranced by the court's graceful *dhoti*-clad men, initiated the occasional kiss and cuddle. 'I must kiss *somebody*,' the Englishman famously replied when the maharaja interrogated him about one of his overtures. His book describes how, during one embrace, a handsome fellow named Narayan promised Ackerley: 'I will come and live with you for always.'

Around the time that Ackerley was in India, homosexuality was being discussed openly in the Indian press for the first time. The debate was sparked by the publication of *Chocolate* (1927), a collection of short stories that had appeared in a Calcutta newspaper in 1924 and were now being reissued as a book. Its author was Pandey Bechan Sharma (1900–1967), a novelist who wrote under the pen name of 'Ugra'. He was also a film-writer and a nationalist whom the British had jailed several times for subversion (nothing is known about his sexuality). Ugra declared that his intention in writing the stories was to combat homosexuality and to promote moral purity, yet they caused a controversy, both because they discussed a taboo subject and for their (discreet) depiction of men embracing and kissing.

Ugra's characters are respected and educated men-about-town who generally are unapologetic about their desires, even if the stories often do not end happily. The tales recognize that the possibilities for homosexual love and sex are widespread in India, and Ugra quotes from traditional Urdu homoerotic verses to underscore the variety of forms that love can take. Oscar Wilde, whom Ugra compares to Krishna for his exaltation of pleasure, is also invoked. 'Chocolate' – a word that Ugra either borrowed from the local slang for homosexual sex or simply settled upon – implies nothing more than a sweet, delicious treat.

A British colonial statute of 1860 made homosexual acts illegal in India, and it remained on the books (even though it was seldom enforced) until 2009, when the Indian High Court declared the law unconstitutional. Three years earlier Manvendra Singh Gohil, who is the heir of the maharajas of Rajpipla, publicly came out as homosexual – the first Indian of royal descent to do so. He is involved in many charitable activities, having founded sexual health programmes and helped organize the first gay conference in India. (In 2009 he also appeared in a BBC reality show, in which, incognito, he had to pick up a man in a Brighton bar.) A growing body of scholarly and creative literature testifies to long-standing homoerotic traditions in Indian history, and it is clear that, eighty years after Ackerley's visit to the Maharaja of Chhatarpur, a new gay culture is now emerging.

Edmund Backhouse 1873–1944

Historically, fantasy has always played a part in the attraction Europeans have felt for Asians. Heterosexual men have long had visions of delicate Oriental women clad in *cheongsam* or kimonos – images popularized by Pierre Loti's book *Madame Chrysanthème* (1887), Puccini's opera on the same theme, *Madama Butterfly*, and in accounts of the Shanghai girls of the 1930s.

Less glamorous reports revealed the bars and brothels of old Saigon or Manila, where sex was available for money, and with or without love. Homosexuals, too, fantasized about the 'Far East'. Frederic Prokosch's novel *The Asiatics* (1935), which takes the form of an imagined travelogue across Asia, from the Levant to the South China Seas, is studded with moments of homoeroticism; and Giovanni Comisso's *Gioco d'infanzia* ('Childhood Game'; 1965), based on the Italian's adventures, follows a world-weary young European man as he immerses himself in the delights of Sri Lanka and China.

The boundaries between sexual fantasies and sexual realities have always been porous, and much literature (notably pornography) has drawn on stereotypes and dreams of desire. Lived experiences, too, become transformed, to the extent that memory and personal narratives often need to be viewed with scepticism.

The problem of veracity is dramatically illustrated by the story of Edmund Backhouse. He was born into a prominent Quaker family; his father was a banker and a baronet, and Edmund's brother served as an admiral in the Royal Navy. Backhouse studied at the elite Winchester College, and then at Oxford. He never took a degree, however, having spent most of his university years dallying in aesthetic and homosexual circles. A nervous breakdown, heavy debts that threatened him with bankruptcy, and family disapproval of his lifestyle prompted him to leave the country for a year, but in

1898 he returned to Britain to spend a few months studying Chinese at Cambridge.

Shortly afterwards Backhouse went to Beijing, where he would live until his death forty-six years later, supported by an allowance from his father, whose title he inherited. After years drifting from job to job, Backhouse began to establish himself as a Sinologist. He co-authored a book on the Dowager Empress Cixi, translated works from Chinese into English, and regularly donated scrolls and other documents to the Bodleian Library. He enjoyed some esteem as a scholar and a philanthropist, and in 1913 the University of London offered him the chair in Chinese studies. Some, however, were unconvinced by his credentials and questioned the authenticity of the scrolls he sent to Oxford, and of the Chinese diary (rescued, he claimed, from the Boxer Rebellion) that served as the basis for *China under the Empress Dowager*.

Several decades after Backhouse's death his biographer, Hugh Trevor-Roper, presented convincing evidence that Backhouse was a fraudster, that many of the sources on which he based his scholarship were unreliable, and that some of the scrolls he gave to the Bodleian were in fact fakes. Trevor-Roper's own reputation was in question (he had authenticated a diary supposedly written by Hitler, which later turned out to be a forgery), but his judgment largely stands. As Robert Bickers, a historian of modern China, comments of Backhouse, 'we know now that not a word he ever said or wrote can be trusted'.

The two unpublished memoirs that particularly incensed Trevor-Roper detailed Backhouse's sex life in Europe – where he claimed to have slept with Lord Alfred Douglas and other celebrities – and in China. Trevor-Roper declared that 'both volumes are grossly, grotesquely, obsessively obscene. Backhouse presents himself as a compulsive pathological homosexual who found in China opportunities for indulgence which, in England ... could be only dangerously and furtively enjoyed.'

One of the volumes – *Décadence Mandchoue*, written at the instigation of a Swiss doctor shortly before Backhouse's death – is a remarkable work, not least for its overwrought style. It is peppered with passages in Chinese, French, Italian and other languages, classical quotations, and precious and antiquated turns of phrase. Even more surprising are Backhouse's descriptions, in pornographic detail, of the gay life of imperial Beijing. Most extraordinary of all is his claim that he was the lover of Empress Cixi, and had sex with her nearly two hundred times. The idea that a middling Englishman such as Backhouse could have enjoyed access to the Forbidden City – much less become the sexual partner and confidant of the empress – beggars the imagination.

In writing about the homosexual milieu of the Middle Kingdom, Backhouse recounts his many and diverse experiences much in the way of a sex manual. He writes about male brothels, the versatile talents of actors and eunuchs, and the attractions of young men like his beloved 'Cassia Flower'. Oral, anal and sadomasochistic sex; sex between two or many men; bestiality – all are described with little left to the imagination.

No one doubts Backhouse's knowledge of China and of the Chinese language. A tradition of same-sex sexual relations certainly did exist in imperial China: actors became the catamites of noblemen and high officials, and in general male prostitution flourished. Not enough historical work has been done to verify or disprove specific facts mentioned in Backhouse's accounts, however; some seem credible, while others are near outlandish. (An anecdote about Cixi visiting a homosexual brothel and ordering its denizens to perform for her, though wonderfully hilarious, strains belief.)

Backhouse's work contains some clues about his intentions. He defends his chronicle as truthful, declaring that readers 'shall not be astonished to learn that in this dissolute company of ancient debauchees and youthful profligates I was among the foremost in unbridled libertinage', but adds that perhaps, in his case, it was 'not wholly unaccompanied by literary allusion and poetical parallelism'. Backhouse further confesses that 'This humble effort is only *une chronique scandaleuse*', and refers to a British diplomat's description of him as 'brilliant in intellect, unbalanced in judgment and amoral in character'. Finally, he muses: 'Is not perverse sexuality, especially such as mine, a form of insanity with lucid intervals …?'

Backhouse's Swiss friend described him as 'a distinguished looking old scholarly gentleman dressed in a shabby black, somewhat formal, suit who had a definite charm and spoke and behaved with exquisite slightly old-style politeness'. Looking back from the age of 70, Backhouse reminisced that 'the sexual act, passive even more than active, afforded to me a ravishing pleasure: the intromission of Cassia's highly militant organ instead of being a prod or a goad, connoted an exquisite, entrancing gratification, *une sensation des plus exquises*; like the first night in heaven'. The memory, real or fabricated, says something about *Décadence Mandchoue* and about Backhouse's life. For an English baronet in war-torn China, implicated in suspect commercial schemes, occasionally rumoured to be a spy and accused of having stolen Chinese treasures, scribbling erotic memoirs provided a way to cock a snook at polite European and Asian mores. The pretence of truthfulness is part of the literary project behind his text, the naughty legacy of an old rake and poseur. The publication of *Décadence Mandchoue* more than half a century after his death represents the recovery of a pseudo-historical documentary on the sex life of imperial China – a *divertissement* that stands as a little gem of erotic literature.

Claude McKay 1889–1948

When Festus Claudius McKay was born, Jamaica was a British colony, dominated by the sugar plantations that covered the whole island. His parents were farmers and had eleven children, of whom Claude was the youngest. At an early age McKay was sent to live with his eldest brother, who had managed to become a teacher, so that he could receive an education – an experience that opened up to him the world of letters.

A chance meeting with an Englishman at the carriage-maker's where he was apprenticed introduced McKay to his future patron and mentor. Walter Jekyll was the son of an army captain; having studied at Harrow and Cambridge, he abandoned a vocation in the Anglican priesthood and studied singing in Milan. In the hope that the tropical climate would help relieve his asthma, Jekyll moved to Jamaica with his intimate friend Ernest Boyle in 1895 – also the year of the Oscar Wilde affair, which was perhaps not a coincidence. Among his other hobbies (he wrote a volume on music and a critique of Christianity, for instance), Jekyll developed an interest in the black peasantry and its culture, and published a collection of Jamaican folktales. McKay availed himself of Jekyll's library, later recalling that Whitman, Carpenter and Wilde were among the authors they read and discussed. Jekyll encouraged the young Jamaican to write poetry in the local creole.

McKay's first book of poems, *Songs of Jamaica*, appeared in 1912. That same year, he left the island, never to return. Jekyll had helped him to enrol as a student of agronomy at Booker T. Washington's pioneering university for African Americans, the Tuskegee Institute in Alabama, but McKay was unhappy there and transferred to a public university in Kansas. Regretting his choice of career, he abandoned tertiary education without taking a degree and in 1914 moved to New York. While there, he worked at odd jobs, married a childhood sweetheart (though they broke up after a year) and began working as a journalist on a black socialist newspaper. According to his biographer, Wayne F. Cooper, McKay had brief passionate affairs with both men and women during this period, and throughout his life, but his orientation was predominantly homosexual. Various names have been circulated, but there is little evidence for who his partners were.

In 1919 McKay moved to England. He would spend most of the next fifteen years in Europe, with the exception of a long stay in Morocco. In London, he found employment with a left-wing workers' newspaper that confirmed him in his socialist (and atheist) perspectives. Three years later he journeyed to Moscow to take part in the fourth congress of the Communist International. He also lived off and on in France for several years, in both Paris and the Midi. During his time in Europe, McKay published novels that count among the most significant in African-American literature: *Home to Harlem* (1928), *Banjo* (1929) and *Banana Bottom* (1933), the last of which he dedicated to Jekyll. The novels were eagerly received, although W. E. B. Dubois, the grand old man of the American black intellectual scene, disapproved strongly of *Home to Harlem* because of its blatant portrayal of sexual licence.

In 1934 McKay himself went 'home' to Harlem. Over the past fifteen years, New York had played host to the Harlem Renaissance – a cultural movement of African Americans and Caribbean migrants loosely connected in the 'black metropolis' (as one of McKay's books described it). Segregation, disenfranchisement and poverty were the lot of most black people in the United States, but Harlem provided a space for greater freedom and sociability, and encouraged the cultural expression of the 'New Negro' poets, essayists and journalists. At the jazz clubs, speakeasies, costume balls and 'rent parties' (private parties held to raise money for cash-strapped tenants), there was also an open attitude towards sexual expression. The first creative writings to have a black homosexual theme, by Richard Bruce Nugent, appeared in the mid-1920s, and a number of other authors linked to the Harlem Renaissance were gay or bisexual: Countee Cullen, Zora Neale Hurston, Langston Hughes, Alain Locke and McKay himself, as well as the sculptor Richmond Barthé and the blues singer Gladys Bentley. White writers like Carl Van Vechten, author of the controversial *Nigger Heaven* (1926), also frequented Harlem to search for literary subjects – and sometimes homosexual pick-ups.

Although most of the black writers remained fairly discreet about their sexual leanings, the novels and jazz songs about Harlem often refer to homosexuality, either openly or in coded form. (The lyrics of 'Sissy Man Blues', 'The Boy in the Boat' and 'Freakish Man Blues' are noteworthy.) Homosocial relationships and homoeroticism feature in McKay's writings in the context of his black characters' energetic sexual appetites. The sex of the partners in his poems is generally unspecified – a curious, if perhaps intentional, omission that allows for varied interpretations. The influence of Edward Carpenter's ideas on sexuality has been discerned in *Home to Harlem*, which contains an overtly gay minor character, a 'pansy' dancer, and a protagonist who, though nominally heterosexual, invites a 'queer' reading.

The theme of friendship between a masculine, working-class man and a gentle, intellectual and politically radical friend – already present in *Home to Harlem* – reappears in *Banjo*, a novel set in the docklands and slums of Marseille. As France's major port, and the gateway to Africa and the colonies, in the inter-war years Marseille had a cosmopolitan population. Africans, West Indians and Arabs populate the book, whose title refers to the charismatic, sexually potent and affable longshoreman who is known for his banjo-playing as much as for his eating, drinking and womanizing. The narrator of the novel, who is manifestly based partly on McKay himself, is a young writer who pals around with the black denizens of the port but almost never shares their penchant for visiting brothels and enjoying flings with the women of the waterfront. His attachment to Banjo, however, is obvious – a brotherly bonding that has strongly erotic overtones.

McKay spent his last years in the United States, becoming an American citizen in 1940. Four years later, suffering from ill health, he converted to Roman Catholicism, and died from cancer in Chicago in 1948. His works had a great influence on later African-American writers, including the openly gay James Baldwin.

Lionel Wendt 1900–1944

Sri Lanka – or Ceylon, as it was known in colonial times – was a serendipitous island for many foreign homosexuals. Edward Carpenter was among those enchanted with its tropical beauty and with the friendliness of its people, and a procession of later expatriates – Paul Bowles, Donald Friend, Arthur C. Clarke – lived there. Lionel Wendt was a Sri Lankan whose modernist photography erotically blends Western and Eastern imagery and allusions. He was also the leading figure in Colombo's avant-garde cultural movement in the years before the Second World War.

Wendt was born into a wealthy Burgher family, of mixed European and Sinhalese ancestry. He grew up immersed in European culture and literature, and had a particular fondness for Proust. Wendt's father was a supreme court judge, a member of the colonial Legislative Council and a founder, in 1906, of the Amateur Photographic Society of Ceylon; his mother, a social worker, came from a family of civil servants. Ceylon was a British outpost, where it was normal for promising young men with private incomes, like Wendt, to travel to England for their education. In 1919 he arrived in London to study law, but also trained at the Royal Academy of Music and became an accomplished pianist. Having qualified as a barrister in 1924, he practised for only a short time before returning to Ceylon. Thereafter Wendt lived a comfortable life in Colombo, giving public recitals but increasingly turning to photography as a mode of expression. That he was homosexual was known to friends and associates, but he was discreet about his liaisons.

In the early 20th century Colombo hosted only a small avant-garde artistic circle. The dominant cultural influences were the ancestral religions of the island's Buddhist and Hindu populations, as well as the starchier contributions of British colonialism. In the late 1920s a group of young figures, including Wendt, his friend the painter George Keyt and other mavericks, attempted to stimulate Ceylon's torpid cultural life and to introduce the more innovative Western styles of art, music and literature. They organized an exhibition of Cubist, Futurist and Post-Impressionist art in the early 1930s, which shocked traditionalists but drew praise from the poet Pablo Neruda, who at that time was Chile's consul in Colombo and a friend of Wendt. Wendt himself gave piano concerts, playing pieces by modernist composers such as Debussy, Poulenc and Bartók to audiences little accustomed to the latest musical developments. He also became fascinated with cinema, and in 1934 narrated the film *Song of Ceylon*, an award-winning documentary made by Basil Wright and sponsored by the Ceylon Tea Propaganda Board. The film lyrically records the religious observances, landscapes and scenes of daily life in Ceylon, and often features slender young men dressed in lungis – images that reflect Wendt's own photographs.

With photography, Wendt found his real *métier*. An exhibition of his works was held in London in 1938, and several made their way into magazines. Much influenced by the experiments undertaken in early 20th-century Europe, he adopted such techniques as multiple exposures and solarization. His cameras – a Rolleiflex and a Leica – captured a variety of subjects: landscape scenes, portraits of Sri Lankan notables and friends, and some very interesting surrealist images. A considerable number are homoerotic, however, and he is certainly one of the earliest non-European photographers to produce such a body of work.

Wendt's photographs of this type document Ceylonese youths going about daily life. Fit young workers climb trees for coconuts, wash at public fountains, tend houses or temples, towel off pet dogs or draw water from a well. Many viewers would not immediately see them as erotic, but a careful observer might note how Wendt dwells on the men's physiques – the strong backs, powerful legs and buttocks of youths shimmying up coconut trees, for instance – which he emphasizes by means of subtle chiaroscuro lighting. Sometimes small details, such as the shimmering water streaming down the torso of one dark-skinned young bather, create particularly sensual motifs. Ceylon's hot climate afforded many opportunities for shooting scantily dressed labourers, domestic servants, dancers, rickshaw-wallahs and boatmen, and his subjects appear in scenes of masculine sociability.

In both his *plein-air* and studio work – aesthetically posed and sexually charged figure studies, generally empty of all but a few props – Wendt places the statuesque bodies of young men centre stage. Some pictures focus insistently on buttocks or loincloth-clad groins. While most of the boys in Wendt's softer, Pictorialist-style images are workers, one especially elegant nude, posed sipping tea, looks very middle class. Overtly sexual imagery is absent, although one boy, asleep on a couch, rests his left hand on his bare chest, stretching the other suggestively across his crotch. Pictures of naked women repeat some of the tropes and camera techniques, but Wendt returns again and again to the male body.

Several of Wendt's more surrealist images vibrate with hints about his private life and desires. One features a comely man who seemingly offers himself to the viewer: lying on his back, with his arms stretched upwards, he is posed against cross-shaped ship masts in a series of multiple exposures. Wendt took the title, *I Heard a Voice Wailing*, from a poem by Christina Rossetti. Called 'A Ballad of Boding', the poem speaks of ships and dreaming and love; it begins: 'There are sleeping dreams and waking dreams / What seems is not always as it seems.' The hazy background in Wendt's photograph is certainly oneiric; and the ship motif promises voyages of discovery (like Rossetti's vessels, sailing to the East), but also the pain of departure and separation.

Another of Wendt's images – a picture of the photographer's desk – sums up his homosexual sensibility. For alongside his camera and ashtray are one of his photographs of a nude Ceylonese man, and a plaster-of-paris statue of a naked Greek god, the Apollo Belvedere. Here Wendt has set up a *mise en scène* of antiquity in the tropics: a classical gay icon in sculpture next to a modern photograph of a beautiful South Asian, set for the purposes of contemplation on an altar-like worktable. A mask and, on the wall, what appears to be a portrait of Wendt himself hint at meanings behind the images.

Wendt died of a heart attack in 1944, at the relatively young age of 44. Although many of his negatives were destroyed after his death, a collection called simply *Lionel Wendt's Ceylon* was published posthumously, in 1950. These pictures were again reproduced, along with further works, in a volume issued to mark the centenary of his birth. The Lionel Wendt Memorial Theatre and Art Gallery in Colombo perpetuate his memory.

Homosexual visitors to exotic parts often voyeuristically photographed the handsome men who caught their fancy. In Wendt's work, however, viewers see the striking efforts of a 'native' photographer to combine allusions full of meaning for homosexuals with scenes drawn from the life around him. The afterword to Wendt's centenary volume notes that he was someone 'born and bred in a small tropical island [who] could move easily and freely in the literary and artistic tradition of Europe'. Part of that tradition was homoerotic, and Ceylon provided a congenial environment for it to take root.

Xuan Dieu 1916–1985

Except for a few rare traders and missionaries, the culture of Vietnam – its indigenous traditions, Buddhist religion and Confucian ethics – was for centuries little known to outsiders. Conquest by the French in the last decades of the 19th century added a layer of European culture, resisted and rejected by some, but assimilated by others. One who absorbed these foreign influences was Xuan Dieu.

Born in northern Vietnam in 1917, Xuan Dieu was the son of a teacher. He was educated at a colonial *lycée* and law faculty. In the 1930s he became a leader of the Tho Moi, or 'New Poetry', movement, whose works showed a familiarity with French writers and the ideas they espoused. The formalism of the old, Sinified schools of literature stressed the importance of mastering and imitating the Confucian classics, as well as the values of a corporatist and hierarchical society. By contrast, the New Poets adopted an individualistic, emotional and romantic outlook. A world-weary melancholy, wilful decadence and aestheticism marked the new modernist poets, much as it had their European counterparts several decades before.

In an essay on poetry, Xuan Dieu wrote admiringly of the impact of French writers on his own work and on Vietnamese cultural life in general, for 'the contact with French literature, especially French poetry, injected a flow of new blood into our society'. The classic French writers he encountered in his schooldays, especially Alphonse de Lamartine, taught him a new way of writing and thinking. Traditionalists in Vietnam thought in terms of 'we' – Confucianism linking together king and subjects, masters and students, fathers and children – but Xuan Dieu claimed that from the French moderns he had learned to use the word 'I' and to behave as an individual. Personal and poetic credos were thus combined. From Alfred de Musset he borrowed an emphasis on sentiment. With Baudelaire, 'I took the full plunge into the heart of modern poetry', while 'Verlaine taught me about sadness … He showed me how to shape my sadness into beautiful poetic expressions.' Verlaine was a particular inspiration, especially in Xuan Dieu's love poetry, as can be seen from an open reference to Verlaine's stormy relationship with Rimbaud in 'Male Love': 'I miss Rimbaud and Verlaine / The two poets dazed by drinking / Intoxicated with exotic poetry, and devoted to friendship'.

Few of Xuan Dieu's 400 poems have been translated into English. A selection of works from the 1930s rendered into English by Huynh Sanh Thong convey a pining desire for love, yet also the knowledge that love is transitory (a reflection of Buddhist views on the transitoriness of all life and sentiments) and often not quite sufficient. 'You love me, but it's still not enough,' he admonishes one lover ('You Must Say It'), and elsewhere laments, 'Without fair warning, flowers bloom and droop: / love comes and goes at pleasure – who can tell?' (from 'Come On, Make Haste'). In another work ('To Love'), he sighed: 'To love is to die a little in the heart.'

Many years later, in the essay on French and Vietnamese poetry, Xuan Dieu quotes from one of his earlier verses, asking: 'How can one explain love? / It doesn't mean anything, a late afternoon / It invades my heart with softening sunlight / With light clouds, with gentle breeze.' And he confided, enigmatically: 'My entire being vibrates like the strings of a violin / While listening to the murmuring of what I have tried to hide.'

Although Xuan Dieu was briefly married, he did not sign the papers validating the union and probably never consummated it. His yearnings were for men. A memoir by a former lover, To Hoai, chronicled Xuan Dieu's long-term partnership with another man: Huy Can, a fellow poet who was also a nationalist, a Marxist and, later, a high-ranking official in independent North Vietnam. Anti-colonial nationalist feeling was increasingly strong among the Vietnamese elite in the inter-war years, and emerged in a more militant form after the Second World War, when Ho Chi Minh led the struggle for independence. (France was ultimately defeated at Dien Bien Phu in 1954.)

Within this context Huy Can converted his lover to Marxist nationalism. Xuan Dieu joined the Viet Minh in 1944, took a job as the editor of a poetry magazine the following year, made radio broadcasts and gave speeches to rouse support for the nationalist cause. In 1946 he accompanied Ho to France for the political negotiations that failed to secure peaceful independence for Vietnam. Once he was fully engaged in politics, Xuan Dieu renounced his individualistic, romantic poetry and dedicated himself to the revolution.

During his campaigning, Xuan Dieu continued to be sexually active and had multiple partners. In 1952 he was subjected to a 'rectification' session by the Communist Party: comrades had criticized him for his 'evil bourgeois thinking', although he decided that it was his homosexuality that caused concern. He subsequently proved an ardent champion of Ho's forces and orthodox ideology, and praised official values in the struggle for the liberation and unification of Vietnam. Many of his later poems are pieces of socialist agitprop. The new regime that followed independence expected loyal cadres to channel their desires to the greater good of nation-building. Lai Nguyen An and Alec Holcombe, both specialists in Vietnamese literature, suggest that there was a trade-off: the poet unquestioningly supported the government, which seemingly turned a blind eye to his homosexuality, and indeed provided a spacious house in Hanoi that he shared with Huy Can. For a time, Xuan Dieu's half-sister lived there too, as Huy Can's wife.

Despite having repudiated his earlier, individualistic poetry, in 1956 Xuan Dieu availed himself of a short period of greater political and cultural openness in Vietnam to publish an article on Walt Whitman, hinting at his empathy with the notion of comradely love.

Some critics still regarded his writing as not sufficiently collectivist and made disobliging comments about his relationship with Huy Can. Nonetheless, several decades after his death the Vietnamese government continues to regard him as a hero: it posthumously awarded him a prestigious prize and named a Hanoi street in his honour.

Xuan Dieu's works embody the intertwining of local and colonial influences, of traditional, modernist and revolutionary perspectives. 'I am an explorer and an importer', Xuan Dieu concluded – an example of migration between cultures.

Jean Sénac 1926–1973

Jean Sénac was a *pied-noir* ('black-foot'): a European in colonial Algeria, which the French had conquered in 1830. The *pied-noir* population was made up of migrants from France, Italy, Malta and, as was the case with Sénac's family, from Spain. His grandfather, a poor miner, had settled in the coastal region of Oran. Sénac grew up in very modest circumstances, raised by his mother, who worked as a cleaner, and by a stepfather; the identity of his biological father was unknown. At the start of the Second World War, when Sénac was an adolescent, France was occupied by Germany, and Algeria came under the control of the Vichy regime. After the war he fulfilled his obligatory military service and spent a period in a sanatorium, suffering from paratyphoid fever and pleurisy. On his recovery, in December 1948, he began to work for the French radio in Algeria.

Throughout the 1940s, when circumstances allowed, Sénac wrote poetry and moved in local artistic circles; and in 1947 he began a correspondence with the writer Albert Camus, a fellow *Français d'Algérie* who would become his friend and mentor. Sénac's first collection of poetry was published in Paris, with a foreword by Camus, in 1954. That year also marked the beginning of the Algerian War of Independence, which would last until its fratricidal and bloody conclusion in 1962.

Several themes marked Sénac's life and work. In the background was always Algeria. Although he never learned Arabic or converted to Islam (few of the French did), he felt viscerally attached to the place. *Algérianiste* writers had talked about a new European race emerging from the various migrant populations that had put down roots in North African soil. They envisaged an easy (if separate) cohabitation with Muslim Algerians and Jews: a hybrid culture drawing on the legacy of the Romans and the Europeans (the Berber and Arabic heritage was seen to play a smaller role) and on the sun-drenched lifestyle of the Mediterranean. Sénac relished this existence, although he was never blind to what it cost the indigenous people and hoped for an enduring multicultural society in the place he always considered his *patrie*, his true home.

Homosexuality was a vital part of Sénac's being. He had his first youthful sexual experiences in Algeria, and wrote evocatively in poetry and prose about his love affair with a Frenchman in the 1950s, and about his casual encounters with the Algerian Arabs he met in cinemas or cafés or at the beach. Finding sexual partners among young Algerians was never difficult, even if many engaged in same-sex relations only furtively. As he grew older Sénac wrote of these meetings, and of the sexual attraction he felt for Algerians, with increasing confidence and in greater detail. In 1957, while on a trip to France, he met a young Parisian named Jacques Miel; they had a brief sexual liaison, and Miel eventually became the writer's closest friend, and his adopted son and heir.

Sénac's experimental poetry is often elliptical and hermetic. He created a new form of poetry: called 'corpoème', it was intended as a metaphorical melding of Sénac's sexual interaction with the body of a lover and his literary reaction to such encounters. The images leave no doubt about his sexual desires and experiences. He explains how social mores, sexual hunger and poverty created possibilities for encounters, 'the handsomest boy taken / for the price of a film ticket'. He recalls moments of sensual pleasure: 'just the memory of such adolescents / provoked a ferocious orgasm'. In a poem entitled 'La Course' (1967), he speaks of thwarted love and of raw, frustrated lust: 'You carry on and on about love. But I understand / only the pain in the balls that have only a mirror / in which to empty themselves'; reciting a litany of Arabic names, he called on the men to bugger him. But he also conjured up beautiful images of the desert, the sea and his partners. In a homage to a lover, called 'Brahim the Generous' (1966), he writes: 'You gave me back light and peace / The curve in the steep path / The science of the well and the bashfulness of the water … / This dessicated heart you have also made your domain.' In poems about Abu Nuwas, Rimbaud, Wilde and Lorca, he invokes other homosexual writers and sets out his hopes for sexual emancipation.

The other major theme of Sénac's life was political engagement. He was an early supporter of the Algerian nationalists who waged an eight-year war of independence. Although he never joined the National Liberation Front, and his activities during the war, which he spent in France, remain somewhat clouded, his writings called on the French to grant independence to Algeria. He begged the *pieds-noirs* to remain in the country and urged the construction of a new, revolutionary society in which Europeans, Arabs and other populations would each have their proper place. In 1962, as a million *pieds-noirs* fled the newly independent Algeria, Sénac returned, full of hope. He resumed his radio broadcasting, helped establish literary journals, wrote literary and art criticism and poetry, and became one of the major figures of French-language cultural life in Algiers. Sénac's writings (including some agitprop poems) lauded the 'citizens of beauty' and the new order, and championed the heroes and causes of the time – Che Guevara and Ho Chi Minh, resistance to capitalism and imperialism, love and sex.

In the mid-1960s Sénac fell out of step with the Algerian government, which was becoming more dictatorial and militaristic, and less congenial to non-Arabs such as himself. As he had once criticized the old colonial system, now he chastised the new regime for its ideological rigidities, failure to attack poverty, lack of development and curtailment of freedom. His poetry, too – with its ever more vivid accounts of homosexual desire – hardly found favour in this prudish climate. Finally dismissed from his post at the radio station in 1972, Sénac sank into poverty. He moved from a beachside suburb to a squalid inner-city basement, and his writings expressed a gloom bordering on despair. In August 1973 he was murdered; some suspected political involvement, but it is more likely that he was killed by a disgruntled hustler or a former sexual partner.

April Ashley 1935–2021

O ver the years, the phrase 'gay and lesbian' has expanded to an ever-lengthening and unpronounceable acronym for all those who do not fit the traditional category of heterosexual – those who identify as lesbian, gay, bisexual, transsexual, intersex, non-binary, queer, asexual and other orientations or identities that fall under the word 'plus'. The terms 'transgender' and more contemporary 'trans' mean different things to different people, encompassing those whose gender identity does not match the sex assigned to them at birth or childhood. Some trans people seek gender reassignment through hormones and surgery, while others do not; not all think of themselves, before or after the transition, as having a same-sex orientation. Once a little-known community subject to derision and discrimination, trans people have now become more prominent and vocal, denouncing transphobia, proclaiming 'trans pride' and demanding the right to legal documents and official recognition of the gender with which they identify.

Gender reassignment surgery, carried out on men and women, dates back to the early 20th century, attracting little attention until the cases of Roberta Cowell, a male-born British racing driver and Second World War fighter pilot who transitioned in 1951, and the American Christine Jorgensen, a former soldier who underwent the surgery the following year. Another of the pioneers to do so was April Ashley. Born in 1930s Liverpool, in a working-class family of six children, to a father who was a British Royal Navy cook and a housewife mother, George Jamieson did not feel a boy or particularly look like a stereotypical lad of his milieu. After suffering from a chronic illness, unhappy family life and gender confusion as a child, George left home to join the merchant marine at the age of 15.

Following several attempts at suicide, George checked himself into a mental hospital and was treated with electric shocks, in cruel and unsuccessful attempts by doctors at producing 'normality'. George moved to London in 1955, but soon left for Paris, there to find work as the presenter of shows at a popular cabaret, Le Carousel, well known for celebrity patrons and its female and male impersonation acts. One of the star performers was 'Coccinelle', who had been considered male at birth but had underground sex-reassignment surgery in Casablanca, Morocco. She recommended the same surgeon to George, who also wanted to transition. Earnings from the cabaret provided the £2,500 needed to go to Casablanca for the operation in 1960. As she awoke from anaesthesia on what she later recalled for *The Guardian* as 'the happiest day of my life', her surgeon greeted her with the words 'Bonjour, Mademoiselle'.

Back in London and with a new name, the tall, pretty and glamorous April Ashley worked as a model, appearing in such magazines as *Vogue*. Some of the photographers, but few readers or members of the fashionable social circles in which she moved, were aware of her history. But in 1961 someone she had considered a friend outed her, for a payment of £5, to *The Sunday People*, which published the exposé. Reaction was hostile, and Ashley was told that her modelling career was over. She made a living from a variety of jobs off and on in London (where she and a friend opened a restaurant in Knightsbridge), Wales and Spain.

In 1963, in Gibraltar, April wed Arthur Corbett, the future third Baron Rowallan – a fortnight later, he ran off with the male heir to a Spanish dukedom. In 1967, Corbett petitioned for divorce. The judge ruled in 1971 that Ashley was still male and thus the marriage was invalid. That view of transgender people set a precedent in British law that survived until the Gender Recognition Act of 2004. Stress contributed to Ashley suffering a heart attack in 1975, after which she moved to California, married again (and subsequently divorced), and found employment in a number of places, from craft shops to Greenpeace.

After passage of the Gender Recognition Act, Ashley returned to Britain, and was able to procure a new birth certificate giving her gender as female. She became active in promoting trans equality, for which she was made a Member of the Order of the British Empire in 2012, invested by the Prince of Wales. Other awards included an honorary doctorate from the University of Liverpool. The Museum of Liverpool devoted a year-long exhibition, 'April Ashley, Portrait of a Lady', to her life and that of other transgender people in Britain. She lived until the age of eighty-six.

At Ashley's simple funeral, three of the pall-bearers shouldering her coffin, covered in the Red Ensign flown on British ships, were uniformed military personnel. The priest spoke of 'a lady of great determination and great courage', an old friend reminisced about her love of opera and ballet, and after a brief valedictory message from Ashley to her friends was read, a bottle of champagne was popped open.

Late in life, still impeccably dressed and groomed, speaking in cut-glass tones – she had 'an aristo voice and a native scouse wit', according to the obituary run in *The Guardian* – Ashley said in an interview with the BBC: 'I know more than anyone how people can judge, but I also know if you are true to yourself, that's all that matters'. Her biggest achievement, she added, was 'becoming me', a sentiment that all LGBTQIA+ people would applaud.

Shi Pei Pu 1938–2009

David Henry Hwang's *M. Butterfly* won the 1988 Tony Award for best play on Broadway, and five years later became a popular movie. It recounted the strange relationship between a French diplomat and a male singer in the Beijing Opera who convinced him that he was a woman. They had a child together, before both were convicted in France for working as Chinese spies. Hwang based his work on a real-life case that is perhaps even more complex than its theatrical counterpart.

Shi Pei Pu, who died in 2009, was born in Shandong, China, in 1938. He moved to Beijing and worked successfully as an actor and singer, then became a writer and teacher of Chinese to diplomats and their families. In 1964, at a Christmas party for diplomats posted to the Chinese capital, Shi met Bernard Boursicot, who had recently arrived to work at France's newly established embassy. Boursicot, who came from a working-class family in Brittany and had neither the bourgeois background nor the university degrees generally held by members of the foreign service, was employed under contract as an accountant. Shi, who spoke French well, told him that he was the son of an academic and had studied literature at the University of Kunming; his father had died, and he lived with his mother. He had two elder sisters, one a table-tennis champion, and the other married to a painter.

Boursicot and Shi became close friends – an intimacy unusual in Maoist China – and Boursicot believed Shi's confidential revelation that he was a woman. Shi (who was later guarded on the point) seems to have convinced him that his parents, who already had two daughters, had decided when he was born to raise him as a boy. Soon after Shi's confession, the two started a sexual relationship; their encounters were brief and fumbling, however, and Shi – who insisted on darkness – refused to appear in the nude. Their relationship continued for a year, until Boursicot resigned from his position and left China.

The details surrounding Shi's life over the next few years, during which China experienced the terrors of the Cultural Revolution, remain unknown. Four years after he had left, Boursicot returned to China, to work once more at the French embassy. He located Shi, and they resumed their sexual relationship (mainly, it seems, involving masturbation and oral intercourse). To the authorities, Boursicot justified his visits to Shi's house as a chance to study the Chinese language and Maoist thought. When another person arrived at Shi's home to tutor Boursicot in revolutionary philosophy, Boursicot agreed to engage in espionage in order to facilitate his contacts with his lover. Shi later claimed that he was absent when Boursicot provided documents and information to the contact, who clearly had been planted by the government. Between 1970 and 1972 Boursicot handed over scores of confidential diplomatic reports, but it seems unlikely that he would have had access to anything other than low-grade intelligence.

In 1972 Boursicot again left China. He returned briefly the following year, as a tourist, when Shi introduced him to their 'son'. Once he was back in France, he began a sexual relationship with Thierry Toulet, and the two moved in together. Boursicot's foreign service took him to the United States, but in 1977 he applied for posting to France's tiny embassy in Mongolia. Since one of his duties was to courier a diplomatic pouch, Boursicot regularly travelled from Ulaanbaatar to Beijing, where he met up with Shi and once more began low-level spying. At the end of his term in Mongolia, in 1979, he returned to Paris, where he arranged for Shi and their 'son', Shi Du Du (also known as Bertrand), to migrate. They arrived in 1982 and settled in with Boursicot and Toulet. The following year, agents from the French security services arrested Boursicot and Shi.

The prosecutors charged both men with espionage. Amid great publicity, the judges convicted them, sentencing each to six years in prison. In the event they were freed after less than a year. When prison doctors revealed that Shi – who was still claiming to be a woman, despite his men's clothes – was in fact a man, Boursicot tried to commit suicide in his cell. Upon their release, they went their separate ways, Shi working as a performer and raising Shi Du Du, and Boursicot living quietly with his partner Toulet. When Shi died, Boursicot commented that he had been so taken in by Shi that he could feel no sadness at his passing. He cut a pathetic figure, gullible and credulous almost beyond belief, and continued to insist that he had believed Shi to be a woman. Perhaps he was a victim of his own Orientalist fantasies, as he is portrayed in Hwang's play.

Understanding Shi's motivations is difficult. Did homosexual feelings propel the provincial Chinese boy towards the opera, where there was a tradition of actors and singers serving as catamites for patrons? Was he really in love with Boursicot, as he claimed? Did he never actually pretend to be a woman, but instead only aim to satisfy Boursicot in female guise (as he also maintained); or was he exceptionally talented at keeping his genitalia out of Boursicot's reach and arguing that his diminutive breasts were the result of hormone treatment? Did he simply see the seduction of the Frenchman as an avenue for social advancement – the small luxuries a diplomat could provide and, ultimately, refuge in France? How could he manage to keep up the pretence and duplicity so well? (Shi's 'son', it transpired, was purchased from an impoverished Uighur family.) What form did Shi's life take without Boursicot, and how much of his own story was a tall tale? How deeply was he implicated in the espionage, and what were his relations with the Chinese authorities? How did he view the *ménage à trois* with his 'husband' and Toulet in Paris?

Europeans' infatuation for Asians has been a trope of history and culture since the first encounters between West and East. Some contacts, such as that between Butterfly and Captain Pinkerton in Puccini's opera (itself based on a real liaison between a British officer and a Japanese woman), were doomed. Most, inevitably, came up against questions of cultural expectations, stereotypes and a measure of fantasy. Literary critics commenting on Hwang's play have focused on its issues of gender, difference and identity. The real-life story, too, makes one wonder about the unfathomable depths of human desire and the extraordinary situations it can produce, the vague boundaries between reality and fantasy, and the muddled intersection of private and public life.

Reinaldo Arenas 1943–1990

Born into grinding poverty in rural Cuba – a destitution so extreme that hunger forced him and other children to eat soil – Reinaldo Arenas was raised by his kindly mother. He never knew his father. In his autobiography, *Antes que anochezca* ('Before Night Falls'; 1992), he recounts his pubescent sexual initiation through intercourse with farmyard animals (common behaviour for young men in the countryside, he affirms) and erotic play with classmates. He evokes provincial Cuba's atmosphere of violent machismo, but also the erotic bonding that occurred between youths.

Like many poor Cubans, Arenas supported the rebellion led by Fidel Castro that overthrew Fulgencio Batista's corrupt government in 1958. Arenas benefited from the changes it brought about, and in 1961 won a scholarship to train as an agricultural accountant in Havana, later studying philosophy and literature at the city's university. The 1960s also offered ample opportunities for sex. Men cruised in parks and on the beach; school and university residences were venues for sexual encounters; and army recruits were ready to provide sexual services. The predominant ethos was that a man who played the active role in intercourse did not compromise his masculinity. The tropical climate, Arenas said, stimulated eroticism, and close physical contact with other men on crowded buses and in shared dormitories, as well as outdoors, made contacts easy. Arenas dived happily into homosexual life. He had versatile sexual tastes and a huge sexual appetite: he calculated, perhaps implausibly but still impressively, that by 1968, when he was 25 years old, he had had sex with 5,000 men; 'I was neither monogamous nor selective,' he wrote. He also fell in love and had several extended relationships.

During this time Arenas made the acquaintance of two of Cuba's leading writers, both of them homosexual: José Lezama Lima and Virgilio Piñera. They both treated homosexual themes more or less openly in their works, and in Havana actively pursued their sexual interests. Their mentorship helped Arenas launch his writing career, and Lezama's argument that beauty subverted dictatorship would provide moral support for Arenas in years to come.

In 1964 Arenas gained coveted, if poorly paid, employment at the National Library. Several years later his first novels, in manuscript form, won awards in literary contests. However, Arenas' literary style – which did not conform to the precepts of socialist realism and was said to lack heroic and morally sound characters – offended the Cuban political authorities. 'Ideological deviation', his writings' failure to fit into a revolutionary mould and the inclusion of homosexual figures brought him under suspicion. The early texts were (illegally) spirited out of the country and published to acclaim overseas. For Arenas, writing and sex went hand-in-hand: he declared that he could never be creative if he abstained. Yet his sexual exploits and increasingly dissident opinions were evidently provoking hostility.

From the 1960s onwards Castro's triumphant revolutionaries had attempted to combat prostitution and homosexuality, and to reform those it considered social misfits, through forced labour. In 1965 – when the gay American poet Allen Ginsberg was expelled from Cuba for repeating a rumour that Fidel Castro's brother, Raúl, was gay, and adding that Che Guevara was cute – Castro declared that homosexuals were not oppressed, but that they could not be true revolutionaries or real Communist militants. By the early 1970s the campaign against homosexuals had gathered strength. Gay men were arrested, interrogated, tortured and imprisoned by the secret police; they were also accused of the crime of being counter-revolutionary. This crackdown was part of the Castro dictatorship's general persecution of intellectuals, Christians and anyone who failed to support the regime. Along with other writers, Arenas was sent for a period to a forced labour camp on a sugar plantation.

Arenas' homosexual activities, although hardly secret, were reported by informers (who included erstwhile friends and even an aunt), and in 1973 he was arrested. His autobiography recounts the horrific treatment he received, including six months of imprisonment before trial on charges of having had sex with minors. The two young men brought to testify against him denied the charges, resulting in a mistrial, but the judge nonetheless sentenced Arenas to two years' incarceration in a hellish jail, where he several times tried to commit suicide. Under duress, he signed a confession admitting that he had sent his writings out of the country. In the meantime, police destroyed many of his remaining manuscripts. An international campaign for his release publicized the case but had little immediate effect.

Arenas was freed in 1976 but found it difficult to get a job, and there was still no possibility of publishing his works in Cuba. Having abstained while he was in prison – despite the opportunities it afforded – he resumed his sex life. Much saddened by the deaths of a beloved grandmother, and of Lezama and Piñera, he tried, daringly and unsuccessfully, to flee Castro's rule by crossing an alligator- and mine-infested swamp to swim to the American military base at Guantánamo. Seeing little future in Cuba, in 1980 he managed to join the 135,000 individuals who left the island during the 'Mariel exodus', whose stated aim was to rid the country of criminals, the insane and perverts.

Arenas landed in Miami. Finding the city's conservative and unintellectual Cuban expatriate community unwelcoming, he decided to move to New York. Although he judged America to be soulless, New York proved stimulating, and he enjoyed the opportunity it gave him to write freely. He completed or rewrote half a dozen novels, established a literary magazine, arranged for his mother to visit for several months, and had 'memorable adventures with the most fabulous black men' in Manhattan. Like many gay men in the 1980s, he contracted HIV; despite periods of debilitating illness and hospitalization, he finished a five-volume sequence of novels that he considered his life's work. In 1990, depressed at his physical condition and inability to write, he took his own life, leaving behind an autobiography and a farewell note encouraging resistance to the Castro government; 'Cuba will be free. I already am', he had written.

His widely translated novels, and the film adaptation of his autobiography released in 2000, have made Arenas the most famous Latin American homosexual of his generation. He was also one of the most forthright of authors in discussing his prolific sexual adventures. A mixture of machismo, Catholicism and conservative attitudes towards sexuality and the family have long characterized South American culture; they have also shaped the vibrant gay cultures of places such as Mexico City, Buenos Aires, Rio de Janeiro and Havana, whether clandestine or public.

Old attitudes, at least, have been changing rapidly. The production in 1993 of an overtly gay film by the celebrated Cuban director Tomás Gutiérrez Alea, *Fresa y chocolate* ('Strawberry and Chocolate') – which tells the story of an artist's obsession with a handsome young Marxist student, who is nominally straight, and his eventual decision to flee the country – was seen as indicative of greater tolerance. In 2010 Castro conceded that his government's treatment of homosexuals had been a 'grave injustice', and in 2022 Cuba legalized same-sex marriage.

Binyavanga Wainaina 1971–2019

'Hey mum. I was putting my head on her shoulder, that last afternoon before she died. She was lying on her hospital bed. Kenyatta. Intensive Care. Critical Care.... I am holding my dying mother's hand.... I am whispering in her ear'. What he told her was: 'I am a homosexual, Mum'. That sentence gave the title to an essay published in 2014 by Binyavanga Wainaina, what he called the 'lost chapter' of his 2011 memoir, *One Day I Will Write About This Place*. In the story, he imagined coming out to his mother on a visit to her deathbed. In reality, he had been living in South Africa when she died and was unable to return to Kenya, and he had never come out to her.

Wainaina was born in Nairobi, and grew up in a middle-class family in Nakuru, in the Kenyan highlands. His Kenyan father was the managing director of an agricultural company and his Ugandan mother the proprietor of a hairdressing salon. After finishing secondary school, he went to South Africa to study accounting at what is now Walter Sisulu University, and he later completed an MPhil at the University of East Anglia. He lived in South Africa for a decade after university, beginning his writing career and also working as a caterer and food critic. Writing a weekly column on food and collecting 13,000 recipes, he quipped: 'I am widely regarded as the leading commentator on African Cuisine in South Africa.... But I would rather describe myself as a dedicated Food Slut'.

In 2002, Wainaina won the Caine Prize for African Writing for his story 'Discovering Home'. With the £10,000 award, he founded a literary magazine, *Kwani?* ('What?'), that served as a launching pad for young African writers. Indeed, as Margaret Busby's obituary in *The Guardian* phrased it, Wainaina was an 'enabler' of African authors, mentoring writers, bringing them to attention and publishing their works. Over the next years, a number of Wainaina's own writings appeared, including pieces in *The New York Times*, *National Geographic* and other publications, though he never published the novel that he planned. He also became a commentator on African affairs, frequently interviewed by international news media as he travelled the world.

In 2005, Wainaina published a satirical essay, 'How to Write about Africa', in *Granta*, a 'piss-job, a venting of steam', he said, written in response to an earlier issue of the journal dedicated to the continent. Wainaina lampooned, with incisiveness, humour and precision, Western writing about Africa, the presuppositions, stereotypes and generalizations that served as common tropes for outsiders' visions of the continent's people, environment and politics. Many of these date back to colonial times, but have remained omnipresent in contemporary commentaries. The provocative essay made Wainaina known to a larger international audience. In coming years, he held fellowships at Union College and Williams College in the United States and served as director of the Chinua Achebe Center for African Writers and Artists at Bard College. In 2014, *Time* magazine placed Wainaina on its list of the 100 most influential people in the world.

In 2011, *One Day I Will Write About This Place* had appeared. It begins with a fond evocation of Wainaina's happy childhood and local life in Nakuru. For Caitlin L. Chandler, on the website Africa is a Country, in language that is lyrical and playful but also non-linear stream-of-consciousness 'Binyavanga mimics how memory constructs our lives from scraps of events and the people we remember'. He writes about his coming of age 'against a backdrop of "development", a nascent religious movement, the rise of popular culture and Kenya's shifting political landscape'.

Only years later did Wainaina come out as gay, though in 'I Am a Homosexual, Mum', he said, 'I swear I have known I am a homosexual since I was five'. At the time of his mother's death in 2000, he had not had sex with a man, and had attempted to sleep with only three women, 'one woman, successfully'. Five years later, he had a paid sexual encounter with a man in London, but 'I cannot say the word gay until I am thirty-nine, four years after that brief massage encounter'. On his forty-third birthday, through this essay, Wainaina outed himself. From then onwards, homosexuality became a theme in many of his interventions in public debate.

Sometimes Wainaina spoke in a personal vein. He framed a TED talk – for which he wore a black skivvy, light blue jacket and bright red tutu-like skirt – as a conversation with his deceased father. 'I need to talk to you', he said, because 'I need to hear from you to be free to love' – adding with a smile that they also 'need to talk about the fact that I've taken to wearing skirts'. (He was always a creative dresser, and sometimes sported multi-coloured hair.) But Wainaina's message was also political at a time of continuing homophobia in many parts of Africa and the adoption of new anti-homosexual legislation in Uganda and Nigeria. This he blamed in part on the self-appointed 'moral brokers' in religious and political groups. Wainaina nevertheless remained hopeful: 'I felt there are enough people who disagreed with what I am, but that agreed that you could not doubt my sense of honour and the work I had done for many years to change this continent'. He affirmed the 'freedom to be diverse', and for gay Africans to live openly and with dignity, as he attempted to do: 'I am living in plain light, not in a dark continent'.

Some conservative leaders in Africa have claimed that homosexuality and other kinds of gender and sexual diversity are Western aberrations that contravene African tradition (despite evidence presented by scholars) and African morality. Anti-queer violence is unfortunately widespread, often with degrees of official tolerance or complicity. In over half of the countries on the African continent, homosexual acts are still considered criminal offences, and in some places homophobic legislation has been reinforced in recent years.

More positively, several countries in which homosexual acts were illegal (in some cases because of colonial-era law codes) have changed their legislation: South Africa (in 1994), Cape Verde (2004), Lesotho (2010), Mozambique (2015), the Seychelles (2016), Botswana (2019), Gabon (2020) and Angola (2021). South Africa enshrines protection against discrimination on the basis of sexual orientation in its constitution and was the first (and so far only) country in Africa to legalize same-sex marriage.

In 2016 Wainaina revealed that he was HIV-positive. Two years later, he said that he had fallen in love and planned to marry his partner. After several strokes, Wainaina died in Nairobi in 2019. A collection of his writings published in 2022 will allow more people to discover his life and ideas.

Sarah Hegazi 1989–2020

On 22 September 2017, Sarah Hegazi (sometimes spelled Hegazy), a 28-year-old Egyptian woman, along with around 35,000 others, attended a concert in Cairo given by Mashrou' Leila, a Lebanese indie rock band. Formed in 2008 by several students at the American University of Beirut, the internationally popular band was known for lively music, satirical lyrics and comments on social issues, including such largely taboo subjects in the Arab world as sex. Hamed Sinno, the lead singer, had indeed come out as gay, a rare and bold move. As 'an act of support and solidarity not only with the vocalist [Sinno] but for everyone who is oppressed', as she put it, Hegazi – who had declared on Facebook that she was a lesbian – and several other fans waved the rainbow flag at the concert. A photograph shows her standing and smiling, holding the banner aloft.

Over the next days, conservative Egyptian journalists and TV presenters mounted an increasingly intense homophobic campaign, condemning Hegazi and the others for the flag-waving, branding them immoral and calling for government action to stamp out such expressions of 'deviance'. Many commentators on social media echoed the views, though others supported those who had publicly affirmed queer rights. Ten days after the concert, a squadron of armed policemen appeared at Hegazi's house, after midnight, to arrest her, but in order not to implicate others she managed to delete the social media on her mobile phone before they carried her away. She was one of seventy-four people, though the only woman, detained in connection with the concert incident.

Although Egyptian law does not criminalize homosexual acts as such, it has wide provisions – often enforced by the censorious and authoritarian government – which can be used against those whose behaviour is deemed immoral or offensive to Islam or the state. Thus, charges of 'debauchery' and 'promoting sexual deviancy' were laid against Hegazi. Taken to a police station, she was bound and gagged, then interrogated, including with questions about her virginity. Hegazi was kept in jail for three months, tortured with electric shocks, and verbally, physically and sexually abused by police officers; women prisoners, she said, were also incited to attack her. When released after paying a fine of around US$56, a not inconsequential sum in Egypt, she found that the hate campaign against her and other queer people was continuing. She decided to flee overseas, receiving asylum in Canada, where she spoke publicly about the repressive political situation in Egypt and pursued her activism. Settling down proved difficult and Hegazi was suffering from severe post-traumatic stress syndrome linked to her incarceration. On 14 June 2020, after sending a final message ('The sky is sweeter than the earth. And I need the sky not the earth'), she took her own life.

Hegazi had grown up, one of four siblings, in a middle-class family; her father, a science teacher in a secondary school, died when she was young. Her mother – who died from cancer soon after Hegazi's flight from Egypt – had been supportive of her sexual identity. Hegazi studied information technology at a local college and the American University in Cairo, and completed several units of study online in overseas universities. Photographs show a happy young woman bicycling in Cairo and enjoying life with her friends. She identified as lesbian, feminist and communist, and opposed the regime of Mohammed al-Sisi, who came to power in a military coup in 2013.

Those who have sex with others of the same gender have faced many problems in Egypt, where one poll showed that fully ninety-five per cent of the population disapprove of homosexuality, and there is sustained persecution of homosexuals. Many queer people consequently live clandestine lives, threatened by denunciation, blackmail, violence and arrest. Infamously, in May 2001, Egyptian police descended on a floating nightclub patronized by gay men, the 'Queen Boat' moored in the Nile, and took into detention more than fifty men who were charged, on the basis of laws dating from 1937 and 1961, with the 'habitual practice of debauchery'; two others were charged with 'contempt of religion'. The police released the identities of the men, and their personal information was published in the local press. After a five-month trial, twenty-three men were convicted (and another was convicted in a juvenile court). A second court overturned the verdicts both of those found guilty and not guilty, and a subsequent ruling imposed sentences of three years in prison on twenty-one men. The case received international condemnation, as well as criticism within the country.

The 2011 revolution brought hope to many gay and lesbian activists, though little changed for sexual minorities. When Omar Sharif, Jr. – actor, model and grandson of the famous Omar Sharif – came out in 2012, for instance, threats caused him to leave Egypt, and he has never returned. In 2020, soon after Hegazi's death, Human Rights Watch reported on persecution of LGBT people in a 'systematic fashion', with arbitrary arrests, torture, forced 'virginity tests' and incarceration in 'inhuman conditions'. According to the organization's LGBT associate Rasha Younes, quoted in *The Washington Post*, 'Egyptian authorities seem to be competing for the worst record on rights violations against LGBT people in the region, while the international silence is appalling'. Hegazi had said from exile that in Egypt, 'Anyone who is different from male, Muslim, Sunni, heterosexual, pro-regime or rich is automatically marginalized and oppressed'.

Activists responded with shock to news of Hegazi's death and anger at the circumstances that ultimately had incited her suicide. Obituaries appeared in the world press, a Toronto artist painted a wall-size mural, and Hamed Sinno turned her words about the sky and the earth into a song. Activists, strengthened by Hegazi's example, still struggle for the rights of queer people around the Arab world.

BIBLIOGRAPHY

General

Robert Aldrich (ed.), *Gay Life and Culture: A World History* (London, 2006)

Robert Aldrich and Garry Wotherspoon (eds), *Who's Who in Gay and Lesbian History: From Antiquity to World War II* (London, 2001)

Robert Aldrich and Garry Wotherspoon (eds), *Who's Who in Gay and Lesbian History: From World War II to the Present Day* (London, 2001)

Louis Compton, *Homosexuality and Civilization* (Cambridge, Mass., 2003)

R. B. Parkinson, *A Little Gay History: Desire and Diversity across the World* (New York, 2013)

Leila Rupp, *Sapphistries: A Global History of Love between Women* (New York, 2009)

Khnumhotep and Niankhkhnum

R. B. Parkinson, '"Homosexual" Desire and Middle Kingdom Literature', *The Journal of Egyptian Archaeology*, vol. 81 (1995), pp. 57–76

Greg Reeder, 'Same-sex Desire, Conjugal Constructs, and the Tomb of Niankhkhnum and Khnumhotep', *World Archaeology*, vol. 32, no. 2 (2000), pp. 193–208

David and Jonathan

Susan Ackerman, *When Heroes Love: The Ambiguity of Eros in the Stories of Gilgamesh and David* (New York, 2005)

The Bible, First and Second Books of Samuel (King James Version)

Michael Vasey, *Strangers and Friends: A New Exploration of Homosexuality and the Bible* (London, 1995)

Sappho

Alastair J. L. Blanshard, *Sex: Vice and Love from Antiquity to Modernity* (Oxford, 2010)

James Davidson, *The Greeks and Greek Love: A Radical Reappraisal of Homosexuality in Ancient Greece* (London, 2007)

Jim Powell, *The Poetry of Sappho* (Oxford, 2007)

Yopie Prins, *Victorian Sappho* (Princeton, N.J., 1999)

Jane McIntosh Snyder, *Lesbian Desire in the Lyrics of Sappho* (New York, 1997)

Socrates

Alastair J. L. Blanshard, *Sex: Vice and Love from Antiquity to Modernity* (Oxford, 2010)

James Davidson, *The Greeks and Greek Love: A Radical Reappraisal of Homosexuality in Ancient Greece* (London, 2007)

David M. Halperin, *One Hundred Years of Homosexuality and Other Essays on Greek Love* (New York, 1990)

Hadrian and Antinous

Royston Lambert, *Beloved and God: The Story of Hadrian and Antinous* (Secaucus, N.J., 1984)

Thorsten Opper, *Hadrian: Empire and Conflict* (London, 2008)

John Addington Symonds, *Sketches and Studies of Italy and Greece* (London, 1879)

Caroline Vout, *Antinous: The Face of the Antique* (Leeds, 2006)

Craig A. Williams, *Roman Homosexuality* (Oxford, 2nd edn, 2010)

Marguerite Yourcenar, *Mémoires d'Hadrien* (Paris, 1951)

Chen Weisong

Brett Hinsch, *Passions of the Cut Sleeve: The Male Homosexual Tradition in China* (Berkeley, Calif., 1990)

Wenqing Kang, *Obsession: Male Same-Sex Relations in China, 1900–1950* (Hong Kong, 2009)

Wu Cuncun, *Homoerotic Sensibilities in Late Imperial China* (London, 2004)

Saints Sergius and Bacchus

John Boswell, *Same-Sex Unions in Premodern Europe* (New York, 1994)

Elizabeth A. R. Brown, Claudia Rapp and Brent D. Shaw, 'Ritual Brotherhood in Ancient and Medieval Europe: A Symposium', *Traditio*, vol. 52 (1997), pp. 259–381

James Davidson, 'Mr and Mr and Mrs and Mrs', *London Review of Books*, vol. 27, no. 11 (2 June 2005), pp. 13–18

Elizabeth Key Fowden, *The Barbarian Plain: Saint Sergius between Rome and Iran* (Berkeley, Calif., 1999)

Aelred of Rievaulx

Aelred of Rievaulx, *Spiritual Friendship*, tr. Mary Eugia Laker (Kalamazoo, Mich., 1977)

John Boswell, *Christianity, Social Tolerance, and Homosexuality* (London, 1980)

Glenn Burger and Steven F. Kruger (eds), *Queering the Middle Ages* (Minneapolis, 2001)

Bernd-Ulrich Hergemöller, *Sodom and Gomorrah: On the Everyday Reality and Persecution of Homosexuals in the Middle Ages* (London, 2001)

Anna Klosowska, *Queer Love in the Middle Ages* (Basingstoke, 2005)

T. Stehling (ed.), *Medieval Latin Poems of Male Love and Friendship* (New York, 1984)

Michelangelo Buonarroti

Michelangelo Buonarroti, *The Poetry of Michelangelo*, ed. and tr. James M. Saslow (New Haven, Conn., 1991)

Lene Østermark-Johansen, *Sweetness and Strength: The Reception of Michelangelo in Late Victorian England* (Aldershot, 1998)

Michael Rocke, *Forbidden Friendships: Homosexuality and Male Culture in Renaissance Florence* (Oxford, 1996)

James M. Saslow, *Ganymede in the Renaissance: Homosexuality in Art and Society* (New Haven, Conn., 1986)

Michel de Montaigne

Alan Bray, *The Friend* (Chicago, 2003)

George E. Haggerty, *Men in Love: Masculinity and Sexuality in the Eighteenth Century* (New York, 1999)

Michel de Montaigne, *The Complete Essays*, tr. and ed. M. A. Screech (London, 2003)

Allan A. Tulchin, 'Same-Sex Couples Creating Households in Old Regime France: The Uses of the *Affrèrement*', *Journal of Modern History*, vol. 79 (2007), pp. 613–47

Antonio Rocco

Louis Asoka, 'Alcibiades the Schoolboy', *Paidika*, no. 2 (1987), pp. 49–54

Giovanni Dall'Orto, 'Antonio Rocco and the background of his *Alcibiade fanciullo a scola*', in Mattias Duyves et al (eds), *Among Women, Among Men* (Amsterdam, 1983)

N. S. Davidson, 'Sodomy in early modern Venice', in Thomas Betteridge, *Sodomy in Early Modern Europe* (Manchester, 2002)

Germaine Greer, *The Boy* (London, 2003)

Antonio Rocco, *L'Alcibiade fanciullo a scola*, ed. Laura Coci (Rome, 1988)

Philippe-Joseph Salazar, 'Rocco, Antonio', in Robert Aldrich and Garry Wotherspoon (eds), *Who's Who in Gay and Lesbian History: From Antiquity to World War II* (London, 2001), pp. 373–75

James Grantham Turner, *Schooling Sex: Libertine Literature and Erotic Education in Italy, France, and England, 1534–1685* (Oxford, 2003)

Benedetta Carlini

Edith Benkov, 'The Erased Lesbian: Sodomy and the Legal Tradition in Medieval Europe', in Francesca Canadé Sautman and Pamela Sheingorn (eds), *Same Sex Love and Desire among Women in the Middle Ages* (London, 2001), pp. 101–22

Judith C. Brown, *Immodest Acts: The Life of a Lesbian Nun in Renaissance Italy* (New York, 1986)

Rosemary Curb and Nancy Manahan (eds), *Lesbian Nuns: Breaking the Silence* (Tallahassee, Fla., 1985)

Susan Schibanoff, 'Hildegard of Bingen and Richardis of Stade: The Discourse of Desire', in Sautman and Sheingorn, pp. 49–84

Michael Sweerts

Albert Blankert, 'Michael Sweerts: Painter of Silence and Secrecy', in *Selected Writings on Dutch Painting: Rembrandt, Van Beke, Vermeer and Others* (Zwolle, 2004)

Vitale Bloch, *Michel Sweerts* (The Hague, 1968)

Guido Jansen and Peter C. Sutton (eds), *Michael Sweerts* (Zwolle, 2002)

Rolf Kultzen, *Michael Sweerts, Brussels 1618–Goa 1664* (Ghent, 1996)

Thomas Röske, 'Blicke auf Männerkörper bei Michael Sweerts', in Mechthild Fend and Marianne Koos (eds), *Männlichkeit im Blick: Visuelle Inszenierungen in der Kunst seit der Frühen Neuzeit* (Cologne, 2004), pp. 121–35

Katherine Philips

Harriette Andreadis, 'The Sapphic Platonics of Katherine Philipps, 1632–1664', *Signs*, vol. 15, no. 1 (1989), pp. 34–60

Graham Hammill, 'Sexuality and Society in the Poetry of Katherine Philips', in Vin Nardizzi, Stephen Guy-Bray and Will Stockton (eds), *Queer Renaissance Historiography: A Backward Gaze* (London, 2009)

Claudia A. Limbert, 'Katherine Philips: Controlling a Life and Reputation', *South Atlantic Review*, vol. 56, no. 2 (1991), pp. 27–42

Arlene Stiebel, 'Subversive Sexuality: Masking the Erotic in Poems by Katherine Philips and Aphra Behn',

in Claude J. Summers and Ted-Larry Pebworth (eds), *Renaissance Discourses of Desire* (Columbia, Mo., 1993), pp. 223–36

Patrick Thomas (ed.), *The Collected Works of Katherine Philips, the Matchless Orinda* (Stump Cross, 1990)

Frederick the Great

Robert Aldrich and Garry Wotherspoon (eds), *Who's Who in Gay and Lesbian History: From Antiquity to World War II* (London, 2001)

Nancy Mitford, *Frederick the Great* (London, 1970)

Voltaire, *La vie privée du roi de Prusse* (Paris, 1784)

Chevalier d'Eon

Simon Burrows et al (eds), *The Chevalier d'Éon and His Worlds: Gender, Espionage and Politics in the Eighteenth Century* (London, 2010)

Anna Clark, 'The Chevalier d'Eon and Wilkes: Masculinity and Politics in the Eighteeenth Century', *Eighteenth-Century Studies*, vol. 32, no. 1 (1998), pp. 19–48

Charles d'Eon de Beaumont, *The Maiden of Tonnerre: The Vicissitudes of the Chevalier and the Chevalière d'Eon*, tr. and ed. Roland A. Champagne, Nina Ekstein and Gary Kates (Baltimore, 2001)

Gary Kates, *Monsieur d'Eon is a Woman: A Tale of Political Intrigue and Sexual Masquerade* (Baltimore, 2001)

Walt Whitman

Maurice Bucke (ed.), *Calamus: A Series of Letters Written during the Years 1868–1880 by Walt Whitman to a Young Friend (Peter Doyle)* (London, 1897, 1972)

Walt Whitman, *Complete Poetry & Selected Prose and Letters*, ed. Emory Holloway (London, 1971)

Walt Whitman archive: www.waltwhitmanarchive.org

Edward Carpenter

Edward Carpenter, *My Days and Dreams: being autobiographical notes* (London, 3rd edn, 1918)

Sheila Rowbotham, *Edward Carpenter: A Life of Liberty and Love* (London, 2008)

Chushichi Tsuzuki, *Edward Carpenter: Prophet of Human Fellowship 1844–1929* (Cambridge, 1980)

André Gide

Jonathan Fryer, *André and Oscar: Gide, Wilde and the Gay Art of Living* (London, 1997)

André Gide, *If It Die: An Autobiography*, tr. Dorothy Bussy (London, 2001)

Michael Lucy, *Gide's Bent: Sexuality, Politics, Writing* (Oxford, 1995)

E. M. Forster

Nicola Beauman, *Morgan: A Biography of E. M. Forster* (London, 1993)

Robert K. Martin and George Piggford (eds), *Queer Forster* (Chicago, 1997)

Arthur Martland, *E. M. Forster: Passion and Prose* (Swaffham, 1999)

Wendy Moffatt, *E. M. Forster: A New Life* (London, 2010)

Radclyffe Hall

Sally Cline, *Radclyffe Hall: A Woman Called John* (London, 1997)

Diana Souhami, *The Trials of Radclyffe Hall* (London, 1998)

Una Troubridge, *The Life and Death of Radclyffe Hall* (London, 1961)

Christopher Isherwood

Chris & Don: A Love Story (documentary film, Arthouse Films, 2007)

Christopher Isherwood, *Christopher and His Kind, 1929–1939* (New York, 1976)

Peter Parker, *Isherwood: A Life* (London, 2004)

Maximilian von Schwartzkoppen and Alessandro Panizzardi

Eric G. Carlston, 'Secret Dossiers: Sexuality, Race, and Treason in Proust and the Dreyfus Affair', *Modern Fiction Studies*, vol. 48, no. 4 (2002), pp. 937–68

Christopher E. Forth, *The Dreyfus Affair and the Crisis of French Manhood* (Baltimore, 2004)

Pierre Gervais, Romain Huret and Pauline Peretz, 'Une relecture du "dossier secret": homosexualité et antisémitisme dans l'Affaire Dreyfus', *Revue d'histoire moderne et contemporaine*, vol. 55, no. 1 (2008), pp. 125–60

Ruth Harris, *Dreyfus: Politics, Emotion, and the Scandal of the Century* (New York, 2010)

Norman L. Kleeblatt, 'The Body of Alfred Dreyfus: A Site for France's Displaced Anxieties of Masculinity, Homosexuality and Power', in Nicholas Mirzoeff (ed.), *Diaspora and Visual Culture: Representing Africans and Jews* (New York, 2000), pp. 76–91

Robert J. Maguire, 'Oscar Wilde and the Dreyfus Affair', *Victorian Studies*, vol. 41, no. 1 (1997), pp. 1–30

Oscar Wilde

Owen Dudley Edwards, 'Wilde, Oscar Fingal O'Flahertie Wills (1854–1900)', *Oxford Dictionary of National Biography* (Oxford, 2004); online edn, Jan. 2010: www.oxforddnb.com/view/article/29400

Richard Ellmann, *Oscar Wilde* (London, 1987)

Wilhelm von Gloeden

Robert Aldrich, *The Seduction of the Mediterranean: Writing, Art and Homosexual Fantasy* (London, 1993)

Sergei Diaghilev

Lynn Garafola, *Diaghilev's Ballets Russes* (New York, 1989)

Tirza True Latimer, 'Balletomania: A Sexual Disorder?', *GLQ*, vol. 5, no. 2 (1999), pp. 173–97

Sjeng Scheijen, *Diaghilev: A Life* (London, 2009)

Jacques d'Adelwärd-Fersen

Jacques d'Adelswärd-Fersen, *Ainsi chantait Marsyas … – Poèmes* (Paris, 1907)

Fausto Esposito, *I Misteri di Villa Lysis: Testamento e morte* (Capri, n.d.)

Roger Peyrefitte, *L'Exilé de Capri* (Paris, 1959)

Wolfram Setz (ed.), *Jacques d'Adelswärd-Fersen, Dandy und Poet: Annäherungen* (Hamburg, 2005)

Karol Szymanowski

Stephen Downes, *Szymanowski, Eroticism and the Voices of Mythology* (Aldershot, 2003)

Hubert Kennedy, 'Karol Szymanowski, his boy-love novel, and the boy he loved', *Paidika*, vol. 3, no. 11 (1994), pp. 26–33

Arthur Rubinstein, *My Many Years* (New York, 1980)

Karol Szymanowski, *Das Gastmahl: Ein Kapitel aus dem Roman Ephebos*, tr. and ed. Wolfgang Jöhling (Berlin, 1993)

Alistair Wightman, *Karol Szymanowski: His Life and Work* (Aldershot, 1999)

Eleanor Butler and Sarah Ponsonby

John Hicklin, *The 'Ladies of Llangollen' as Sketched by Many Hands; with Notices of Other Objects of Interest in 'That Sweetest of Vales'* (London, 1847); e-book on www.guttenberg.org/files/20810/20810-h/20810.h.htm

Elizabeth Mavor, *The Ladies of Llangollen: A Study in Romantic Friendship* (London, 1971)

Martha Vicinus, *Intimate Friends: Women Who Loved Women, 1778–1928* (Chicago, 2004)

Anne Lister

Anna Clark, 'Anne Lister's Construction of Lesbian Identity', *Journal of the History of Sexuality*, vol. 7 (1996), pp. 23–50

Jennifer Frangos, '"I love and only love the fairer sex": The Writing of a Lesbian Identity in the Diaries of Anne Lister (1791–1840)', in Linda S. Coleman (ed.), *Women's Life-Writing: Finding Voice/Building Community* (Bowling Green, Oh., 1997), pp. 43–61

Jill Liddington, *Female Fortune: Land, Gender and Authority – The Anne Lister Diaries and Other Writings, 1833–36* (London, 1998)

Anne Lister, *No Priest but Love: The Journals of Anne Lister, 1824–1826*, ed. Helena Whitbread (New York, 1992)

Martha Vicinus, *Intimate Friends: Women Who Loved Women, 1778–1928* (Chicago, 2004)

Helena Whitbread (ed.), *The Secret Diaries of Miss Anne Lister* (London, 2010)

Eva Gore-Booth

Dictionary of Irish Biography (Cambridge, 2009)

Gifford Lewis, *Eva Gore-Booth and Esther Roper: A Biography* (London, 1988)

Sonja Tiernan, *Eva Gore-Booth: An Image of Such Politics* (Manchester, 2012)

Sylvia Townsend Warner

Claire Harman, *Sylvia Townsend Warner: A Biography* (London, 1989)

Susanna Pinney (ed.), *I'll Stand by You: The Letters of Sylvia Townsend Warner and Valentine Ackland* (London, 1998)

Claude Cahun

Claude Cahun, Photographe (Paris, 1995)

Louise Downie (ed.), *Don't Kiss Me: The Art of Claude Cahun and Marcel Moore* (London, 2006)

Gen Doy, *Claude Cahun: A Sensual Politics of Photography* (London, 2007)

Shelley Rice (ed.), *Inverted Odysseys: Claude Cahun, Maya Deren, Cindy Sherman* (New York, 1999)

BIBLIOGRAPHY

Suzy Solidor

Marie-Hélène Carbonel, *Suzy Solidor: une vie d'amours* (Paris, 2007)

Tirza True Latimer, *Women Together/ Women Apart: Portraits of Lesbian Paris* (New Brunswick, N.J., 2005)

Martin Pénet, 'L'expression homosexuelle dans les chansons françaises de l'entre-deux-guerres: entre dérision et ambiguïté', *Revue d'histoire moderne et contemporaine*, vol. 53, no. 4 (2006), pp. 106–27

Annemarie Schwarzenbach

'Dossier Annemarie Schwarzenbach', *Inverses*, no. 6 (2006)

Dominique Laure Miermont, *Annemarie Schwarzenbach, ou le mal d'Europe* (Paris, 2004)

Carson McCullers

Virginia Spencer Carr, *The Lonely Hunter: A Biography of Carson McCullers* (Athens, GA., 2003)

Richard M. Cook, *Carson McCullers* (New York, 1975)

Carlos L. Dews (ed.), *Illumination and Night Glare: The Unfinished Autobiography of Carson McCullers* (Madison, Wis., 1999)

Jan Whitt (ed.), *Reflections in a Critical Eye: Essays on Carson McCullers* (Lanham, Md., 2008)

Richard Schultz

Karl-Heinz Steinle, *Der Literarische Salon bei Richard Schultz* (Berlin, 2002)

Federico García Lorca

Paul Binding, *Lorca: The Gay Imagination* (London, 1985)

Federico García Lorca, *Collected Poems*, ed. Christopher Maurer (New York, 2nd edn, 2002)

Ian Gibson, *'Caballo azul de mi locura': Lorca y el mundo gay* (Barcelona, 2009)

Ian Gibson, *Federico García Lorca: A Life* (London, 1989)

Angel Sahuquillo, *Federico García Lorca y la cultura de la homosexualidad. Lorca, Dalí, Cernuda, Gil-Albert, Prados y la voz silenciada del amor homosexual* (Alicante, 1991)

Newton Arvin

Micki McGee (ed.), *Yaddo: Making American Culture* (New York, 2008)

Barry Werth, *The Scarlet Professor: Newton Arvin – A Literary Life Shattered by Scandal* (New York, 2001)

Lilly Wust and Felice Schragenheim

Aimée & Jaguar (film directed by Max Fäberböck, 1999)

Murial Cormican, *'Aimée and Jaguar* and the Banality of Evil', *German Studies Review*, vol. 26, no. 1 (February 2003), pp. 105–19

Erica Fischer, *Aimée and Jaguar: A Love Story, Berlin 1943* (New York, 1995)

Eugène Jansson

Eugène Jansson (1862–1915): Nocturnes suédois (exh. cat., Musée d'Orsay, Paris, 1999)

Magnus Enckell

Harri Kalha, *Tapaus Magnus Enckell* (Helsinki, 2005)

Juha-Heikki Tihinen, 'Enckell, (Knut) Magnus', in Robert Aldrich and Garry Wotherspoon (eds), *Who's Who in Gay and Lesbian History: From Antiquity to World War II* (London, 2001), pp. 148–49

Donald Friend

Ian Britain (ed.), *The Donald Friend Diaries: Chronicles & Confessions of an Australian Artist* (Melbourne, 2010)

Anne Gray (ed.), *The Diaries of Donald Friend* (Canberra, 4 vols, 2001–6)

Barry Pearce, *Donald Friend, 1915–1989: Retrospective* (Sydney, 1990)

Alair Gomes

Alair Gomes (London, 2001)

Bhupen Khakhar
Timothy Hyman, *Bhupen Khakhar*
(Bombay, 1998)

Abu Nuwas
Ahmad al-Tifashi, *The Delight of Hearts*, tr.
Edward A. Lacey (San Francisco, 1988)
Joseph A. Massad, *Desiring Arabs*
(Chicago, 2007)
Vincent-Mansour Monteil (ed. and
tr.), *Abû-Nuwâs: le vin, le vent, la vie*
(Paris, 1979)
Stephen O. Murray and Will Roscoe
(eds), *Islamic Homosexualities: Culture,
History, and Literature* (New York, 1997)
J. W. Wright Jr. and Everett K. Rowson
(eds), *Homoeroticism in Classical Arabic
Literature* (New York, 1997)

Constantine Cavafy
C. P. Cavafy, *Collected Poems*, tr. Edmund
Keeley and Philip Sherrard, ed. George
Savidis (Princeton, N.J., revised edn,
1992)
C. P. Cavafy, *The Unfinished Poems*,
tr. and ed. Daniel Mendelsohn
(New York, 2009)
Michael Haag, *Alexandria: City of
Memory* (New Haven, Conn., 2005)
Robert Liddell, *Cavafy: A Critical
Biography* (London, 1974)

T. E. Lawrence
Michael Asher, *Lawrence: The Uncrowned
King of Arabia* (London, 1998)
Philip Knightly and Colin Simpson,
The Secret Lives of Lawrence of Arabia
(London, 1969)
T. E. Lawrence, *Seven Pillars of Wisdom*
(London, 1926)

Yannis Tsarouchis
Niki Gripari and Adam Szymczyk (eds),
Yannis Tsarouchis: Dancing in Real Life
(London: Sternberg Press, 2021)
Nicos Hadjinicolaou, 'Introduction',
in *Theophilos, Kontoglou, Ghika,
Tsarouchis: Four painters of 20th century*

Greece (exh. cat., Wildenstein Gallery,
London, 1975), p. 36
Athena Schina, 'The Painting of Yannis
Tsarouchis and his Multiple Copies', in
Tsarouchis, 1936–1989: Multiple Copies
(Athens, 1989), pp. 28–29
Tsarouchis: peintures et gouaches (exh. cat.,
Galerie Claude Bernard, Paris, 1997)
Yannis Tsarouchis, 1910–1989 (exh. cat.,
Benaki Museum, Athens, 2010)
Yannis Tsarouchis Foundation website:
www.tsarouchis.gr

Ali al-Jabri
Amal Ghandour, *About This Man Called
Ali: The Purple Life of an Arab Artist*
(London, 2009)
Brian Whitaker, *Unspeakable Love: Gay
and Lesbian Life in the Middle East*
(London, 2006)

Ihara Saikaku
Gary P. Leupp, *Male Colors: The
Construction of Homosexuality in
Tokugawa Japan* (Berkeley, Calif., 1995)
Gregory M. Pflugfelder, *Cartographies of
Desire: Male–Male Sexuality in Japanese
Discourse, 1600–1950* (Berkeley, Calif.,
1999)
Ihara Saikaku, *The Great Mirror of Male
Love*, tr. and ed. Paul Gordon Schalow
(Stanford, Calif., 1990)

Nobuko Yoshiya
Gregory M. Pflugfelder, '"S" is for Sister:
Schoolgirl Intimacy and "Same-Sex
Love" in Early Twentieth-Century
Japan', in Barbara Molony and
Kathleen Uno (eds), *Gendering Modern
Japanese History* (Cambridge, Mass.,
2005), pp. 133–90
Jennifer Robertson, 'Yoshiya Nobuko:
Out and Outspoken in Practice and
Prose', in Anne Walthall (ed.), *The
Human Tradition in Modern Japan*
(Wilmington, Del., 2002), pp. 155–74
Michiko Suzuki, 'Writing Same-Sex Love:
Sexology and Literary Representation

in Yoshiya Nobuko's Early Fiction', *The Journal of Asian Studies*, vol. 65, no. 3 (2006), pp. 575–99

William Plomer
Peter F. Alexander, *William Plomer: A Biography* (Oxford, 1989)
Louis Allen, 'William Plomer (1905–1974 [*sic*]) and Japan', in Hugh Cortazzi and Gordon Daniels (eds), *Britain and Japan, 1859–1991: Themes and Personalities* (London, 1991)
Sumie Okada, *Western Writers in Japan* (Basingstoke, 1999)
William Plomer, *The Autobiography of William Plomer* (London, 1975)

Yukio Mishima
Yukio Mishima, *Confessions of a Mask*, tr. Meredith Weatherby (New York, 1958)
Yukio Mishima, *Forbidden Colors*, tr. Alfred H. Marks (New York, 1978)
John Nathan, *Mishima: A Biography* (London, 1975)
Donald Richie, *The Japan Journals, 1947–2004* (Berkeley, Calif., 2004)

Tamotsu Yato
Donald Richie, 'Sacred Desire: Notes on Tamotsu Yato: Photographer', *Kyoto Journal*, no. 44 (2000), pp. 35–41
Tamotsu Yato, *Young Samurai: Bodybuilders of Japan* (Grove Press, New York, 1967); published in Japanese as *Taidō*
Tamotsu Yato, *Naked Festival* (Tokyo, 1968; New York, 1969)
Tamotsu Yato, *Otoko: Photo Studies of Young Japanese Males* (Tokyo and New York, 1972)

John Henry Newman
John Cornwell, *Newman's Unquiet Grave: The Reluctant Saint* (London, 2010)
David Hilliard, 'UnEnglish and Unmanly: Anglo-Catholicism and Homosexuality', *Victorian Studies*, vol. 25, no. 2 (1982), pp. 181–210

Anthony Kenny, 'Cardinal of conscience', *Times Literary Supplement*, 30 July 2010, pp. 3–5

Rosa Bonheur
Dore Ashton, *Rosa Bonheur: A Life and a Legend* (London, 1981)
Sandra Buratti-Hasan and Leïla Jarbouai, eds, *Rosa Bonheur (1822–1899)* (Paris, 2022)

Hubert Lyautey
Robert Aldrich, *Colonialism and Homosexuality* (London, 2003)
Christian Gury, *Lyautey-Charlus* (Paris, 1998)
Douglas Porch, *The French Foreign Legion* (New York, 1991)

Frieda Belinfante
Los Angeles Times, 7 March 1995 (obit.)
Klaus Müller, 'The Holocaust in the Netherlands: A Reevaluation', paper given at the United States Holocaust Memorial Museum, Washington, D.C., 1 May 1997
Klaus Müller, '"Ik wilde het gevaar in het gezicht kijken": De levens van Frieda Belinfante', in Klaus Müller and Judith Schuyf (eds), *Het begint met nee zeggen: Biografieën rond verzet en homoseksualiteit 1940–1945* (Amsterdam, 2006), pp. 93–127

Ronnie Kray
Tom Driberg, *Ruling Passions* (London, 1977)
Ronald Kray, *My Story* (London, 1994)
Reg and Ron Kray, with Fred Dinenage, *Our Story* (London, 1989)
Laurie O'Leary, *Ronnie Kray: A Man Among Men* (London, 2002)
John Pearson, *Profession of Violence* (London, 1973)

Yves Saint Laurent
Farid Chenoune and Florence Muller, *Yves Saint Laurent* (New York, 2010)

Robert Murphy and Ivan Terestchenko, *The Private World of Yves Saint Laurent and Pierre Bergé* (London, 2009)

Yves Saint Laurent (exh. cat., Metropolitan Museum of Art, New York, 1984)

Magnus Hirschfeld

Elena Mancini, *Magnus Hirschfeld and the Quest for Sexual Freedom: A History of the First International Sexual Freedom Movement* (London, 2010)

James D. Steakley, *The Homosexual Emancipation Movement in Germany* (New York, 1975)

Charlotte Wolff, *Magnus Hirschfeld: A Portrait of a Pioneer in Sexology* (London, 1986)

Del Martin

Marcia M. Gallo, *Different Daughters: A History of the Daughters of Bilitis and the Birth of the Lesbian Rights Movement* (Berkeley, Calif., 2007)

New York Times, 27 August 2008 (obit.)

Harvey Milk

Elizabeth A. Armstrong, *Forging Gay Identities: Organizing Sexuality in San Francisco, 1950–1994* (Chicago, 2002)

Randy Shilts, *The Life and Times of Harvey Milk: The Mayor of Castro Street* (New York, 1982)

Guy Hocquenghem

Guy Hocquenghem, *Le Désir homosexuel* (Paris, 1972)

Bill Marshall, *Guy Hocquenghem: Theorising the Gay Nation* (London, 1996)

Simon Nkoli

Marc Epprecht, *Hungochani: The History of a Dissident Sexuality in Southern Africa* (Montreal, 2004)

Simon Nkoli, 'Wardrobes: Coming out as a black gay activist in South Africa', in Mark Gevisser and Edwin Cameron (eds), *Defiant Desire: Gay and Lesbian Lives in South Africa* (Braamfontein, 1994)

Maharaja of Chhatarpur

J. R. Ackerley, *Hindoo Holiday* (London, 1932)

Hoshang Merchant (ed.), *Yaraana: Gay Writing from India* (New Delhi, 1999)

Peter Parker, *Ackerley: The Life of J.R. Ackerley* (London, 1989)

Pandey Bechan Sharma ('Ugra'), *Chocolate and Other Stories on Male– Male Desire*, tr. and ed. Ruth Vanita (New Delhi, 2006)

Ruth Vanita, *Queering India: Same-Sex Love and Eroticism in Indian Culture and Society* (New York, 2002)

Edmund Backhouse

Robert Bickers, 'Backhouse, Sir Edmund Trelawny', *Oxford Dictionary of National Biography* (Oxford, 2004); online edn, Jan 2008: http://www. oxforddnb.com/view/article/30513

Derek Sandhaus (ed.), *Décadence Mandchoue: The China Memoirs of Sir Edmund Trelawny Backhouse* (Hong Kong, 2011)

Hugh Trevor-Roper, *A Hidden Life: The Enigma of Sir Edmund Backhouse* (London, 1976)

Claude McKay

Wayne F. Cooper, *Claude McKay: Rebel Sojourner in the Harlem Renaissance – A Biography* (Baton Rouge, La., 1987)

Gary E. Holcomb, 'Diaspora Cruises: Queer Black Proletarianism in Claude McKay's *A Long Way Home*', *Modern Fiction Studies*, vol. 49, no. 4 (2003), pp. 714–45

Eric Garber, 'A Spectacle in Color: The Lesbian and Gay Subculture of Jazz Age Harlem', in Martin Duberman, Martha Vicinus and George Chauncey, Jr (eds), *Hidden from History: Reclaiming the Gay and Lesbian Past* (New York, 1989), pp. 318–31

Michael Maiwald, 'Race, Capitalism, and the Third-sex Ideal: Claude McKay's *Home to Harlem* and the Legacy of Edward Carpenter', *Modern Fiction Studies*, vol. 48, no. 4 (2002), pp. 825–57

Lionel Wendt
Lionel Wendt's Ceylon (London, 1950)
Lionel Wendt: A Centennial Tribute (Colombo, 2000)
Robert Aldrich, *Cultural Encounters and Homoeroticism in Sri Lanka: Sex and Serendipity* (London, 2014)

Xuan Dieu
Huyn Sanh Thong (tr. and ed.), *An Anthology of Vietnamese Poems: From the Eleventh through the Twentieth Centuries* (New Haven, Conn., 1996)
Lai Nguyen An and Alec Holcombe, 'The Heart and Mind of the Poet – Xuan Dieu: 1954–1958', *Journal of Vietnamese Studies*, vol. 5, no. 2 (2010), pp. 1–90
Nguyen Quoc Vinh, 'Deviant Bodies and Dynamics of Displacement of Homoerotic Desire in Vietnamese Literature from and about the French Colonial Period (1858–1954)', www. https://www.academia.edu/6610063/ Deviant_Bodies_and_Dynamics_of_ Displacement_of_Homoerotic_Desire_ in_Vietnamese_Literature_from_ and_about_the_French_Colonial_ Period_1858_1954_
Harriet M. Phinney, 'Objects of Affection: Vietnamese Discourses on Love and Emancipation', *Positions*, vol. 16, no. 2 (2008), pp. 329–58
Xuan Dieu, 'Influence of French Poetry on Modern Vietnamese Poetry: A Poet's Account', *Vietnamese Studies*, no. 124 (1997), pp. 41–74

Jean Sénac
Robert Aldrich, *Colonialism and Homosexuality* (London, 2003)
Jamel-Eddine Bencheikh and Christiane

Chaulet-Achour, *Jean Sénac: Clandestin des deux rives* (Paris, 1999)
Jean Sénac, *Oeuvres poétiques* (Arles, 1999)
Jean Sénac, *Selected Poems*, tr. Katia Sainson and David Bergman (Riverdale, N.Y., 2010)

April Ashley
The Guardian, 19 January 2022 (obit.)
BBC News, 29 December 2021 (obit.): https://www.bbc.com/news/ entertainment-arts-59816881
Duncan Fallowell and April Ashley, *Avril Ashley's Odyssey* (London: Jonathan Cape, 1982)

Shi Pei Pu
David Henry Hwang, *M. Butterfly* (New York, 1988)
Dorinne K. Kongo, '"M. Butterfly": Orientalism, Gender, and a Critique of Essentialist Identity', *Cultural Critique*, no. 16 (1990), pp. 5–29
Joyce Wadler, 'The True Story of M. Butterfly; The Spy Who Fell in Love with a Shadow', *New York Times*, 15 August 1993
Joyce Wadler, obituary of Shi Pei Pu, *New York Times*, 1 July 2009

Reinaldo Arenas
Reinaldo Arenas, *Before Night Falls*, tr. Dolores M. Koch (New York, 1993)
Emilio Bejel, *Gay Cuban Nation* (Chicago, 2001)
Rafael Ocasio, 'Gays and the Cuban Revolution: The Case of Reinaldo Arenas', *Latin American Perspectives*, vol. 29, no. 2 (2002), pp. 78–98

Kenneth Binyavanga Wainaina
Africa is a Country website, with articles on Wainaina: https://africasacountry. com/search?query=binyavanga+wai naina
Binyavanga Wainaina, *One Day I Will Write About This Place: A Memoir* (London, 2012)

Binyavanga Wainaina, *How to Write About Africa* (London, 2022)

Bart Luirink and Madeleine Maurick, *Homosexuality in Africa: A Disturbing Love* (Soesterberg, 2016)

Sarah Hegazi

'Arrests and torture of gays, lesbians in Egypt are "systematic," rights report says', *The Washington Post*, 1 October 2020

The New Arab, 16 June 2020 (obit.)

'The Queer Revolution in the Middle East: one good song can do more than 500 protests', a 2022 documentary film by Michael Collins for *The Guardian*: https://www.youtube.com/watch?v=_DQYwBhgOxk

Elias Jahshan, ed., *This Arab is Queer: An Anthology by LBTQ+ Arab Writers* (London, 2022)

Omar Sharif, Jr., *A Tale of Two Omars: A Memoir of Family, Revolution, and Coming Out During the Arab Spring* (Berkeley, Calif., 2021)

SOURCES OF ILLUSTRATIONS

I The Metropolitan Museum of Art, New York. The Howard Mansfield Collection, Purchase, Rogers Fund, 1936

II Brady-Handy Photograph Collection/ Library of Congress, Washington, D.C.

III J. Paul Getty Museum, Los Angeles

IV Calderdale Museums, Yorkshire

V Musée des Beaux Arts, Nantes

VI Russian Museum, St. Petersburg

VII Photo Tord Lund/Thielska Galleriet, Stockholm

VIII Photo Wilhelm von Gloeden

IX Fondation Cartier pour l'art contemporain, Paris

X Courtesy Chemould Prescott Road, Mumbai

XI Private Collection/Courtesy Chemould Prescott Road, Mumbai

XII David Collection, Copenhagen

XIII National Portrait Gallery, London

XIV Château de Versailles et de Trianon, Versailles

XV Courtesy Toni Boumans/United States Holocaust Memorial Museum, Washington, D.C.

XVI Gordon Rainsford/Gay and Lesbian Memory in Action (GALA), Johannesburg

XVII Musée Guimet, Paris

XVIII Private Collection

XIX George Grantham Bain Collection/ Library of Congress, Washington, D.C.

XX PA Photos

INDEX

Roman numerals refer to plate illustrations